Picture : Muhammad Ali —

A Rare Glimpse Into the Life of The Champ by the Photographers of the Courier Journal

2 —

"I've wrestled with alligators. I've tussled a whale. I done handcuffed lightning. And thrown thunder in jail."

Table of Contents

Foreword	7
Young Ali	11
Miami	73
Home	107
Deer Lake	139
vs Spinks	195
Retirement	221
Bahamas	247
The Later Years	263

- 6 -

Sharell Caldwell was eight hours early. She arrived at Freedom Hall at 2 a.m. for a 10 a.m. ticket distribution, armed with a lawn chair, prepared to be patient, determined to attend a Muslim prayer service for Muhammad Ali.

"My grandmother had a sister with polio and people used to pick on her," Caldwell explained on the morning of June 7, 2016. "She'd always be the one sticking up for her. She was out there scrapping with some girls who were picking on my aunt in front of a barbershop on West Broadway. Muhammad Ali came and pulled her off the girl and told her that she was too pretty to be fighting.

"Then HE becomes the greatest fighter of all time."

For most of his extraordinary life, Louisville's most famous son was also one of its most familiar. He was a traveling circus with a big tent, an international icon full of sound and fury and cultural significance, yet he never lost touch with the loud kid from Grand Avenue or the town that sprung him on an unsuspecting planet.

"Muhammad Ali belongs to the world, but he only has one hometown," Louisville Mayor Greg Fischer said. "The Louisville Lip spoke to everyone, but we heard him in a way that no one else could, as our brother, our uncle and our inspiration."

Born, bred and now buried in Louisville, Ali left a lasting imprint on the city and made vivid, individualized memories for many of its residents.

"No matter what stage he was on, how big it was, if there was someone from Louisville there, he'd always recognize you," said former Courier Journal columnist Billy Reed. "He might not know our names."

Maj. Kelly Jones, special operations commander for Louisville Metro Police, prefaced a briefing on Ali's funeral by recounting his own brush with The Greatest.

Happening on Ali at the Charlotte airport, Jones deliberately kept his distance until the champ spotted his 3-year-old daughter, dropped to his knees, clapped his hands and spread his arms to invite an embrace.

"I don't know anybody's life that he didn't touch throughout his lifetime here in Louisville," Jones said.

Born Cassius Marcellus Clay Jr., Ali made his entrance at Louisville General Hospital at 6:35 p.m. on Saturday, January 17, 1942, and he made his exit with a funeral procession befitting royalty.

By profession, he was a boxer, but no ring could contain his outsized personality and only a handful of his contemporaries could equal his impact.

"There are people in the middle of Africa and Asia who haven't the slightest idea who the president of the United States is, but they know Muhammad Ali," writer John Schulian told Thomas Hauser for Muhammad Ali: His Life and Times. "He was more important than any athlete has a right to be or could expect to be.

"He was important in the antiwar movement; he was important in matters of racial pride; he was important in teaching people how to love. He was such an extraordinary person that, when I think of him, I have to remember almost as an afterthought, 'Oh, yeah, besides everything else, he was a great fighter.'"

If some of these sentences sound slightly hyperbolic, consider the fawning prose of renowned tough guy Norman Mailer as he reflected on the power of Ali's presence in The Fight.

"Women draw an audible breath," Mailer wrote. "Men look down. They are reminded again of their lack of worth. If Ali never opened his mouth to quiver the jellies of public opinion, he would still inspire love and hate. For he is the Prince of Heaven – so says the silence around his body when he is luminous."

The man moved among us for 74 years – floating, for the most part, like a butterfly – and he moved so gracefully that his fights were often compared to ballet recitals. As his public persona gained complexity, the cartoonish braggart gradually giving way to a man of weighty and polarizing principles, Ali's bouts would transcend boxing in ways that scarcely seem possible today.

"Do you have any idea what Ali meant to black people?" Hall of Fame baseball player Reggie Jackson asked in 2001. "He was the leader of a nation, the leader of Black America. As a young black, at times I was ashamed of my color; I was ashamed of my hair. And Ali made me proud …

"Do you know what it did for Black Americans to know that the most physically gifted, possibly the most handsome, and one of the most charismatic men in the world was black? Ali helped raise black people in this country out of mental slavery. The entire experience of being black changed for millions of people because of Ali."

When Ali fought Joe Frazier for the first time in their 1971 unification bout, Mailer worked ringside for Life magazine. The magazine's cover photograph was taken by Frank Sinatra.

Ali elevated his sagging sport to levels it can no longer glimpse. As of July, 2018, boxing's primary sanctioning bodies recognized either Anthony Joshua or Deontay Wilder as the heavyweight champion of the world. Neither man is in imminent danger of being mobbed.

"Now that Ali is gone, boxing is the same as it was before, a boring brawl, with a bit of excitement here and there," German author Jan Phillip Reemtsma wrote in More Than a Champion. "…(Ali) compelled people who had never before had any interest in boxing to pay attention to prizefights."

Much as the still photographs published in these pages capture his moods and his muscles, the essential Ali was a three-dimensionsal figure in fluid motion, a sculpted body with a hyperactive mouth.

Though striking in repose, "so pretty that I can hardly stand to look at myself," Ali cannot be fully appreciated without video or volume. He was, indisputably, something to see. And to hear.

From the Ali anthology:

"I've wrestled with alligators,
I've tussled with a whale.
I done handcuffed lightning
And throw thunder in jail.
You know I'm bad.
Just last week, I murdered a rock,
Injured a stone, hospitalized a brick.
I'm so mean, I make medicine sick."

Drawn mainly by Ali's magnetism, and conscious that there might not be another chance to see him fight in the flesh, I covered his final bout in the Bahamas on Dec. 11,

1981. He lost a 10-round unanimous decision to Trevor Berbick.

"Against (Larry) Holmes, I had excuses," Ali said the morning after. "I was too light. I had trouble breathing. But I had no excuses this time. I had 10 rounds to do what I wanted to do, but I couldn't do it. . .Father Time caught up with me. I'm finished. I've got to face the facts. For the first time, I could feel that I'm 40 years old."

Father Time would exact an aggressive toll on Ali. Appearing at the Opening Ceremonies for the 1996 Summer Olympics in Atlanta, he was so enfeebled by Parkinson's disease that watching him light the ceremonial flame was as much an exercise in apprehension as it was closure.

Long reviled for his boasts, his beliefs and his conscientious objection to the Vietnam war, Ali would find greater acceptance through his infirmities. Near the end of his life, the Louisville Lip was seldom seen and rarely heard in public, but increasingly regarded with reverence.

"Even the ones that disliked the statements, even the ones who disliked his boxing style, even the ones who disliked what they would consider to be arrogance – speaking out at a time when most colored people were afraid to – I think most if not all respect the man," former middleweight champion Bernard Hopkins said at the prayer service preceding Ali's funeral. "To speak as boldly and proudly as he did, I wish we had that spirit in a lot of people today."

Wishing will not make it so. Louisville's most famous son left footprints too large to be duplicated.

Tim Sullivan
Courier Journal sports columnist

10 —

Young Ali

1954
— 1969

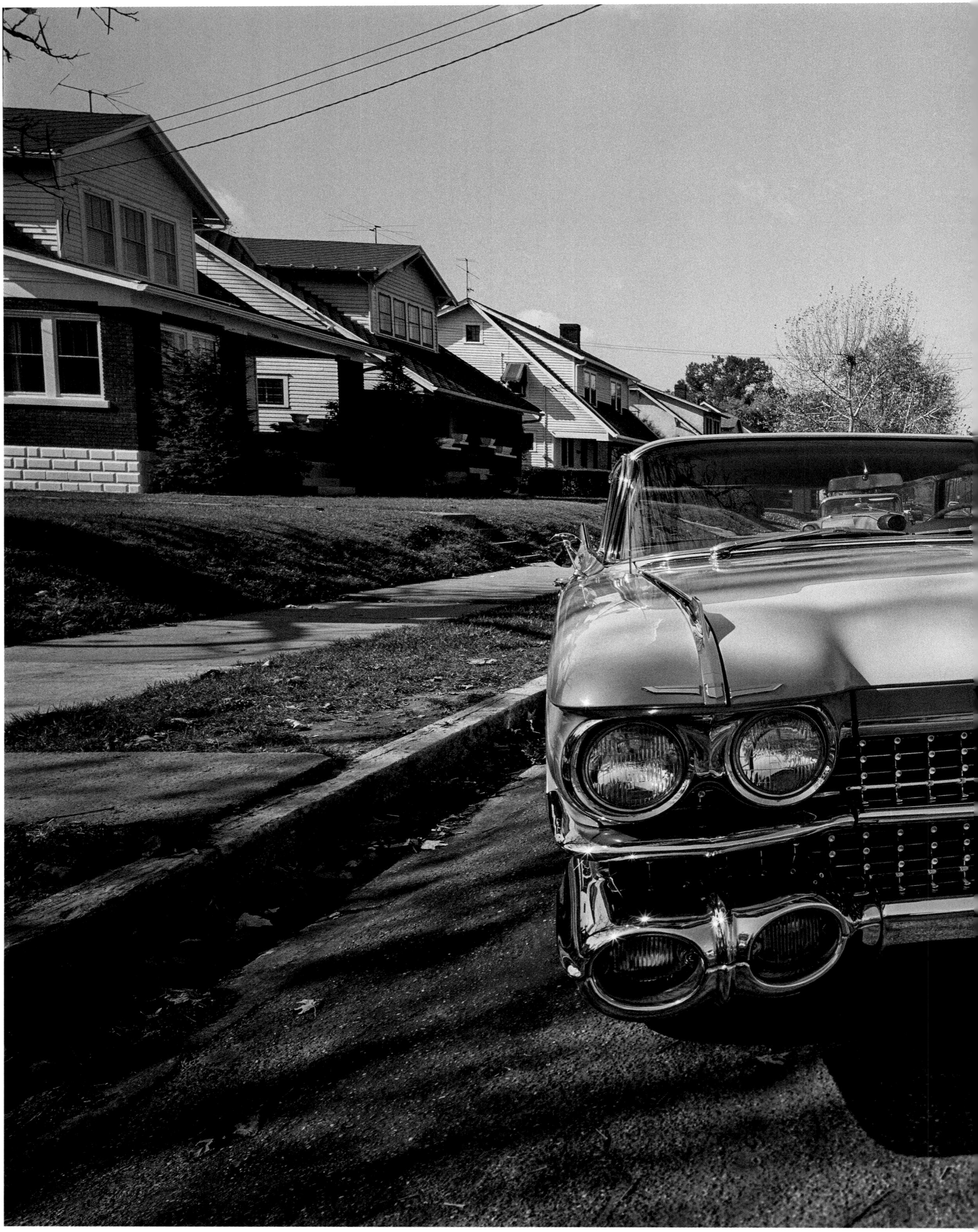

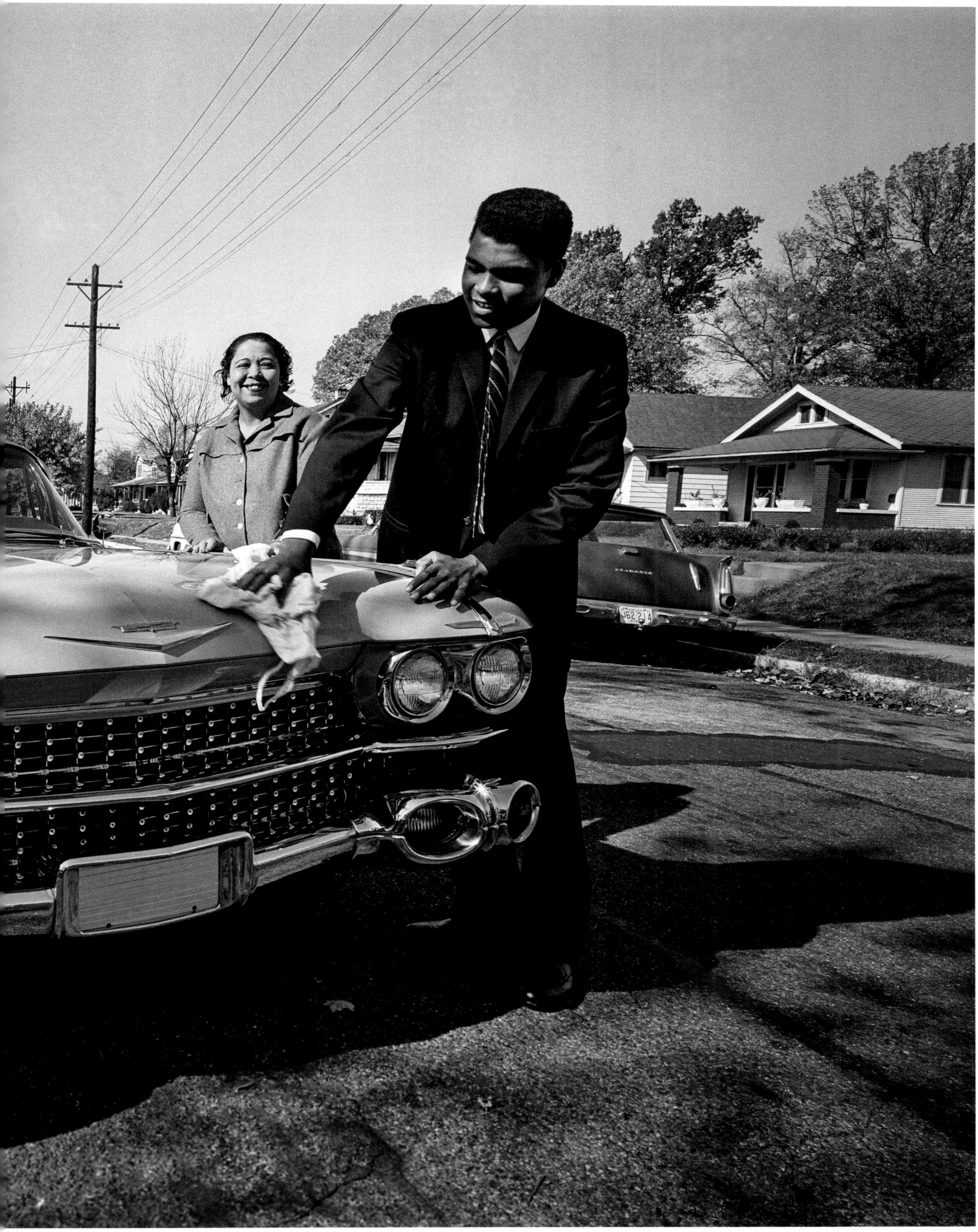

"I'M YOUNG, I'M HANDSOME, I'M FAST. I CAN'T POSSIBLY BE BEAT."

16 —

Page 12–13

Gean A. Baron
Cassius Clay shows off a new pink Cadillac to his mother Odessa Clay, left. He bought the automobile for his parents following his first professional fight.

November 1, 1960

It begins with a bicycle. The 12-year-old Cassius Clay parked his red and white Schwinn outside the Columbia Auditorium in October, 1954, went inside to attend a bazaar, and came back to discover his bike had been stolen.

Directed to a policeman who was training boxers in the basement, the young boy tearfully vowed to "whup" the perpetrator. Officer Joe Martin, destiny's instrument, told him he needed to learn how.

The child who would become a global celebrity and a political cause as Muhammad Ali found his path and his purpose in that chance meeting.

Physically blessed and exceedingly brash, the young Ali reminded his mother of a March wind, "blowing every which way." Boxing brought him direction, structure and, soon, success. It focused his energies, filled his days, tapped his deep reservoir of athletic talent and provided a platform conducive to an era's most ebullient personality.

"He stood out because, I guess, he had more determination than most boys, and he had the speed to get him someplace," Martin told Ali biographer Thomas Hauser. "He was a kid willing to make the sacrifices necessary to achieve something worthwhile in sports. I realized it was almost impossible to discourage him. He was easily the hardest worker of any kid I ever taught."

He would catch the attention of some of Louisville's most prominent people even before beating Poland's Zbigniew Pietrzykowski for the light heavyweight gold medal at the 1960 Rome Olympics.

According to a 1963 account published in Sports Illustrated, the idea for the Louisville Sponsoring Group developed during a bridge game at the home of investment counselor William Faversham, once a sparring partner of the actor Spencer Tracy.

Three days before he made his professional debut at Freedom Hall on Oct. 29, 1960, Cassius Clay signed a managerial contract with 11 investors who paid him a $10,000 signing bonus, guaranteed him a monthly income against earnings and eased his tax burden by deferring a portion of his income for retirement.

This was 40 months before Clay would fight Sonny Liston for the heavyweight title. It did not take much foresight, though, to see he was bound for bigger things.

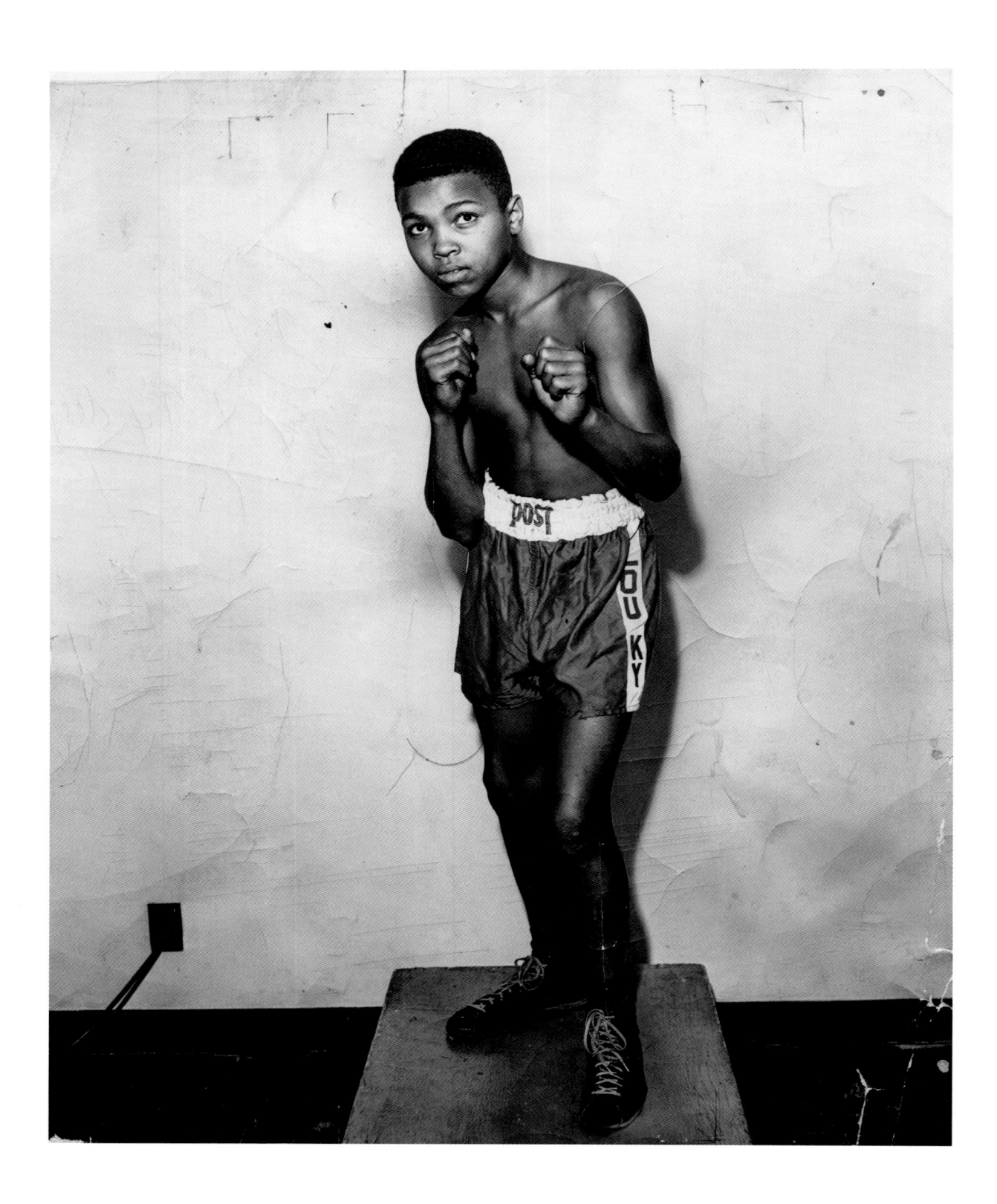

1 Charley Pence
This is the first known photo taken of Muhammad Ali, who was then known as Cassius Clay. It shows the flyweight before his fight against Ronnie O'Keefe on the WAVE-TV amateur boxing program, "Tomorrow's Champions.

November 11, 1954

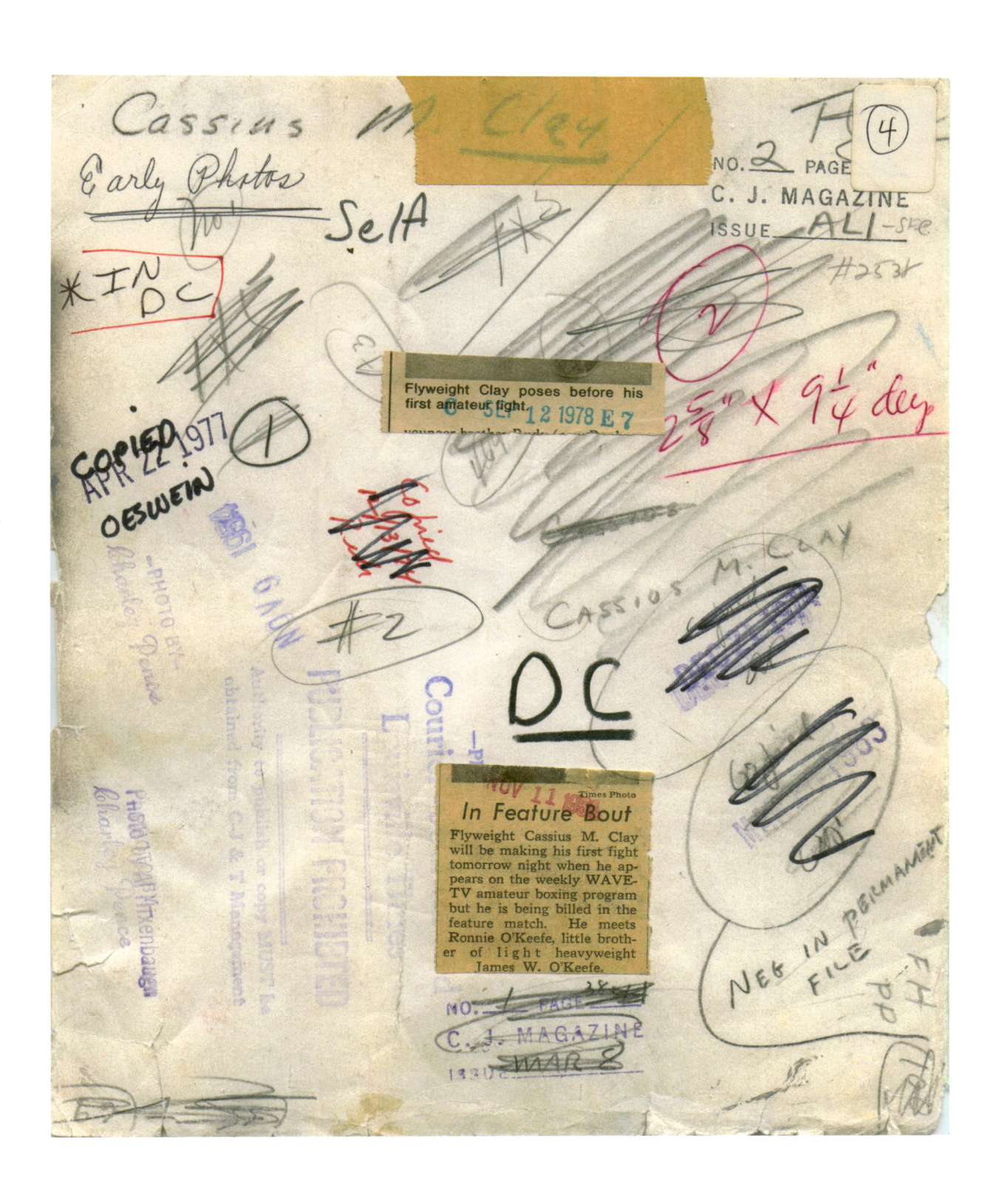

1
The back of the photo at left, from the original print in the Courier Journal archives, shows the multiple times the photo was used in the newspaper.

20

↑ **Courier Journal Archive**
Golden Gloves boxing winner Cassius Clay beams as referee Don Asbury held up his hand in victory.

February 5, 1957

→ **Gean Baron**
Young boxers weigh in for a Golden Gloves tournament. Dr. F. Albert Olash checks Newman Cosby's blood pressure, while Dave Striegal, left, and Clay look on.

Janaury 15, 1957

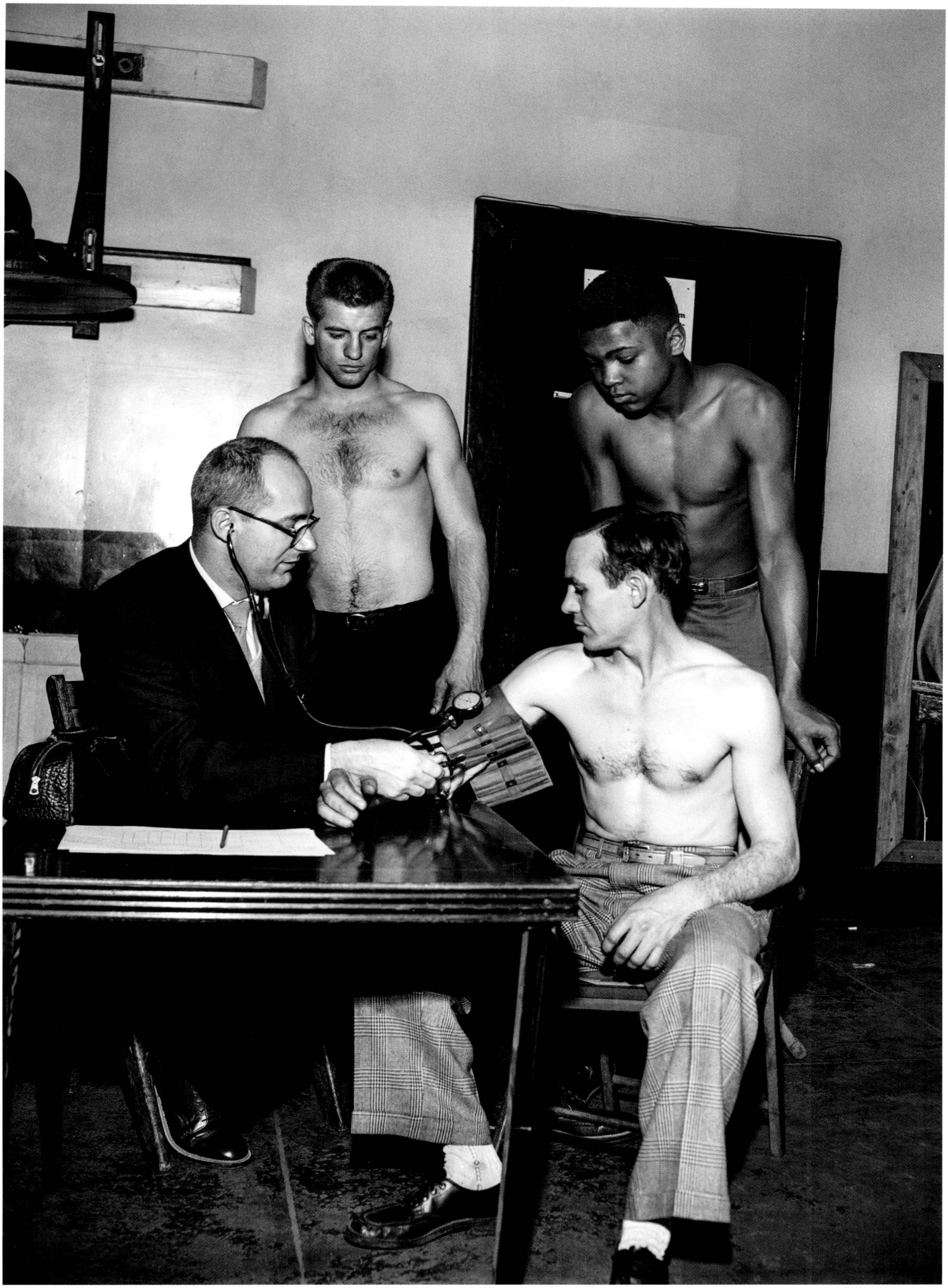

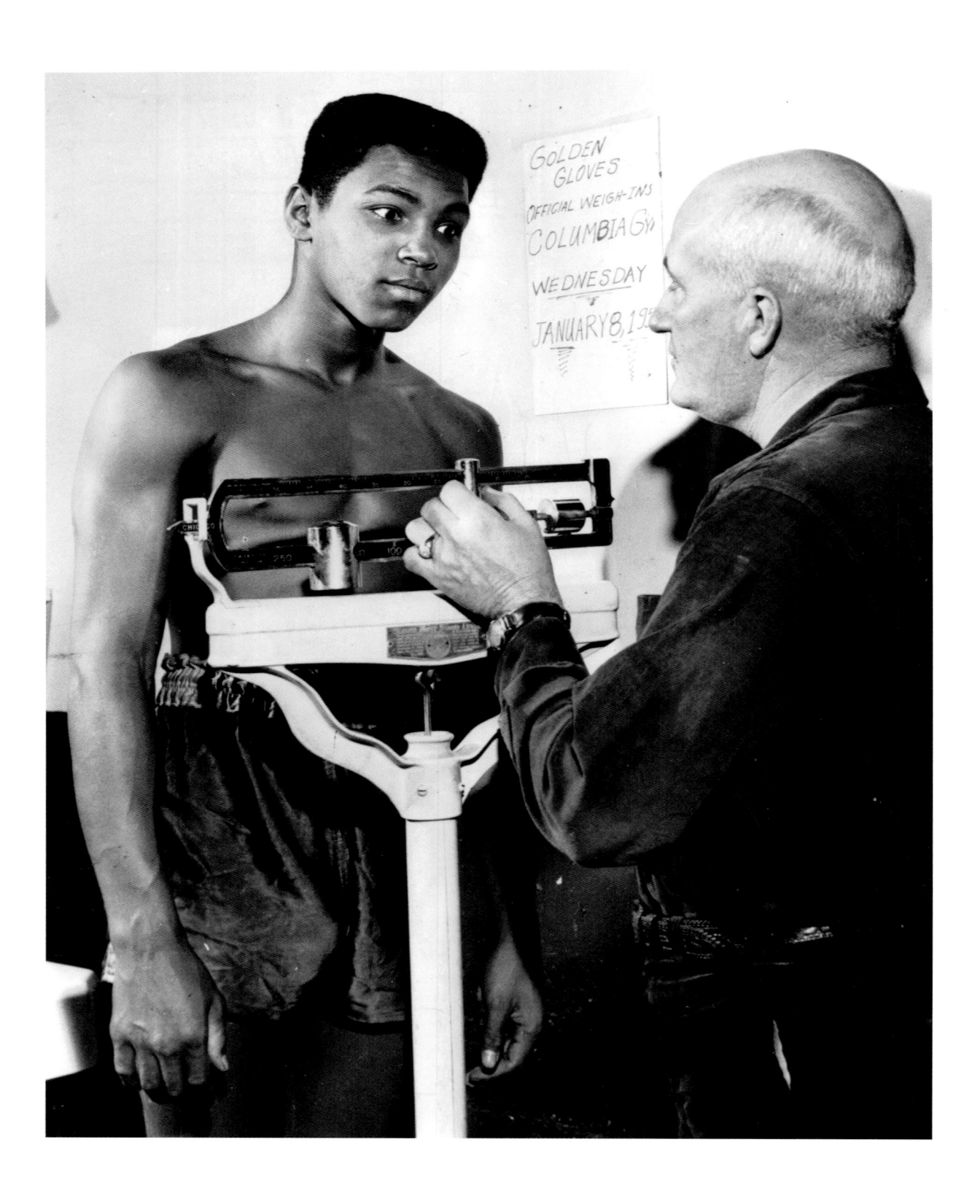

1 Tom Easterling
Louisville police officer Joe Martin, director of youth boxing, with a young Cassius Clay. Martin became Clay's mentor, getting him involved in boxing.

January 8, 1959

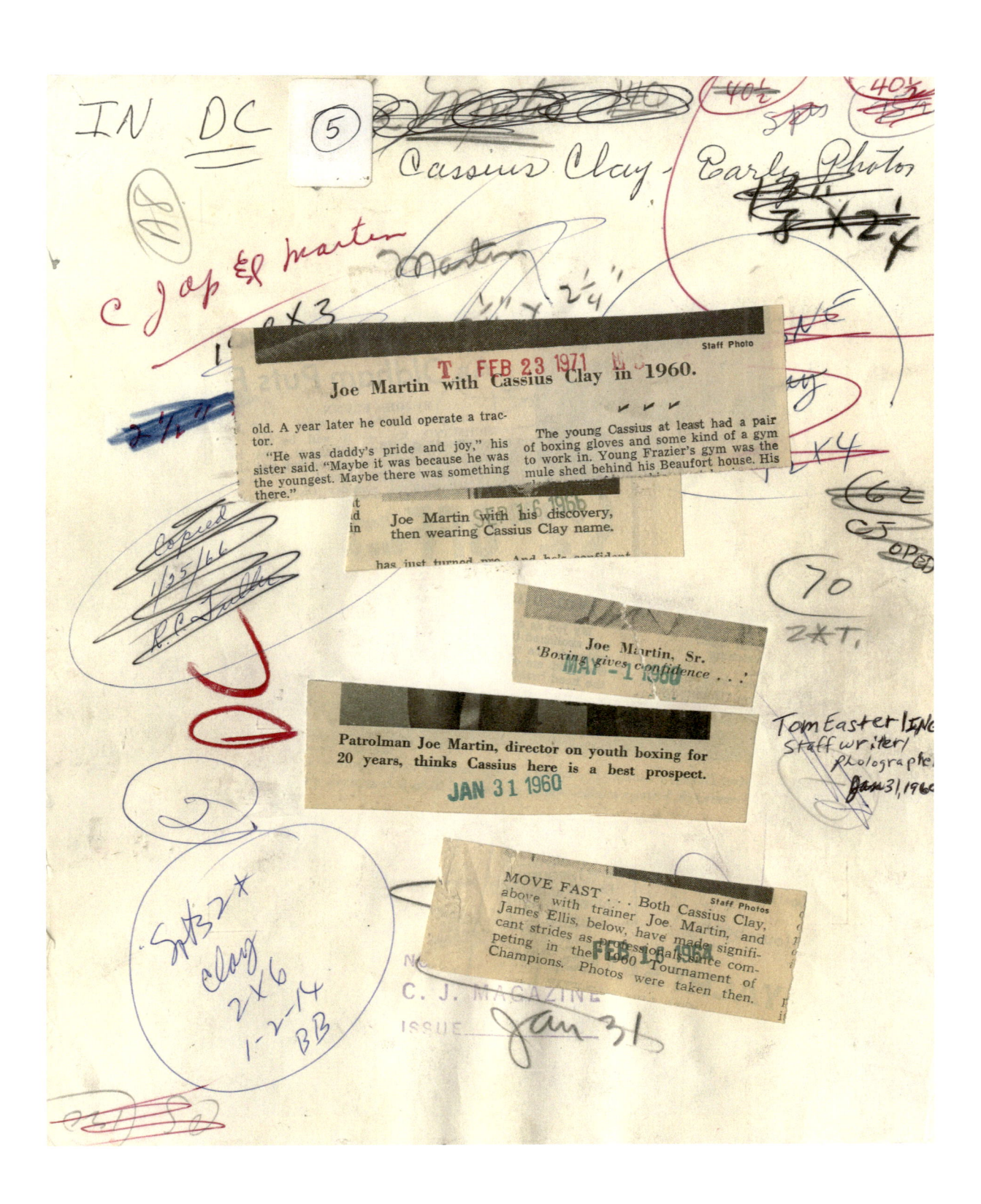

1
The back of the photo at left, from the original print in the Courier Journal archives.

→ **Courier Journal Archive**
Policeman and mentor Joe Martin inspects Clay's Golden Gloves ring.

1959

24 —

25

1 Charles Fentress Jr.
The family of 18-year old Boxing champion Cassius Clay Jr. gathers around him at Standiford Field to admire the gold medal he won at the Olympics in Rome. At left is brother Rudolph, age 17, and at right are his parents, Cassius and Odessa Clay.

September 9, 1960

↑ Thomas V. Miller
Clay works out on a punching bag at Bruner's Headline Gym.

October 5, 1960

→ Warren Klosterman
Clay trains for his first professional fight against Tunney Hunsaker.

October 10, 1960

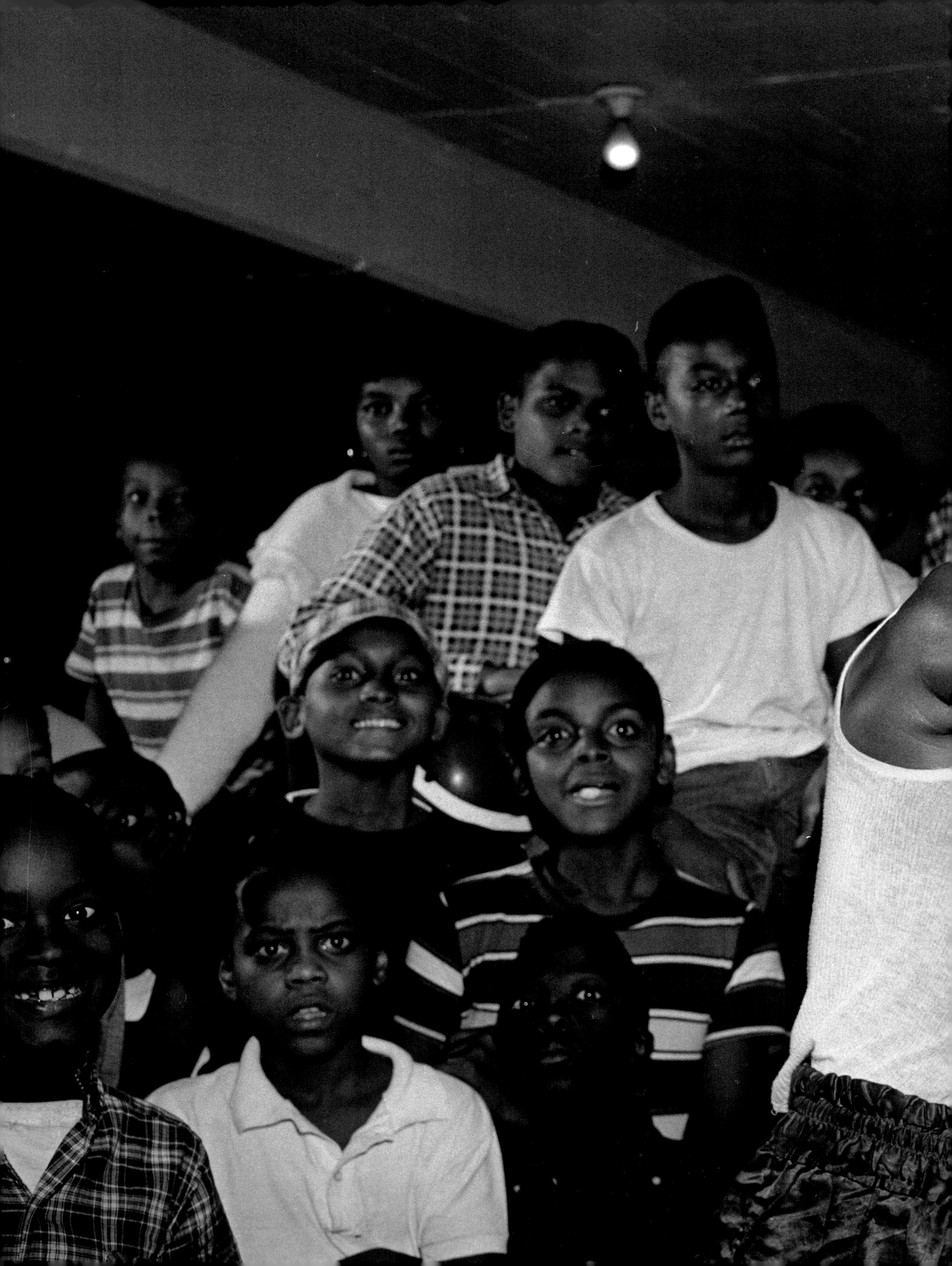

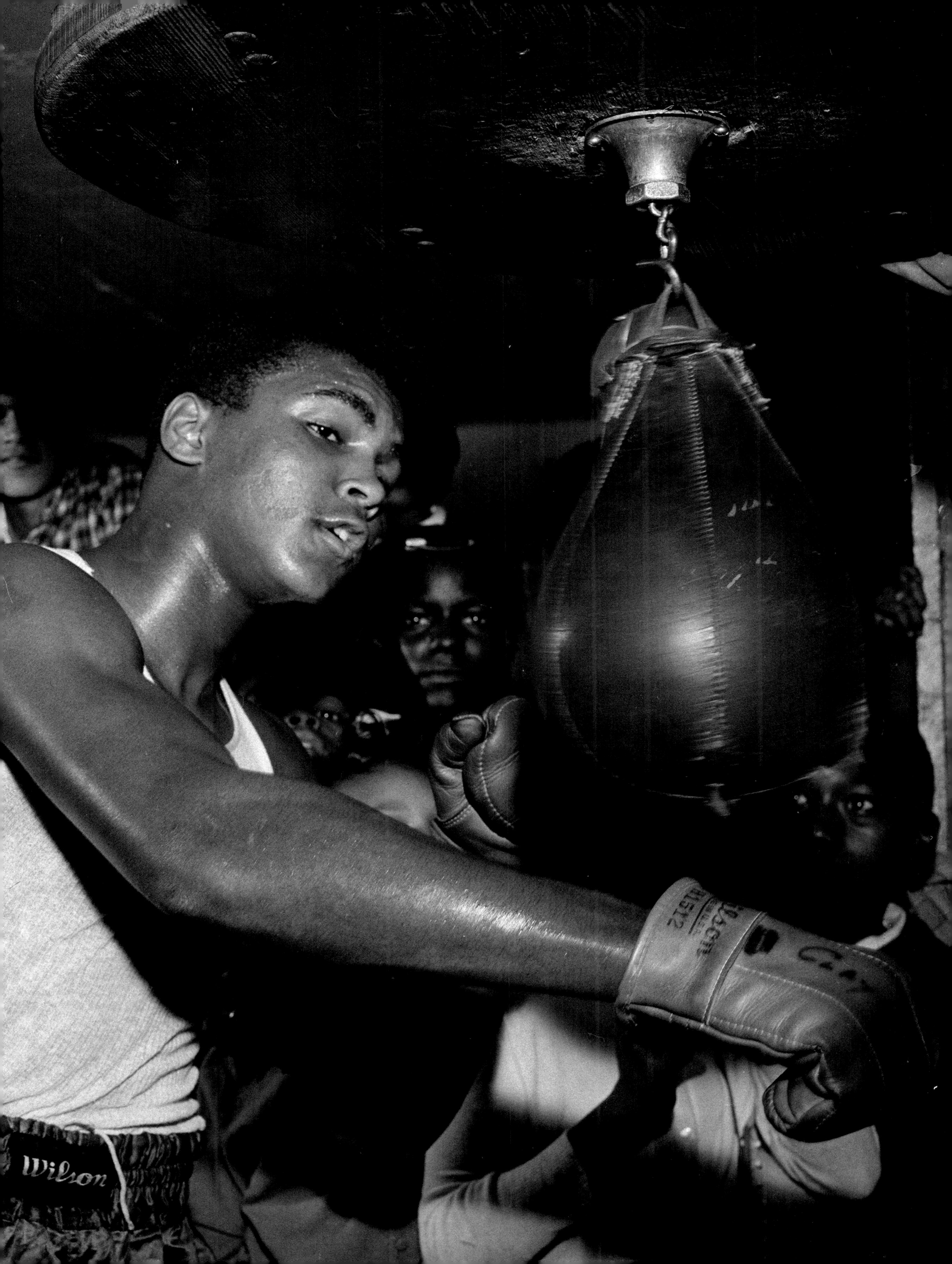
Wilson

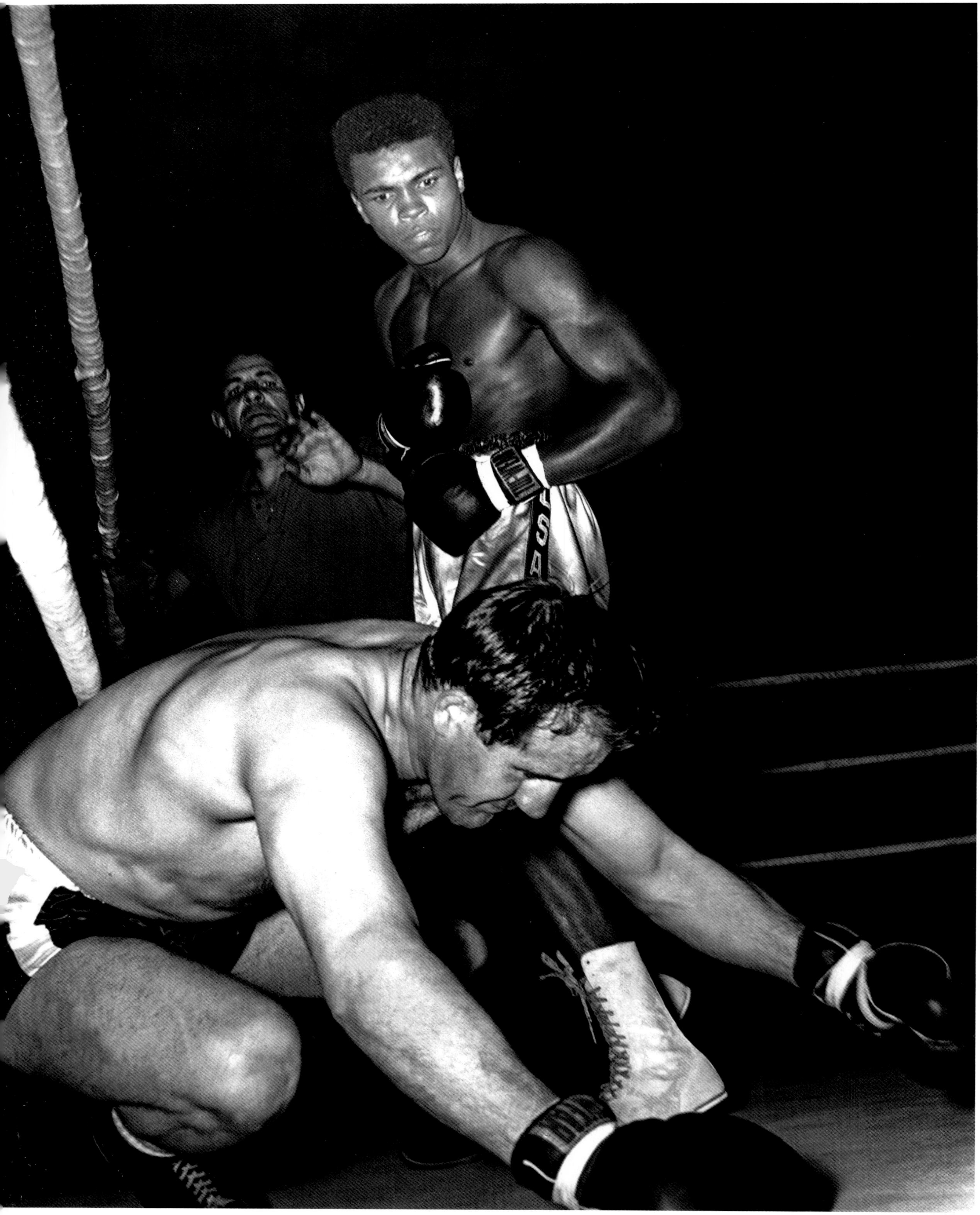

← **Robert Steinau**
Cassius Clay and referee Don Asbury watch as LaMar Clark sank to the canvas for the second time in the first round of their heavyweight fight at Louisville's Freedom Hall. Clay went on to knock out Clark in the second round of the eight-round match.

April 19, 1961

↑ **Warren Klosterman**
Clay, right, in his first professional bout with Tunney Hunsaker, left, at Freedom Hall in Louisville. Hunsaker was the chief of police in Fayetteville, West Virginia. Hunsaker had this to say following the fight: "Clay was as fast as lighting. I tried every trick I knew to throw him off balance, but he was just too good."

October 30, 1960

"Braggin' is when a person says something and can't back it up. I do what I say."

→ Courier Journal Archive
Cassius Clay, left, and Angelo Dundee discuss a document that Dundee was typing. Dundee trained the heavyweight champion during his professional boxing career.

October 10, 1961

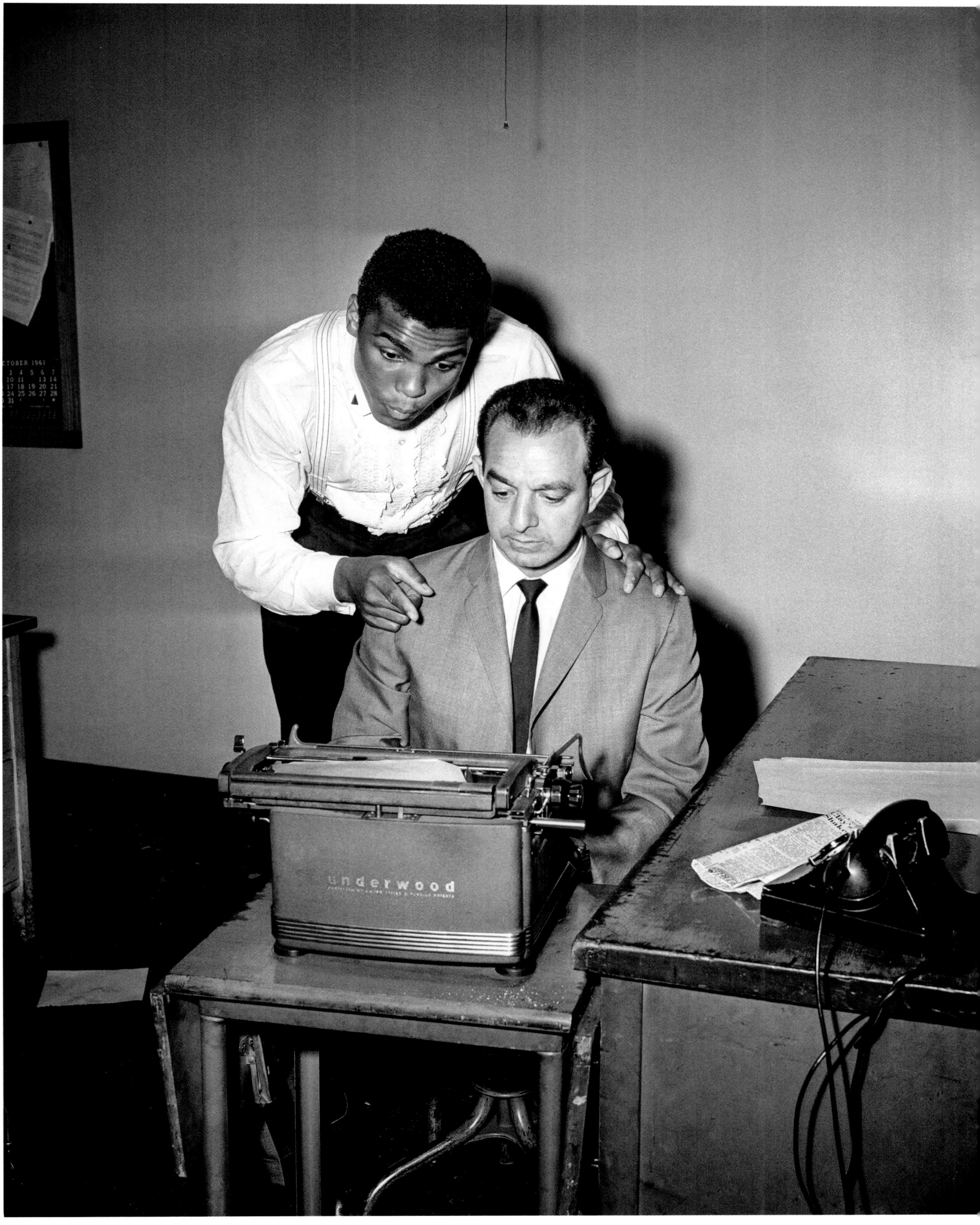
underwood

1 Robert Steinau
Trainer Angelo Dundee, right, and Jimmy Ellis, center, watch as Cassius Clay works out in Louisville.

April 15, 1961

— 35

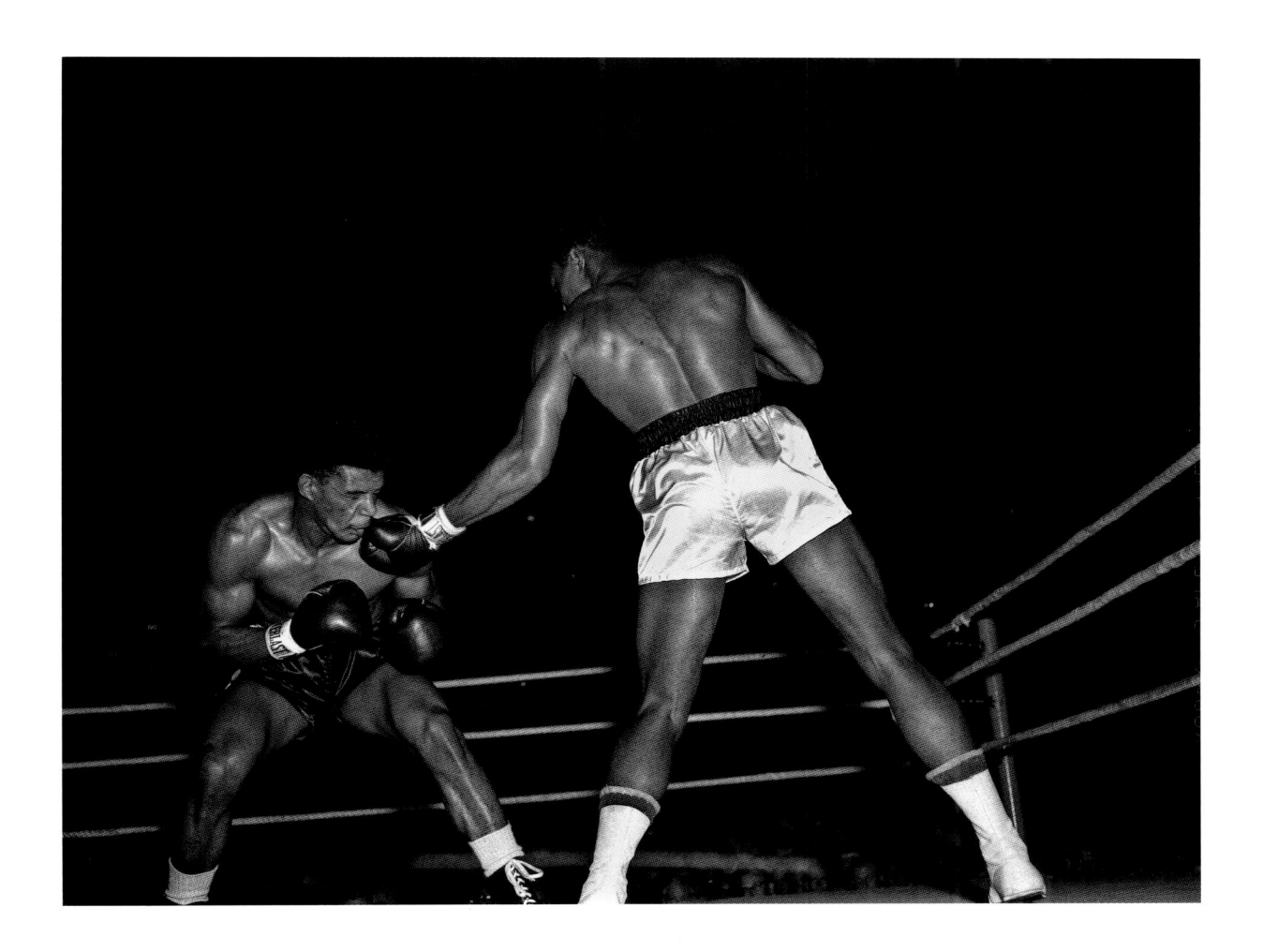

↑ R.C. Fuller
Clay defeats Alonzo Johnson, left, in a 10-round unanimous decision.

July 22, 1961

→ Warren Klosterman
Cassius Clay, left, looks over business documents with William Faversham, who came up with the idea of putting together The Louisville Sponsoring Group, a syndicate of 11 businessmen to back Clay's professional boxing career.

February 28, 1961

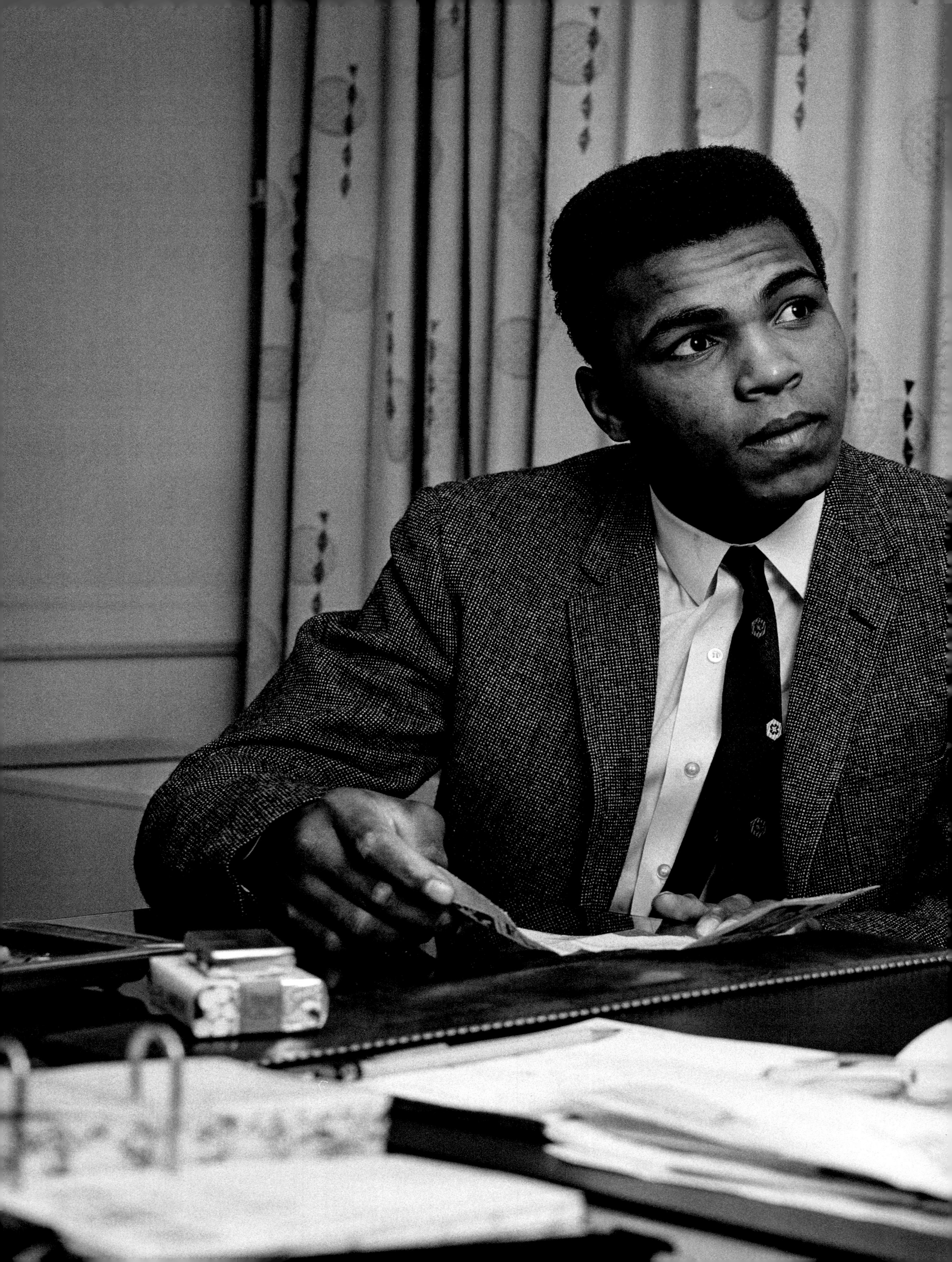

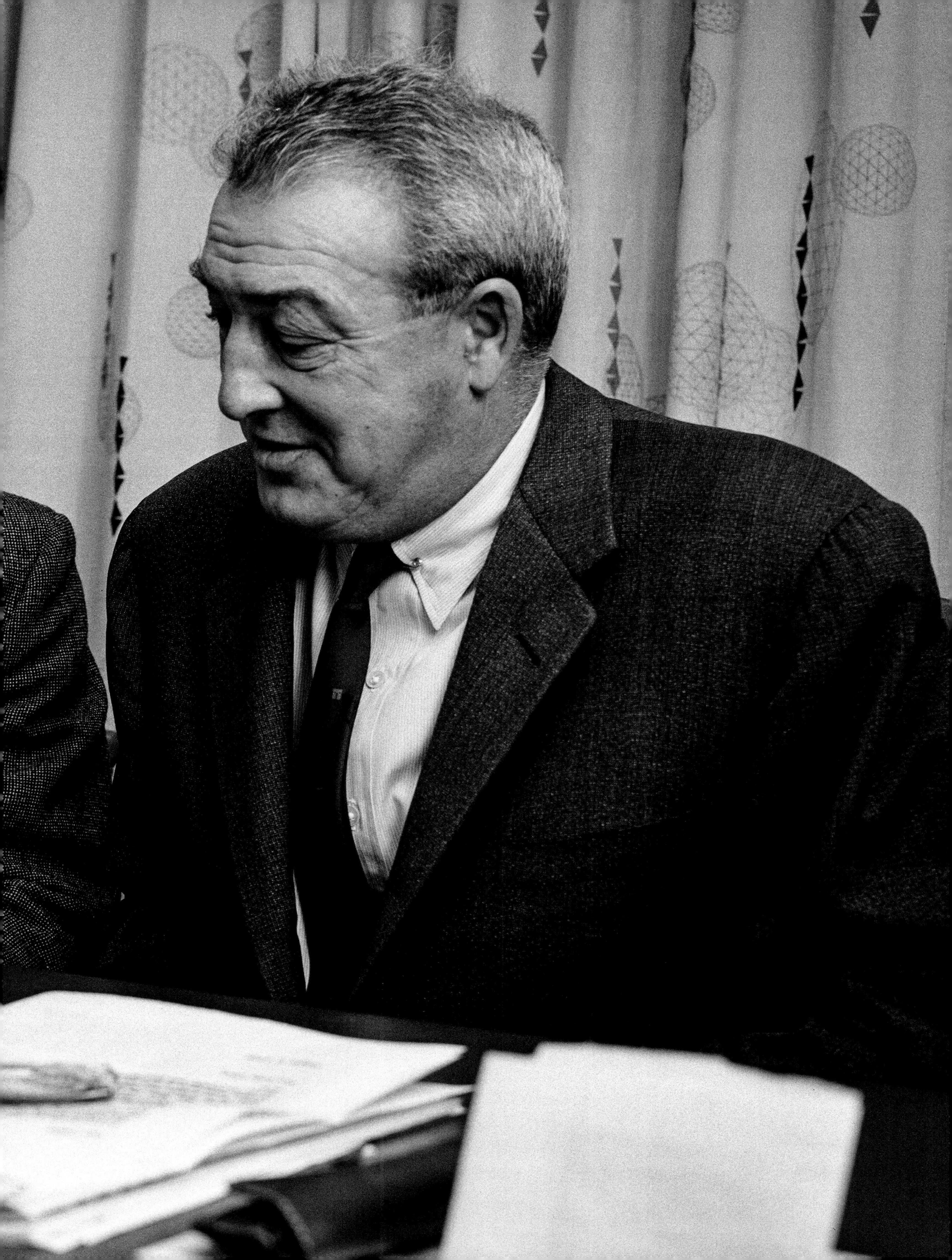

1 Bud Kamenish
Cassius, left, chats with a caller while on the air with WHAS Radio personality Milton Metz.

November 29, 1962.

— 39

1 Bill Strode
Clay shows off his new Cadillac at the corner of 4th Street and Broadway in Louisville.

March 23, 1963

1 Charles Pence
George Chuvalo, left, and Mike DeJohn, right, feel Cassius Clay's muscles before the DeJohn and Chuvalo fight in Louisville.

September 1963

→ Charles Darneal
Clay, foreground, and brother Rudy arrive home last night after a week in New York where he defeated Doug Jones.

1963

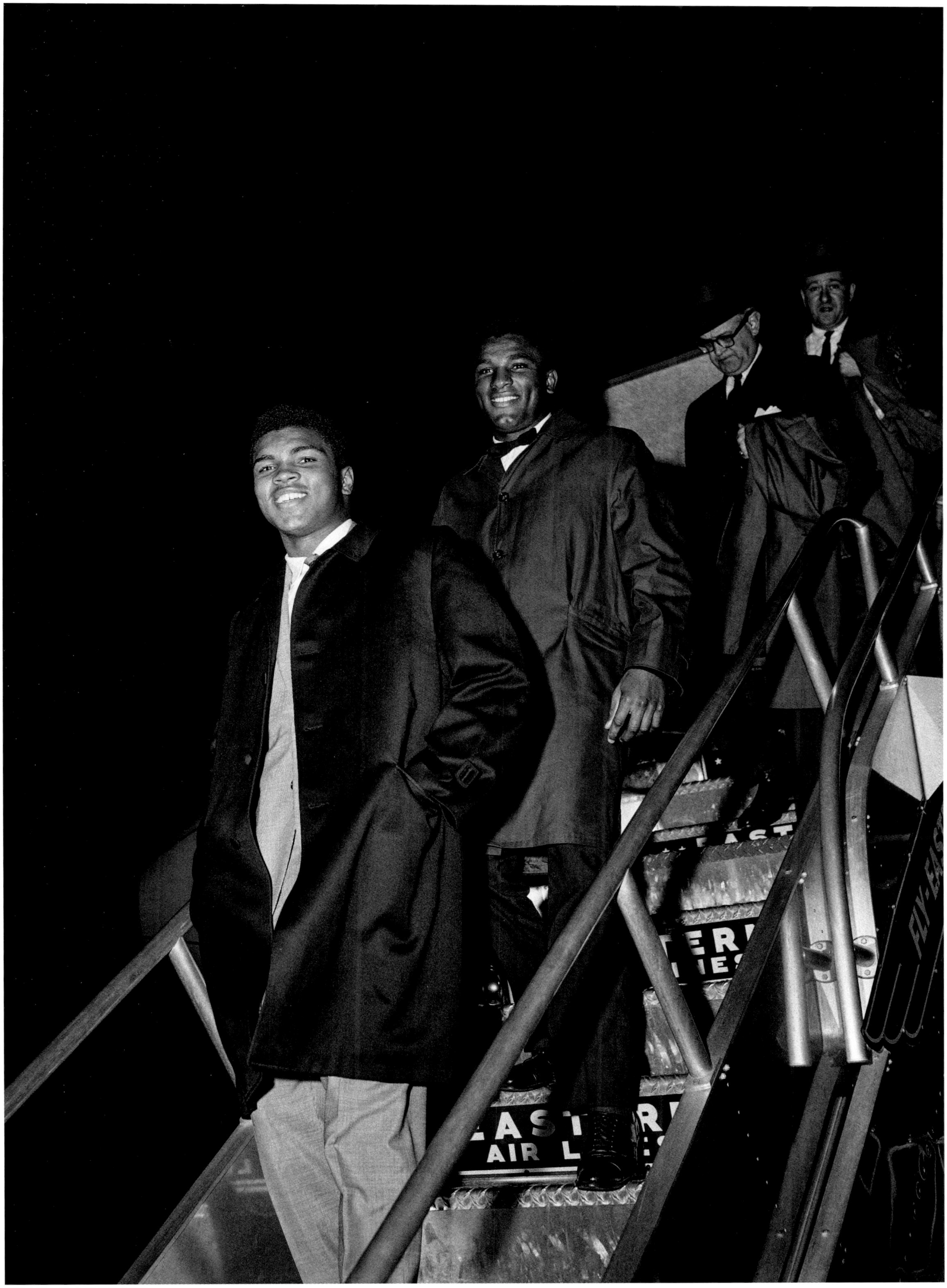

1 Charles Fentress
Cassius Clay, left, and his brother Rudy, right, takes their 99-year-old great-grandmother Betsy Jane Greathouse for a walk.

July 7, 1963

1 R. C. Fuller
Odessa Clay, mother of Cassius Clay, who later became known as Muhammad Ali.

March 21, 1963

1 Courier Journal Archive
An early family photo of Cassius Clay, right, and his brother Rudy.

1 Warren Klosterman
Clay, right, and his brother Rudy stand
outside their parent's new home.

November 21, 1962

→ Bud Kamenish
Clay wears a toy crown on his return to Louisville alongside his
mother Odessa Clay, center, and Cassius Clay Sr., right, after
winning the heavyweight boxing title against Sonny Liston.

March 7, 1964

46

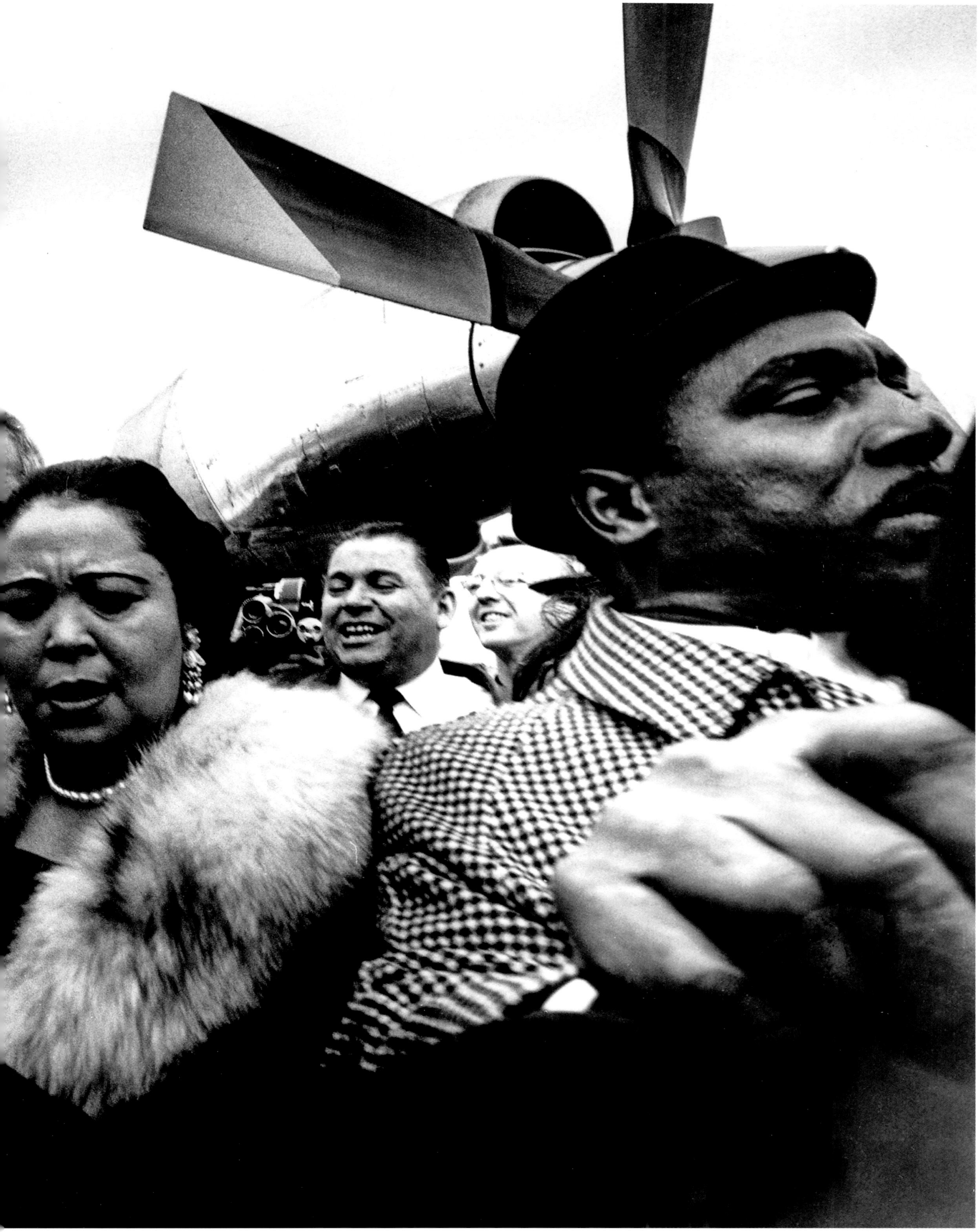

1 Robert Steinau
Neighborhood youngsters, who idolize Cassius Clay, give him a big welcome home with signs they made themselves. From left: John Sheldon Lightsy, age 5; Terrance White, age 9; Rodney Kaufman, age 12; Roosevelt Lightsy, age 12, partially obscured by "Welcome Home" sign; and LeRoy Wright, age 12.

June 26, 1965

1 Bud Kamenish
Clay gave a victory sign as he posed
behind the wheel of his 1963 convertible.

March 29, 1963

1 Robert Steinau
Muhammad Ali, formerly Cassius Clay, had little to say as he arrived at the Selective Service headquarters in Louisville to protest his reclassification as 1-A from his previous draft-exempt 1-Y status.

March 17, 1966

↑ Robert Steinau
Ali shakes hands with a supporter outside the Selective Service headquarters in Louisville.

March 17, 1966

→ Thomas Hardin.
Ali signs a cast for a young boy during a visit to the Louisville's Children's Hospital.

October 26, 1966

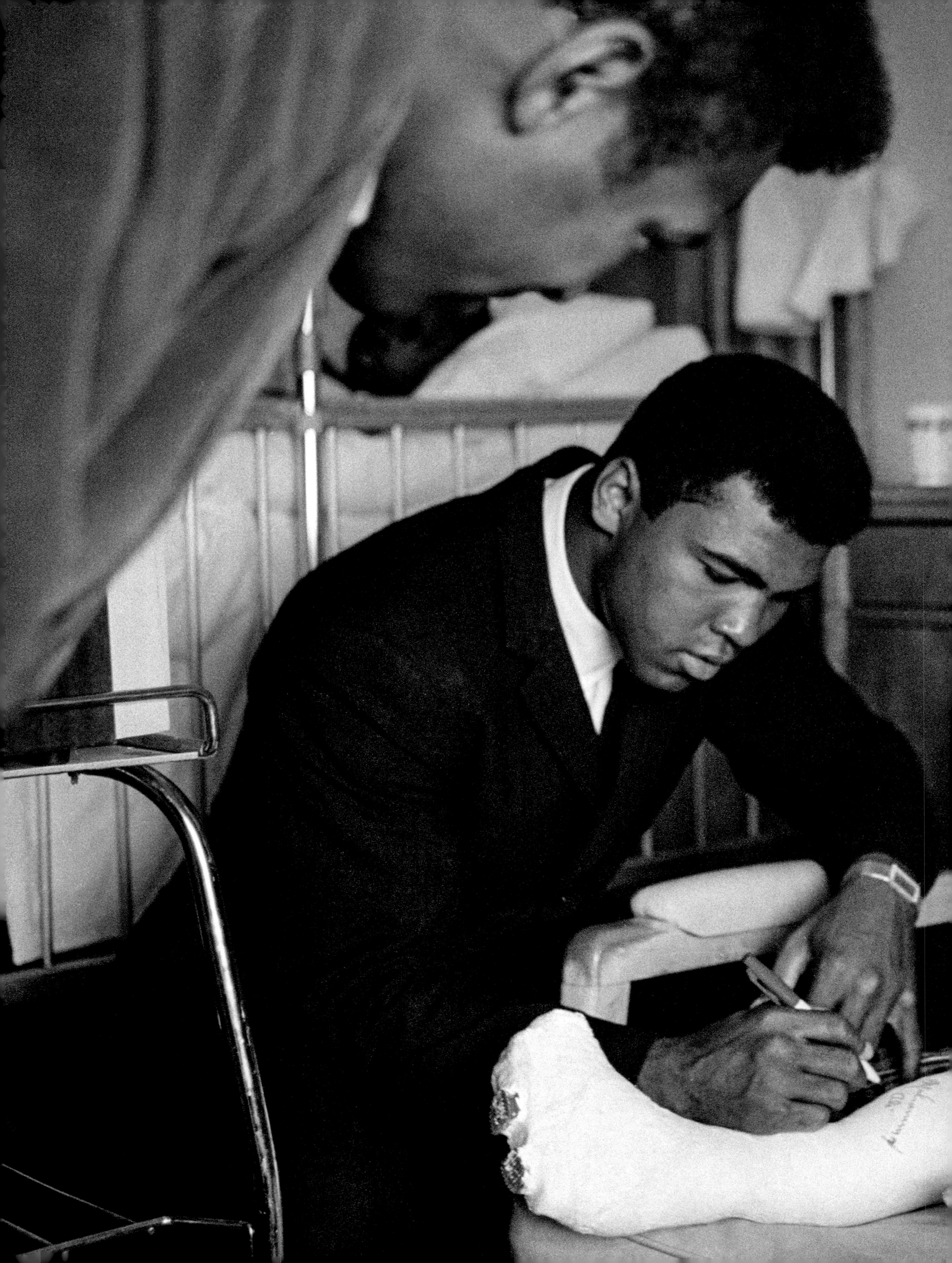

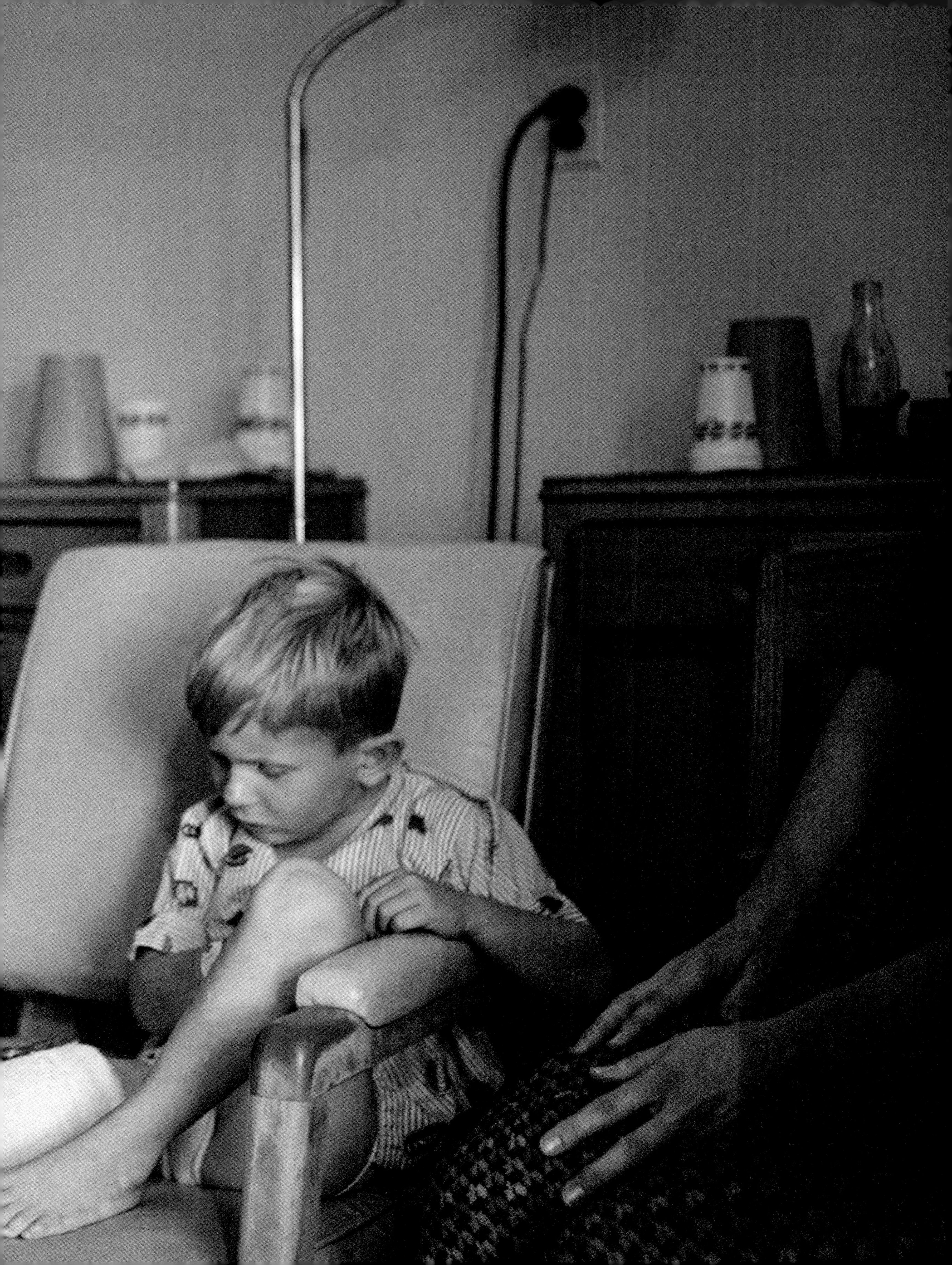

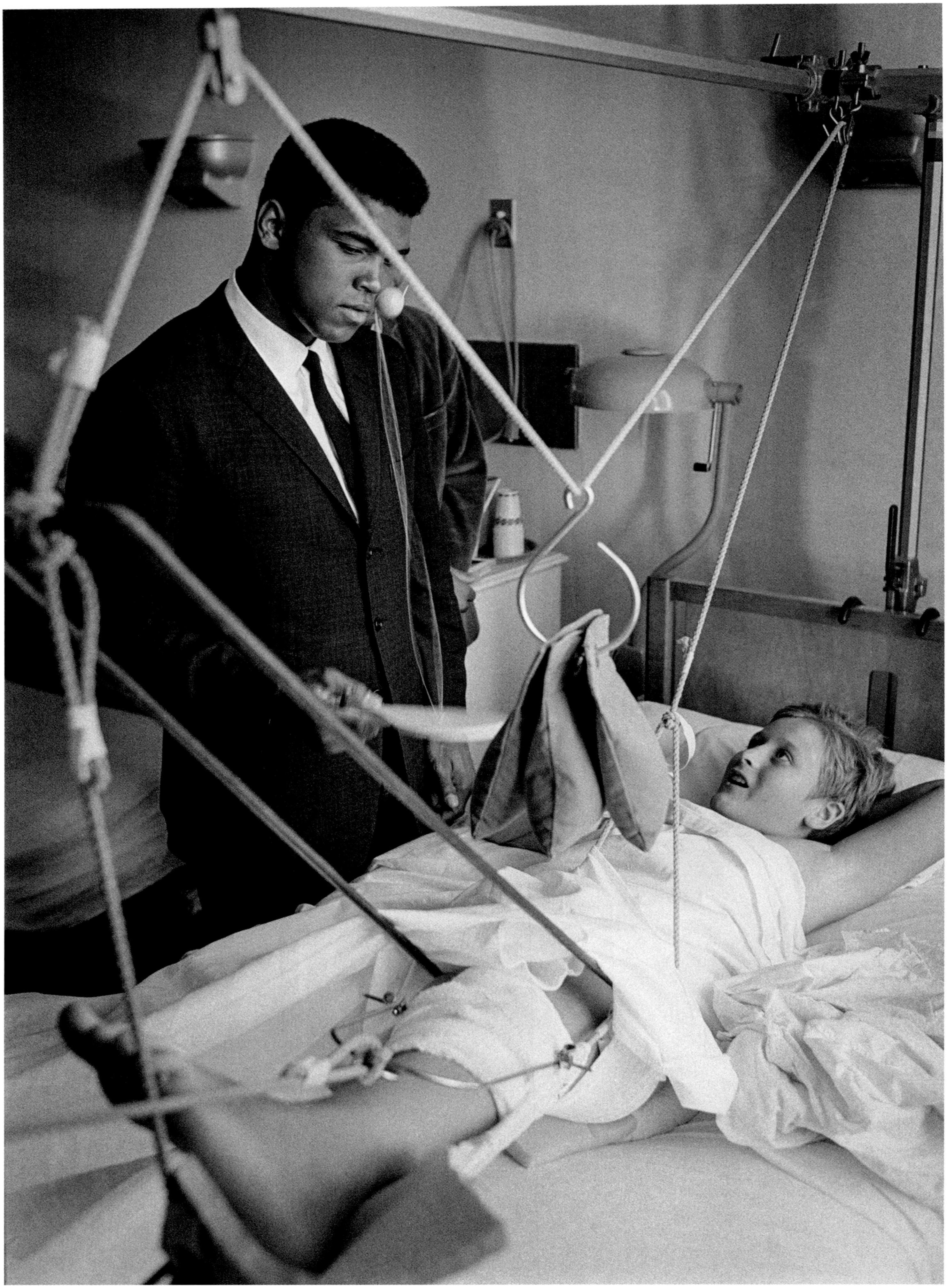

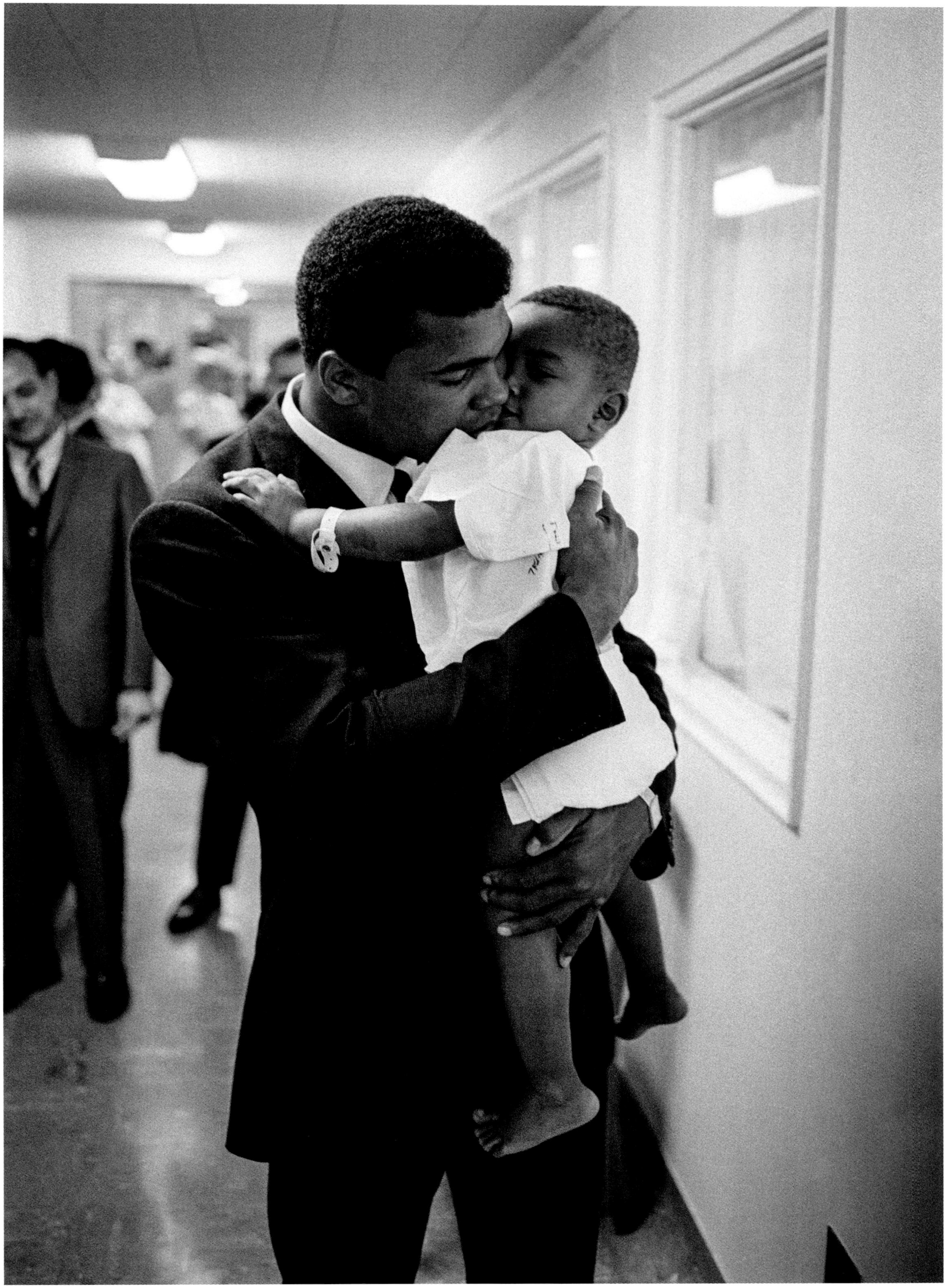

← C. Thomas Hardin
Left : Muhammad Ali entertains a young
boy with a paddle ball while visiting
Louisville's Children's Hospital.

Right : Ali gives a hug and a kiss to
Mike Abell, 22 months, during a visit to
Louisville's Children's Hospital.

October 26, 1966

↑ Thomas V. Miller
Heavyweight champion Ali, left, confers with Dr.
Martin Luther King, right. Ali was in court to try and
stop his induction into the Army.

March 3, 1967

1 Charles Fentress
Muhammad Ali spoke in support
of open housing legislation
during a rally in Louisville.

March 29, 1967

→ Charles Fentress
Ali spoke in support of open housing
legislation during a rally in Louisville.

March 29, 1967

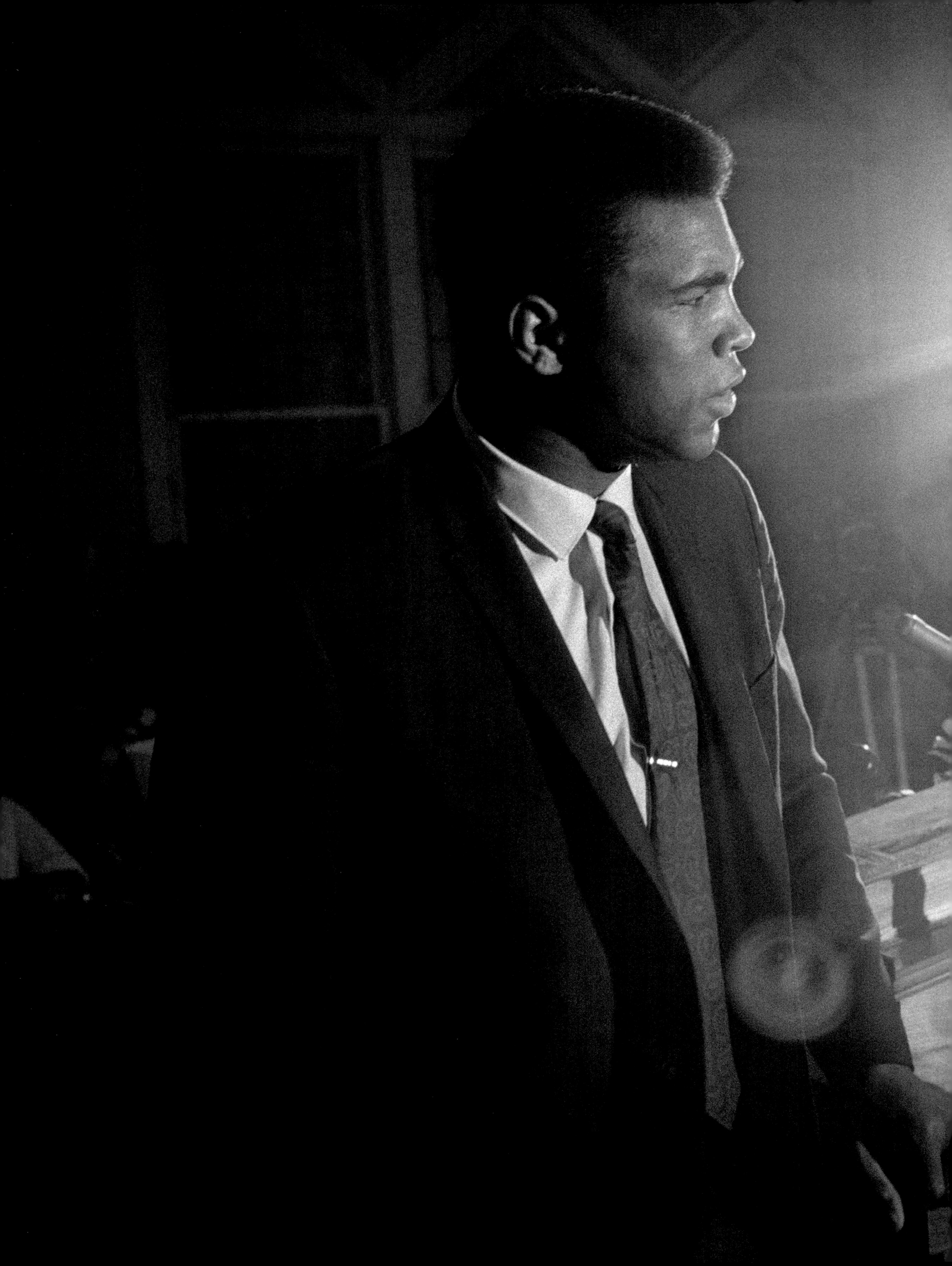

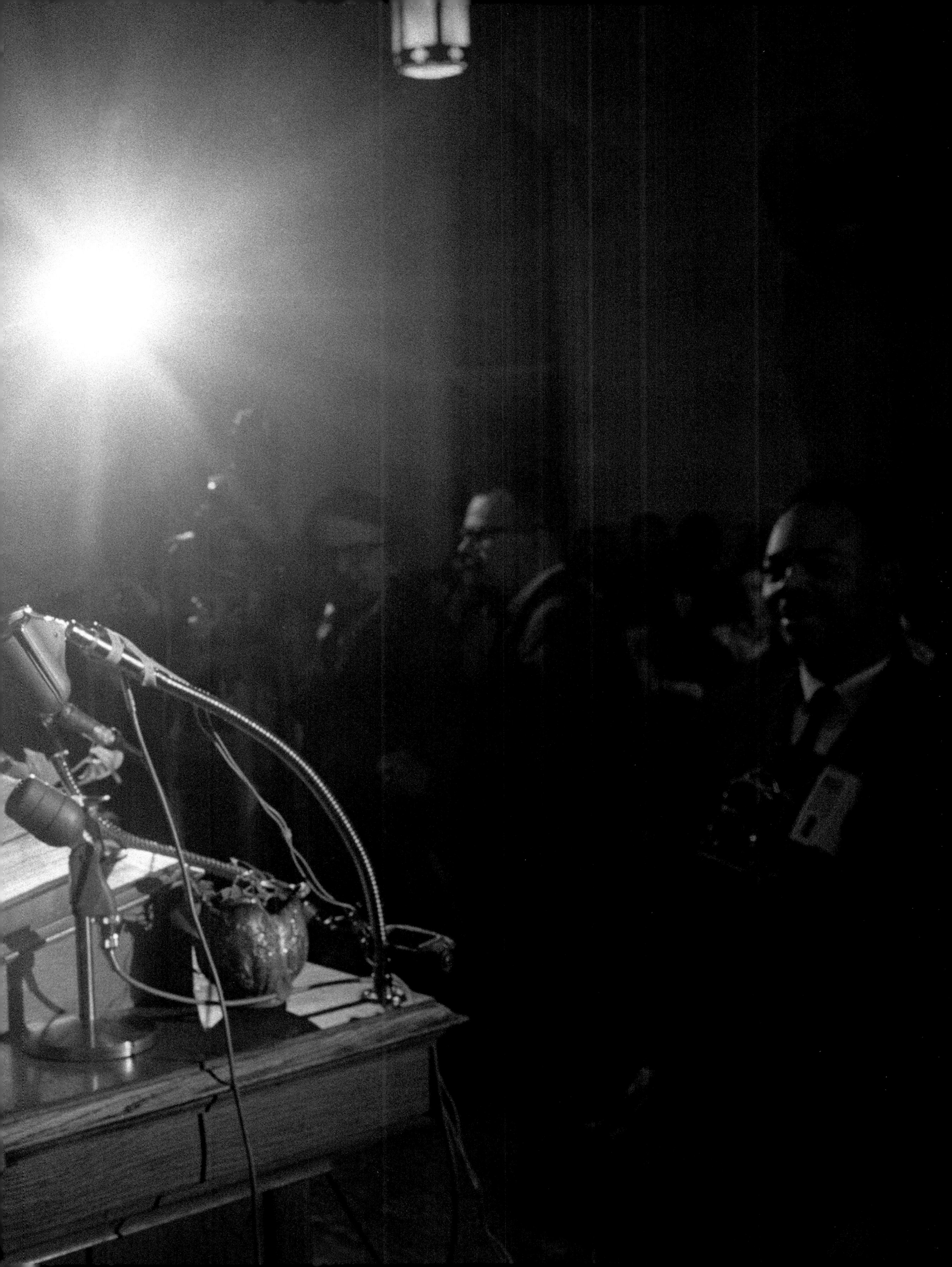

1 Jay Thomas
Muhammad Ali looks through photos during an interview with the Courier Journal.

August 9, 1969

— 61

1 Jay Thomas. 1969.
An intense Ali talks with the Courier Journal about his faith and his refusal to be drafted into the United States Army.

August 9, 1969

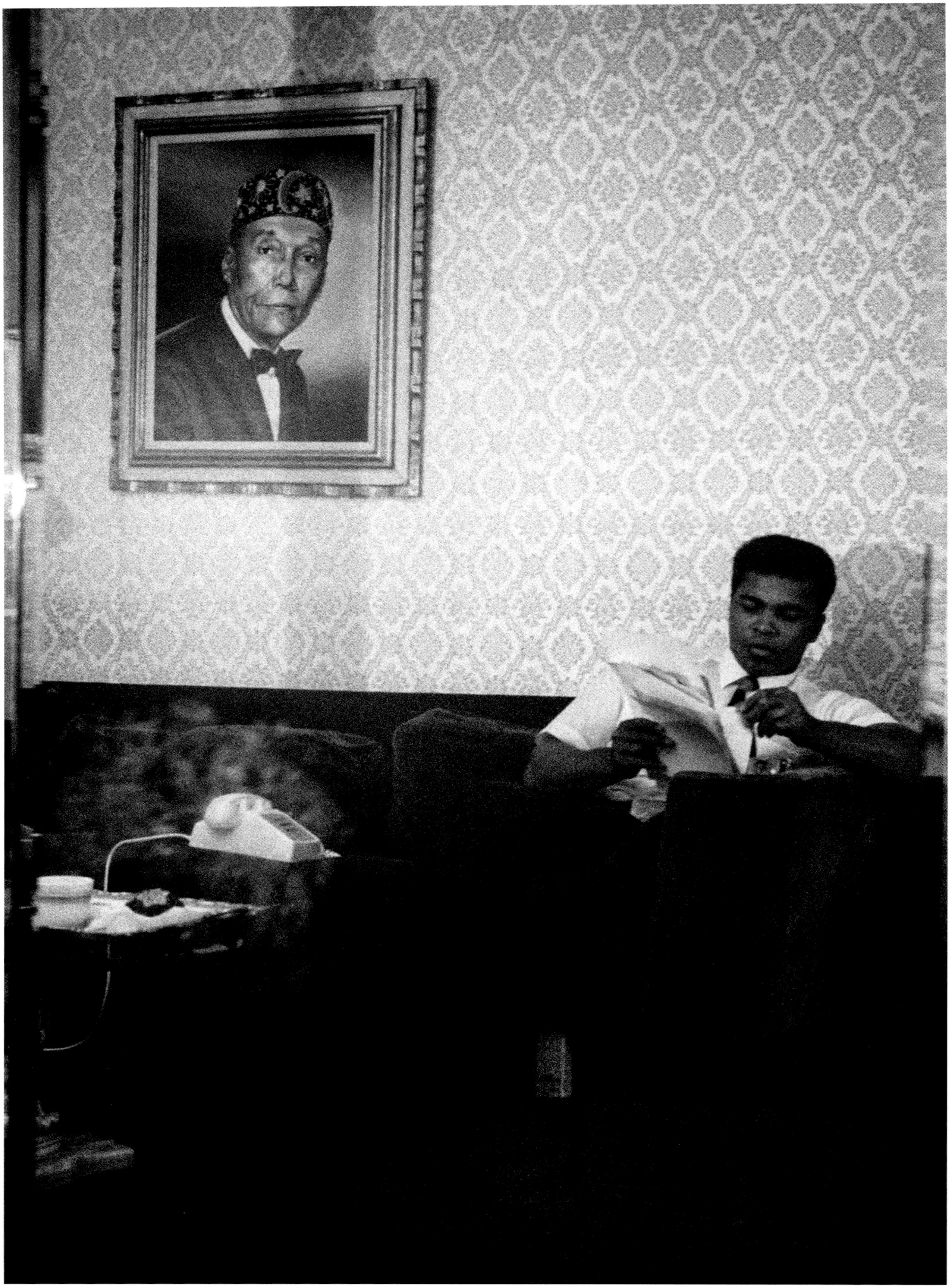

> "The word 'Islam' means 'peace'. The word 'Muslim' means 'one who surrenders to God.' But the press makes us seem like haters."

← Jay Thomas
Muhammad Ali looks through papers on a couch under a painting of Nation of Islam leader Elijah Muhammad.

1969

↑ Jay Thomas
Ali answered questions during an interview with the Courier Journal about the turbulent state of his life.

1969

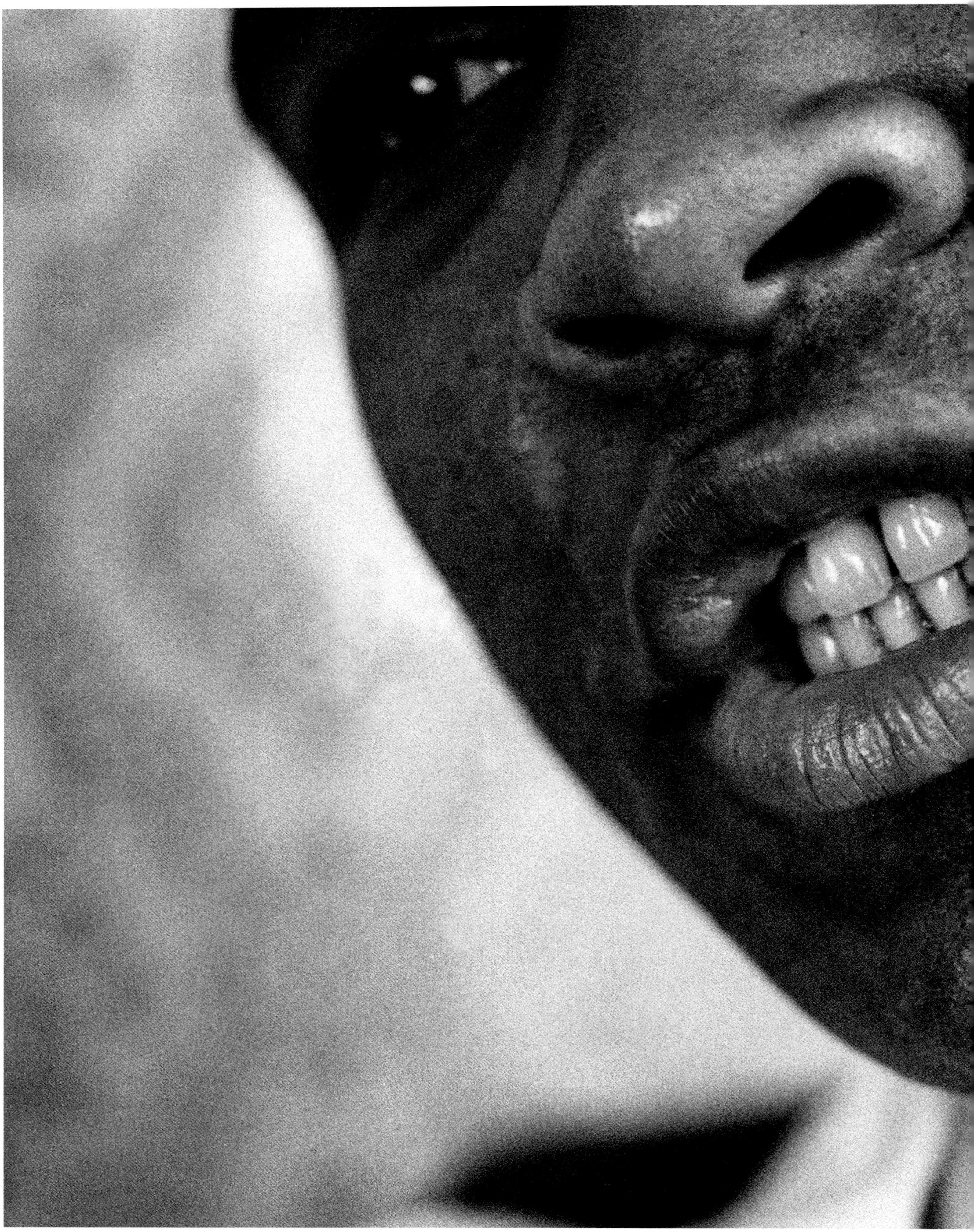

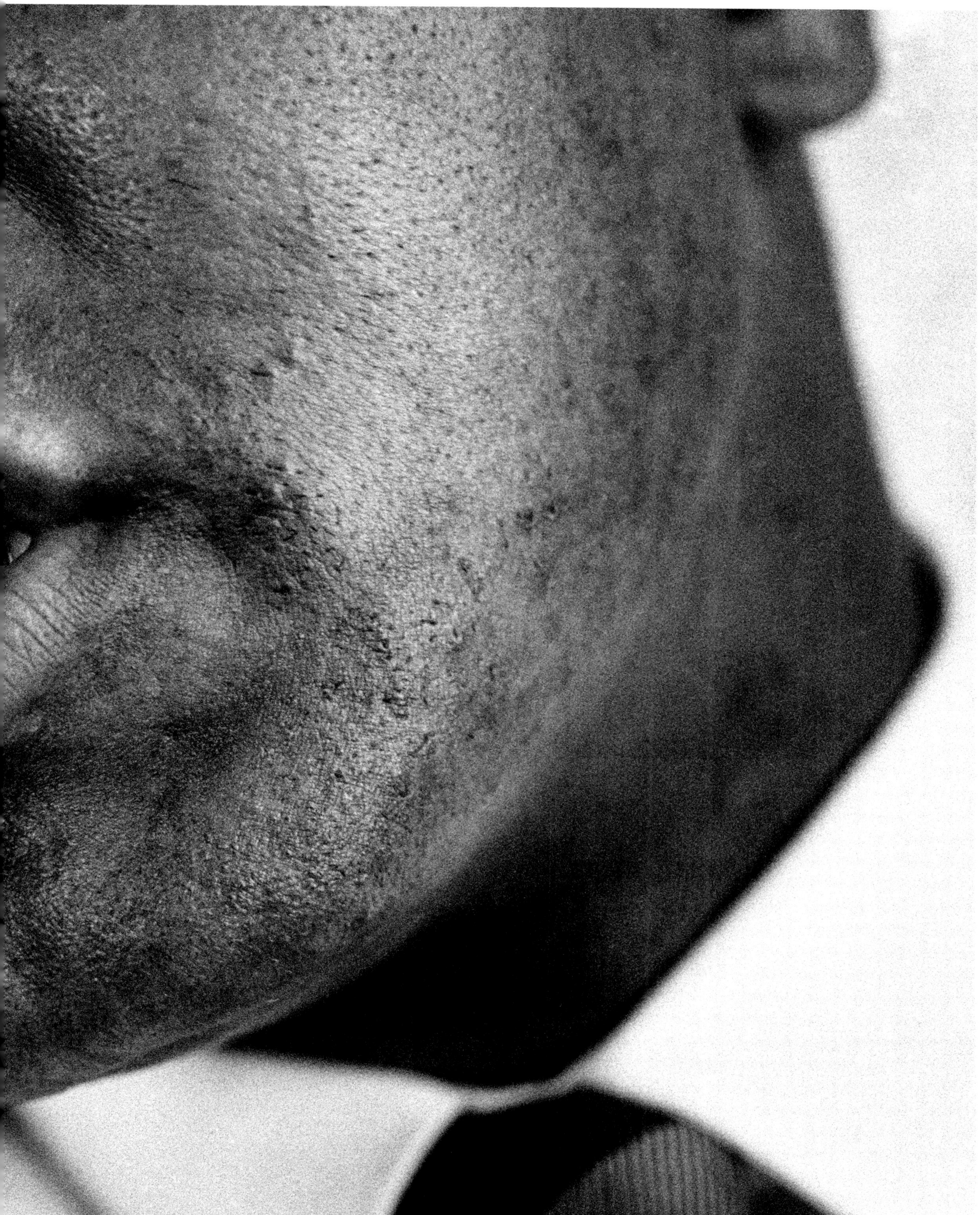

1 C. Thomas Hardin
At home in Pennsylvania, Muhammad Ali enjoys painting when not in the ring.

December 1970

1 C. Thomas Hardin
Ali shows off a painting of a cruise ship at his home in Cherry Hill, N.J.

December 1970

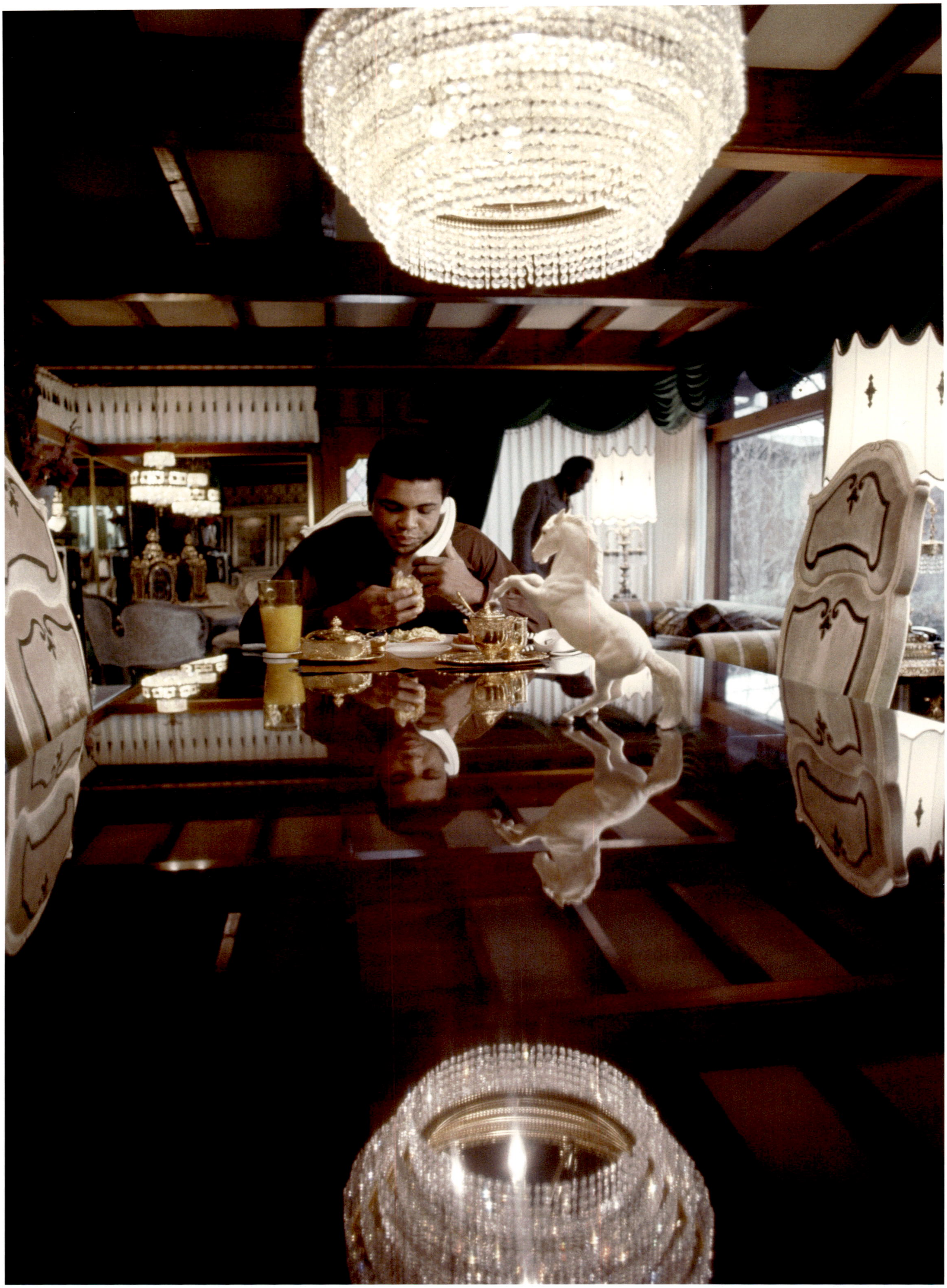

← **C. Thomas Hardin**
Muhammad Ali talks on the phone while eating a meal at his Cherry Hill, N.J. home.

December 1970

↑ **C. Thomas Hardin**
Ali spends time with his twin babies Jamillah and Rasheda at his home in Pennslyvania.

December 1970

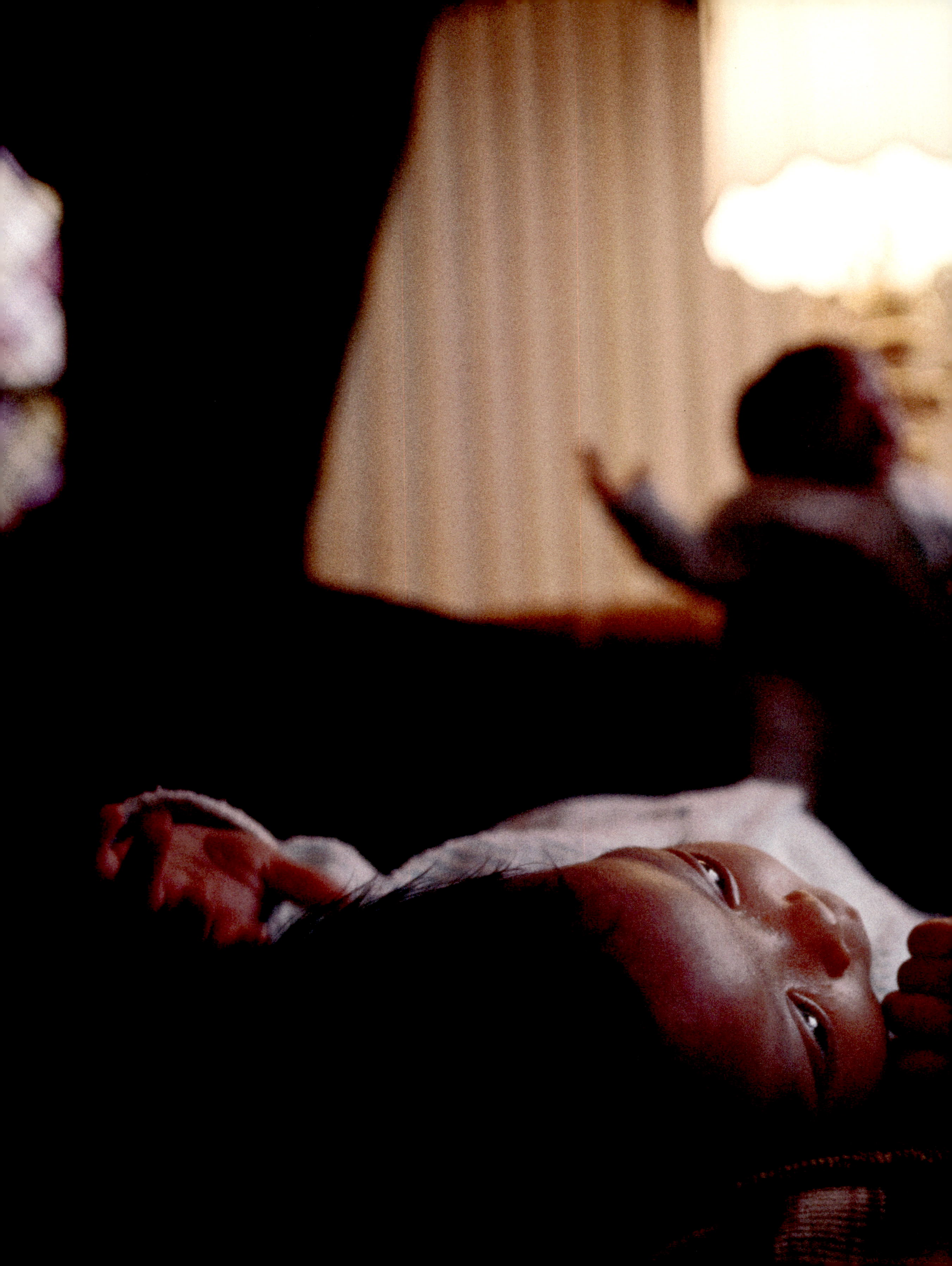

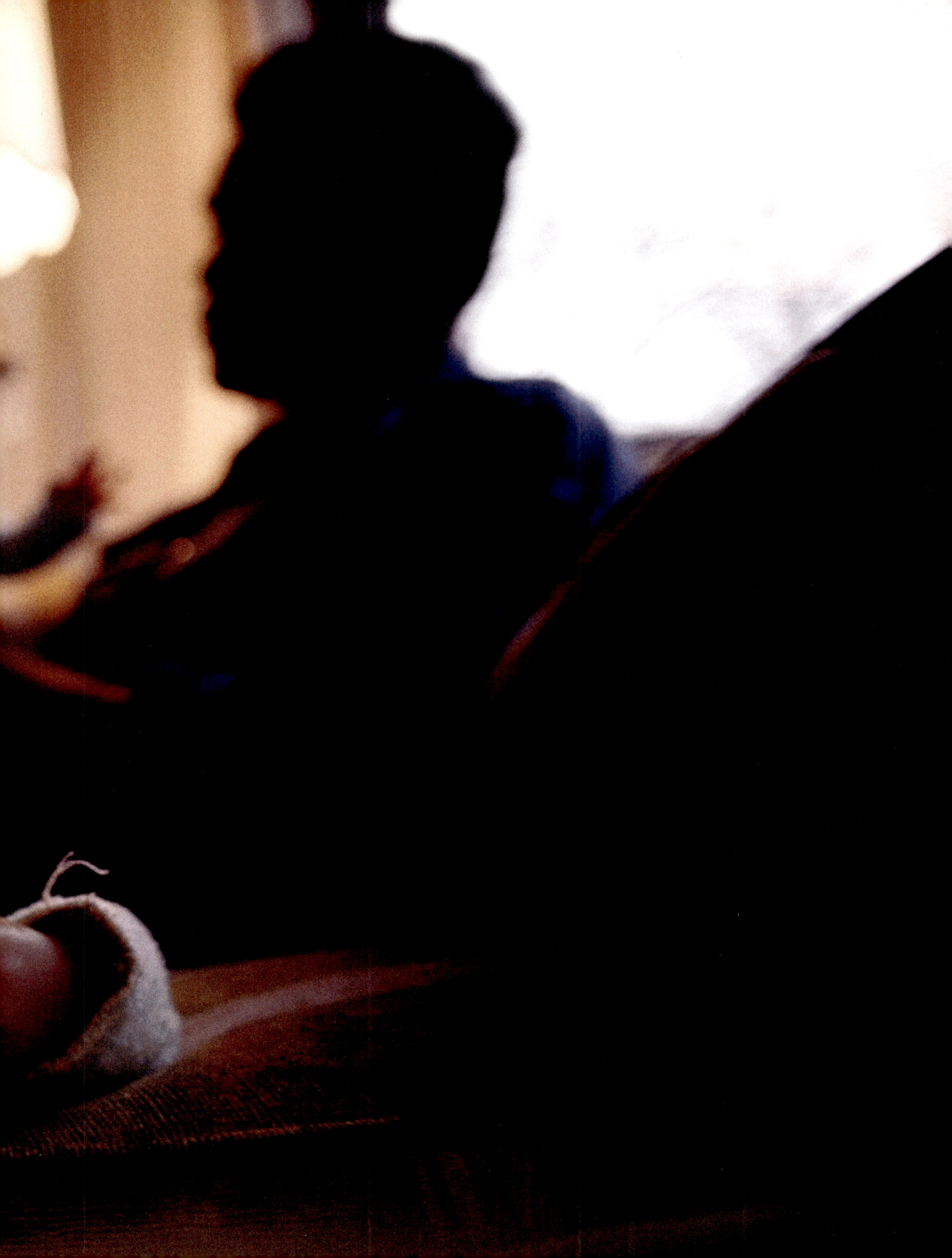

72 —

Miami

1971

"IT'S JUST A JOB. GRASS GROWS, BIRDS FLY, WAVES POUND THE SAND. I BEAT PEOPLE UP."

Cassius Clay came of age in Miami. He "shocked the world" in taking the heavyweight title from Sonny Liston on Feb. 25, 1964, and then touched off a series of aftershocks by converting to Islam, changing his name to Muhammad Ali and announcing, "I ain't got no quarrel with them Viet Cong."

Still brash, still loud, still a prolific source of comic verse and self-promotion, the nimble young boxer was also on the move beyond the ring.

The clown, it turned out, had serious convictions. The showman was becoming a symbol of racial pride and opposition to the war in Vietnam. More than any athlete before or since, Muhammad Ali embodied cause and conscience and controversy at a turbulent hour in American history.

"I don't have to be what you want to be," he said. "I'm free to be what I want."

He had returned to Louisville from the 1960 Summer Olympics in Rome with a gold medal and enough potential to persuade 11 local businessmen to invest in his future. The Louisville Sponsorship Group decided to entrust his development to Miami-based trainer Angelo Dundee.

"I'm slow, I don't rush the fighters," Dundee told Boxing News before he died in 2012. "It was October, 1960 and they asked when did I want him to start training with me. I said, 'Let him stay home for the holidays, there's no rush, he's an 18-year-old kid.' I got a call later that day telling me he would be with me the next day. He wanted to fight. He got on a train and he came down – that was him all over."

Dundee's Fifth Street Gym, a loft above a drug store, is where the young fighter sharpened his skills and refined his theatrics. It was there, a week before the first Liston fight, that he posed for the famous photograph of the Beatles being knocked out collectively by a "domino" punch.

An 8-1 underdog against Liston, Clay nonetheless predicted "a total eclipse of the Sonny," and then demonstrated that he was much more than mouth. Too quick for the fearsome puncher he called, "The Bear," Clay would dance beyond the range of Liston's blows and then punish him with his longer reach and lightning jab.

When the ball rang for the seventh round, Liston sat on his stool.

The following day, the new champion said he had joined the Nation of Islam and would be known, for the time being, as Cassius X. The name Muhammad Ali would come later, and it would endure.

→ **Larry Spitzer**
Muhammad Ali stands in the street outside the 5th Street Gym in Miami Beach as he prepares for his world heavyweight title bout with Joe Frazier.

February 1971

TROPICAL
SHOE REPAIR
LADIES HEEL LIFTS
LEATHER
RUBBER
NYLON
MEN & BOYS
RUBBER
HEELS
HALF SOLES
RUBBER
MIAMI
5TH ST.
UPSTAIRS

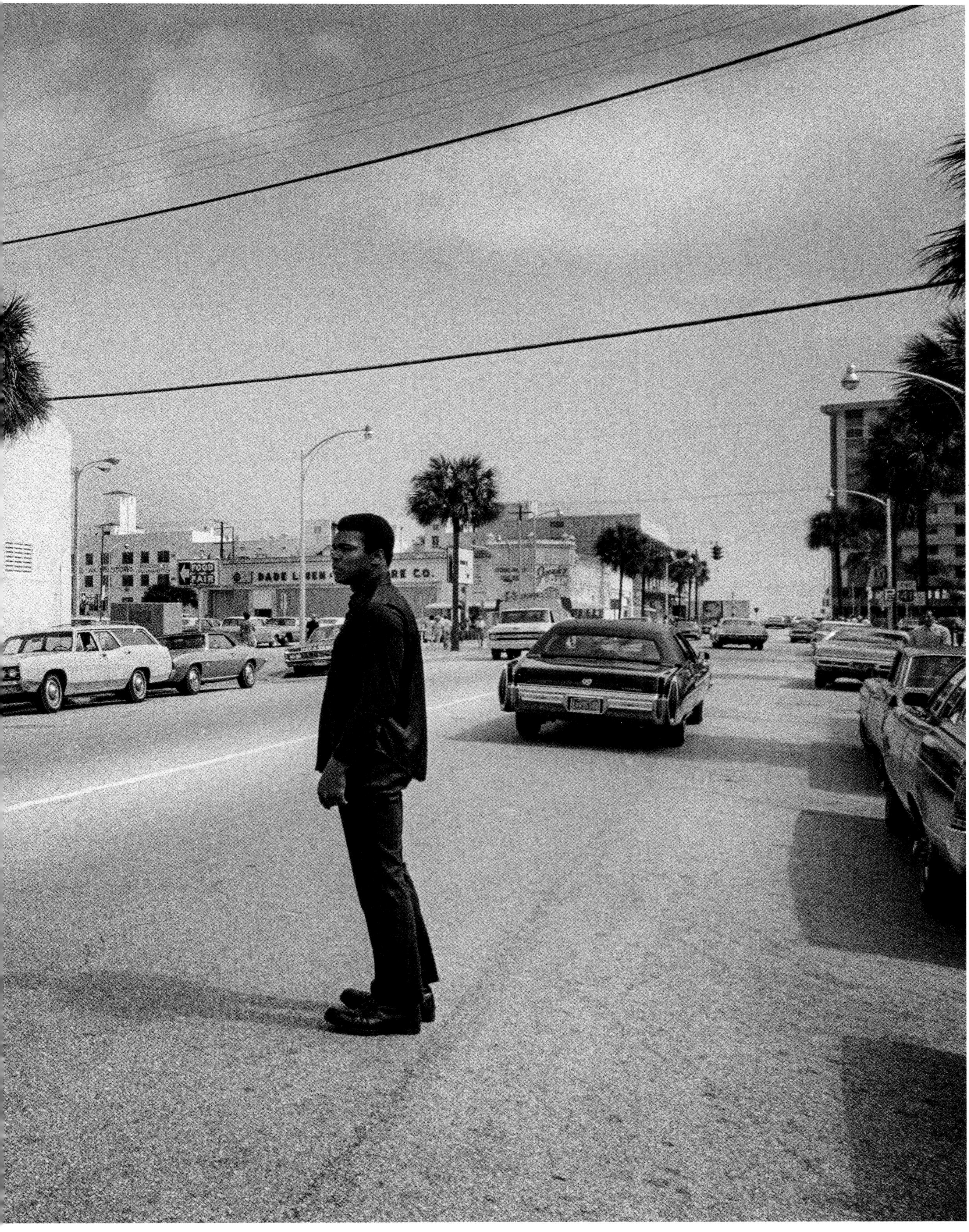
FOOD
FAIR

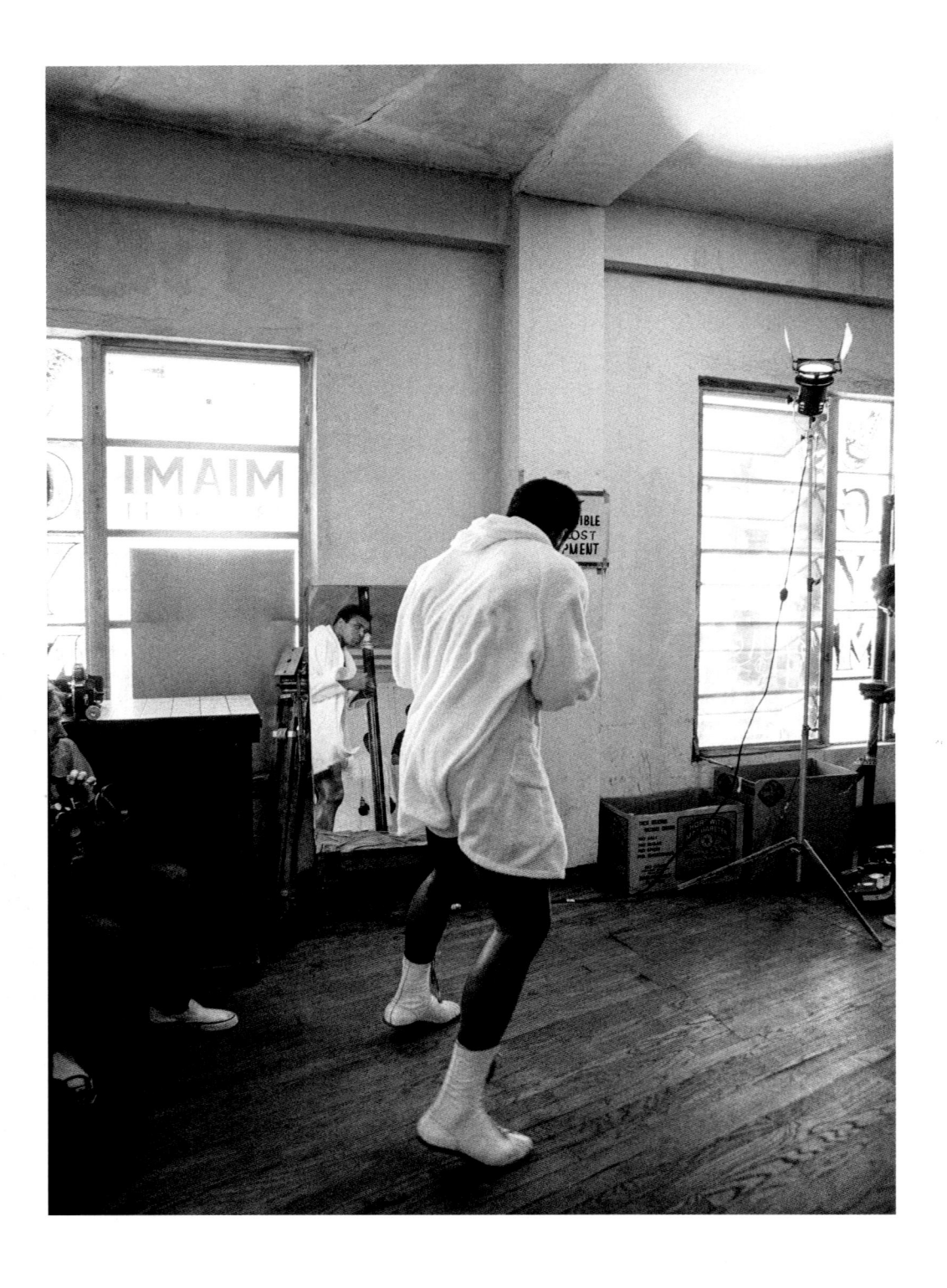

1 Larry Spitzer
Muhammad Ali watches himself in a mirror while training in Miami Beach.

February 1971

→ Larry Spitzer
Ali jumps rope while in training for his heavyweight title bout with Joe Frazier.

February 1971

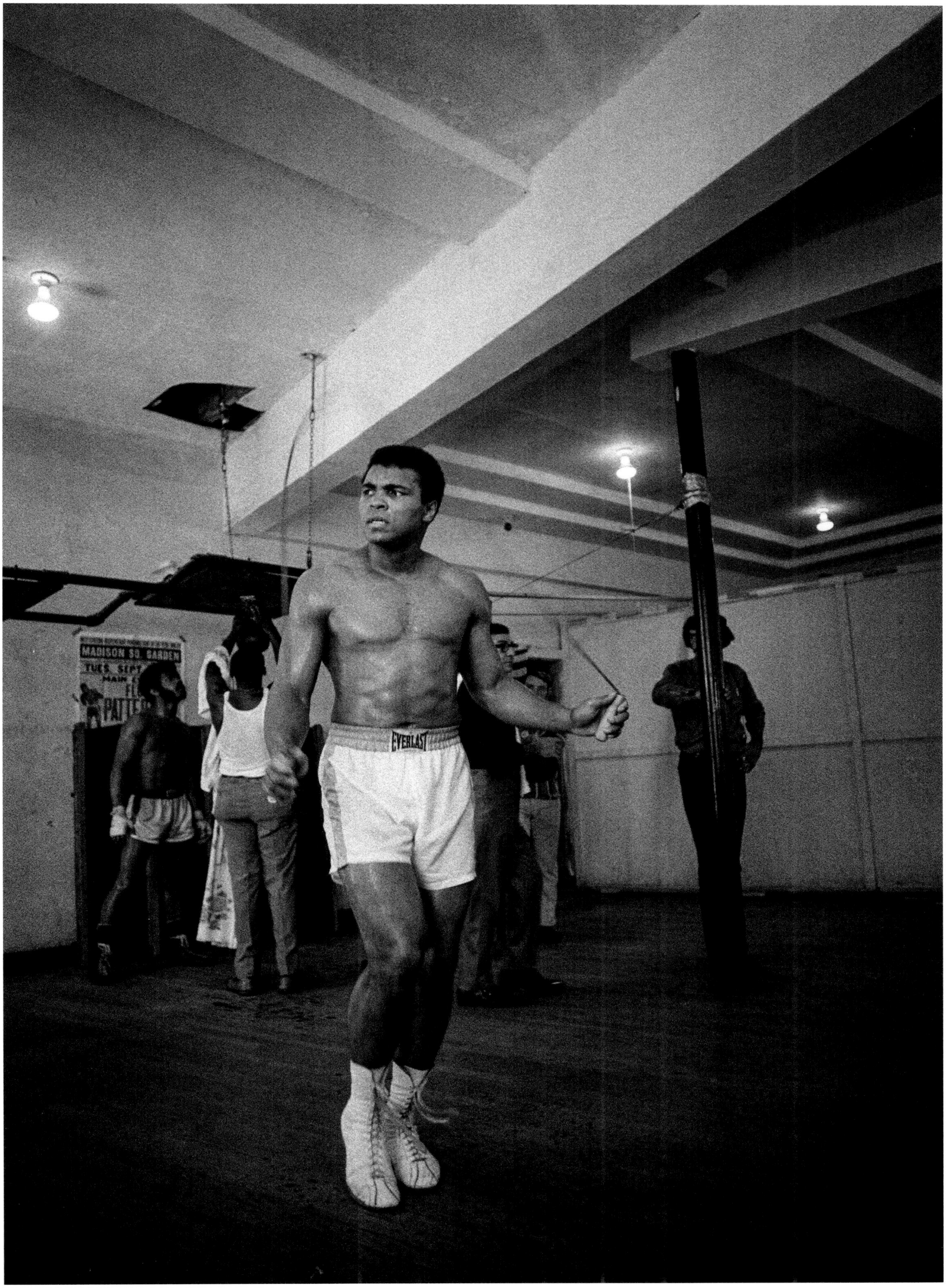
MADISON SQ. GARDEN
EVERLAST

↑ Larry Spitzer
A crowd watches in the background as
Muhammad Ali trains at the 5th Street
Gym in Miami Beach.

February 1971

→ Larry Spitzer
Ali swings at a heavy bag while in training
to fight Joe Frazier.

February 1971

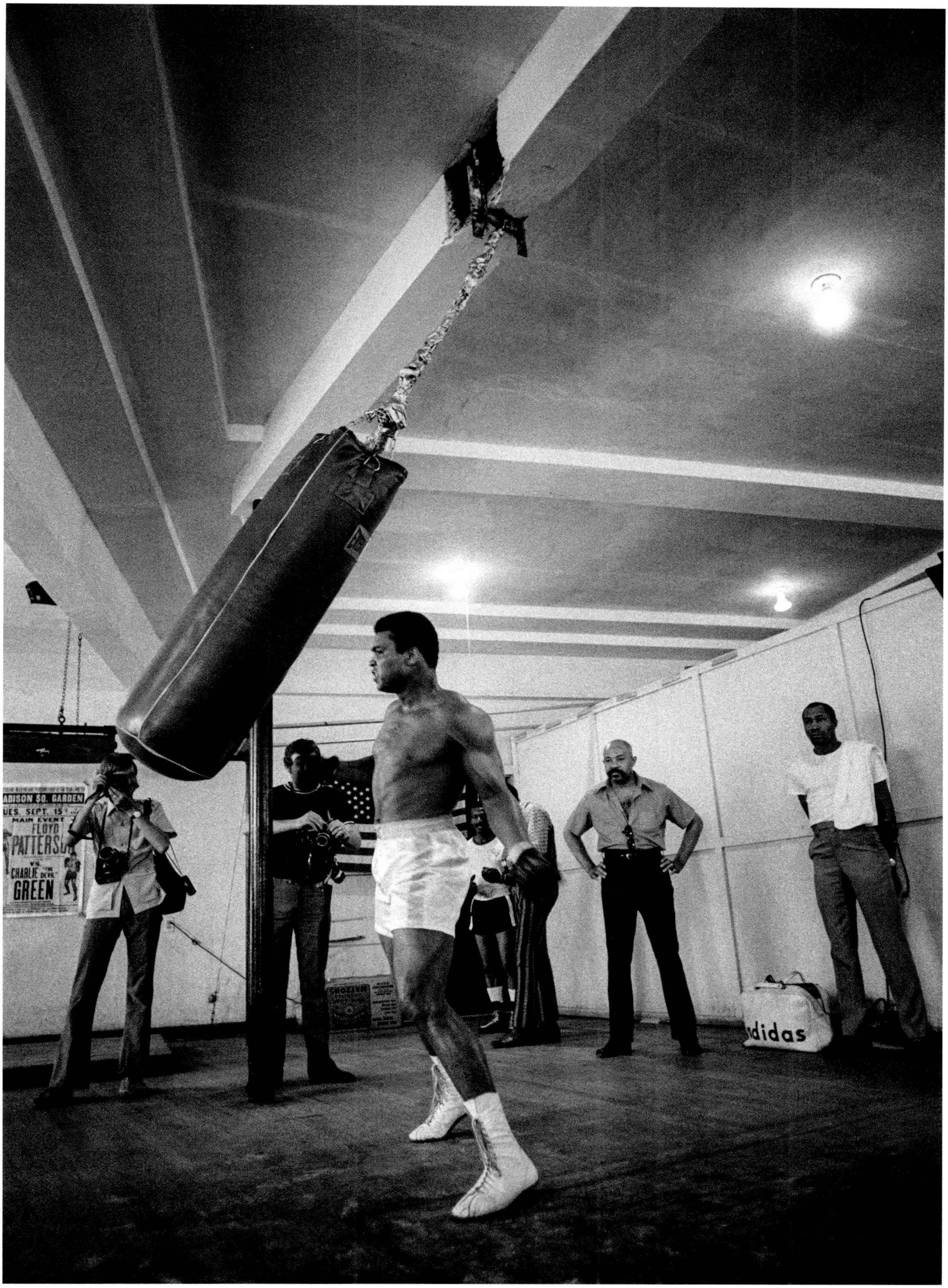
ADISON SQ. GARDEN
FLOYD
VS
CHARLIE
GREEN

1 Larry Spitzer
Muhammad Ali hones his skills on a speed bag while training in Miami Beach.

February 1971

1 Larry Spitzer
Ali snarls as he works out with a heavy bag.

February 1971

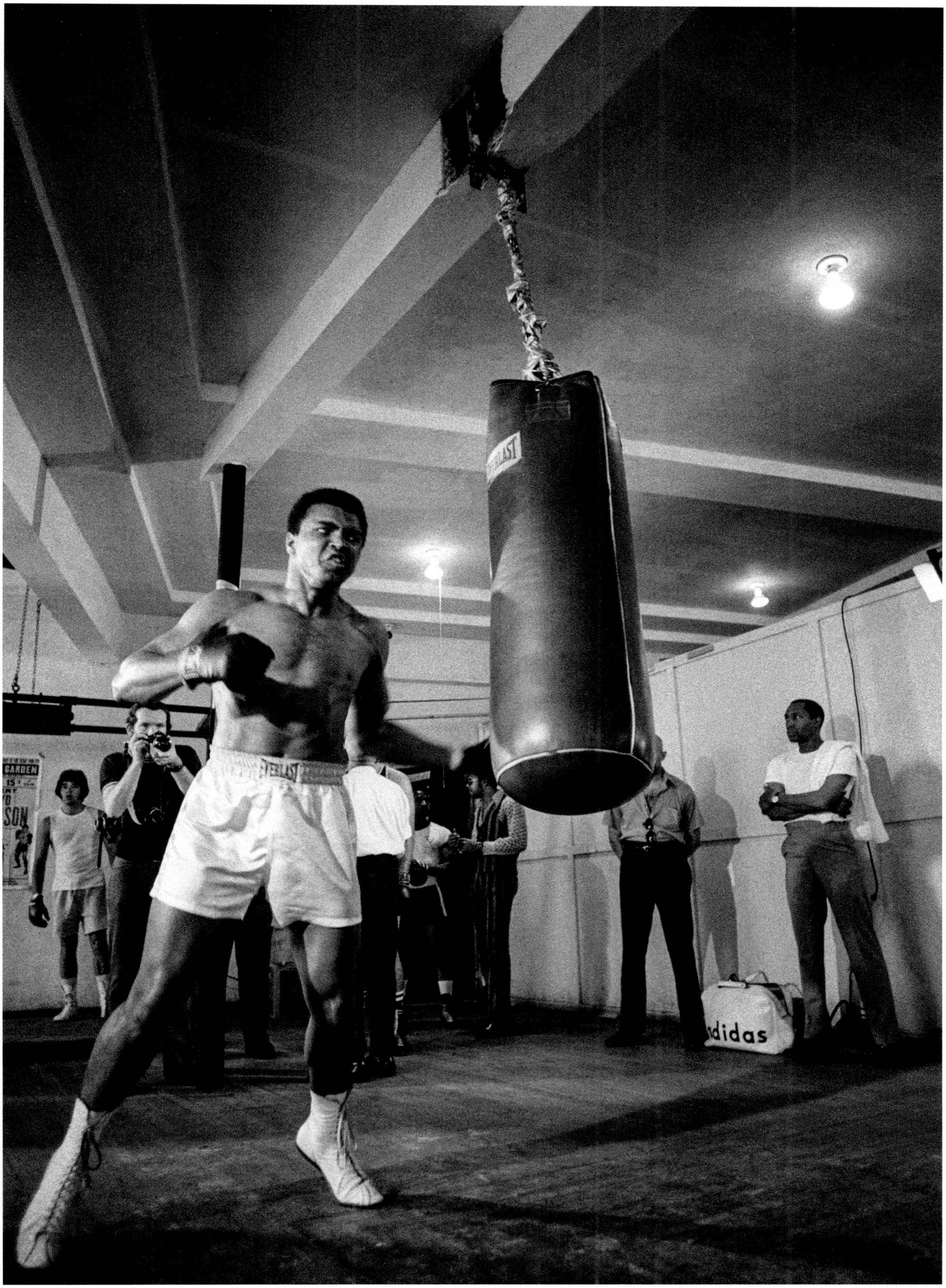
EVERLAST
EVERLAST
GARDEN

1 Larry Spitzer
Muhammad Ali cools off while training in Miami Beach.

February 1971

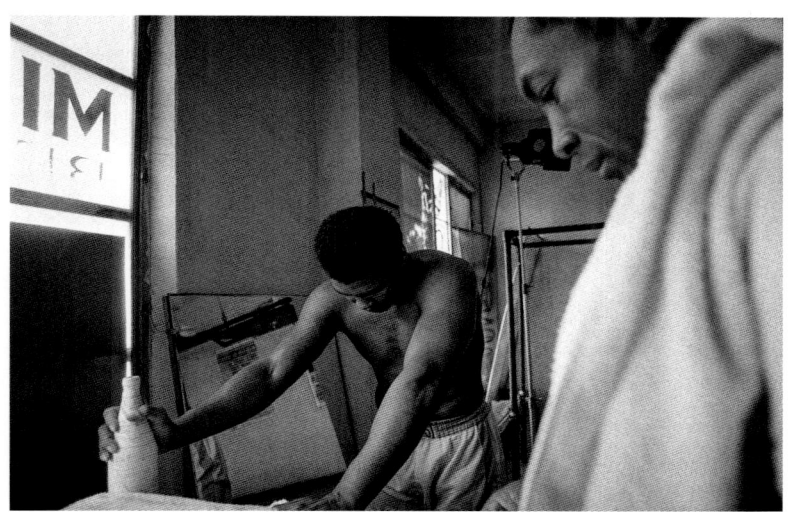

1 Larry Spitzer
Ali takes a break from his intense training
for his upcoming title bout with Joe Frazier.

February 1971

1 Larry Spitzer
Muhammad Ali playfully prepares to fight a young admirer.

February 1971

1 Larry Spitzer
Photographers surround Ali and children in the boxing ring while training in Miami.

February 1971

1 Larry Spitzer
Trainer Angelo Dundee wraps
Muhammad Ali's hand while training in
Miami Beach.

February 1971

→ **Larry Spitzer**
Ali is surrounded by media while training for his heavyweight title match against Joe Frazier.

February 1971

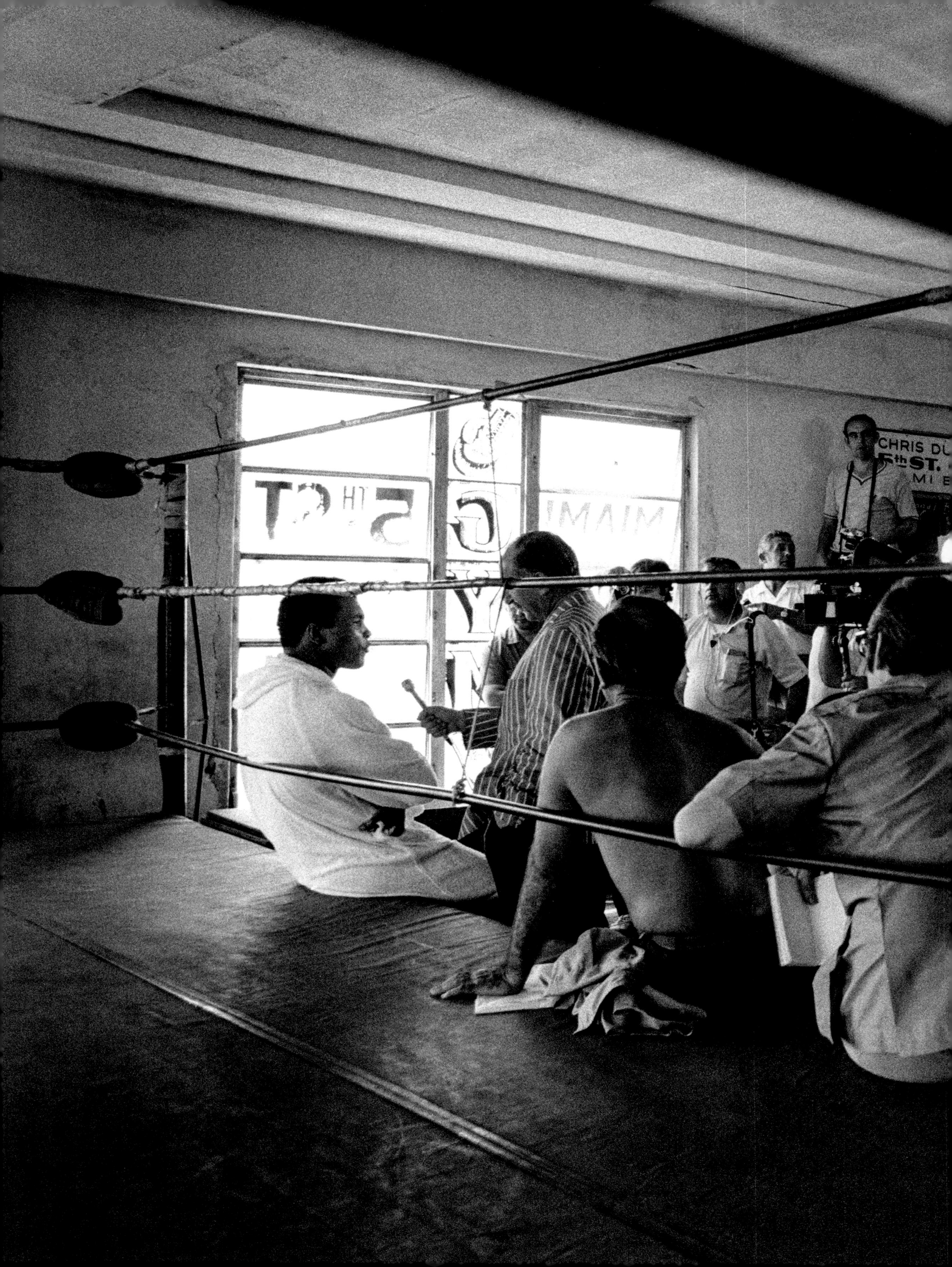
CHRIS DU
5th ST.

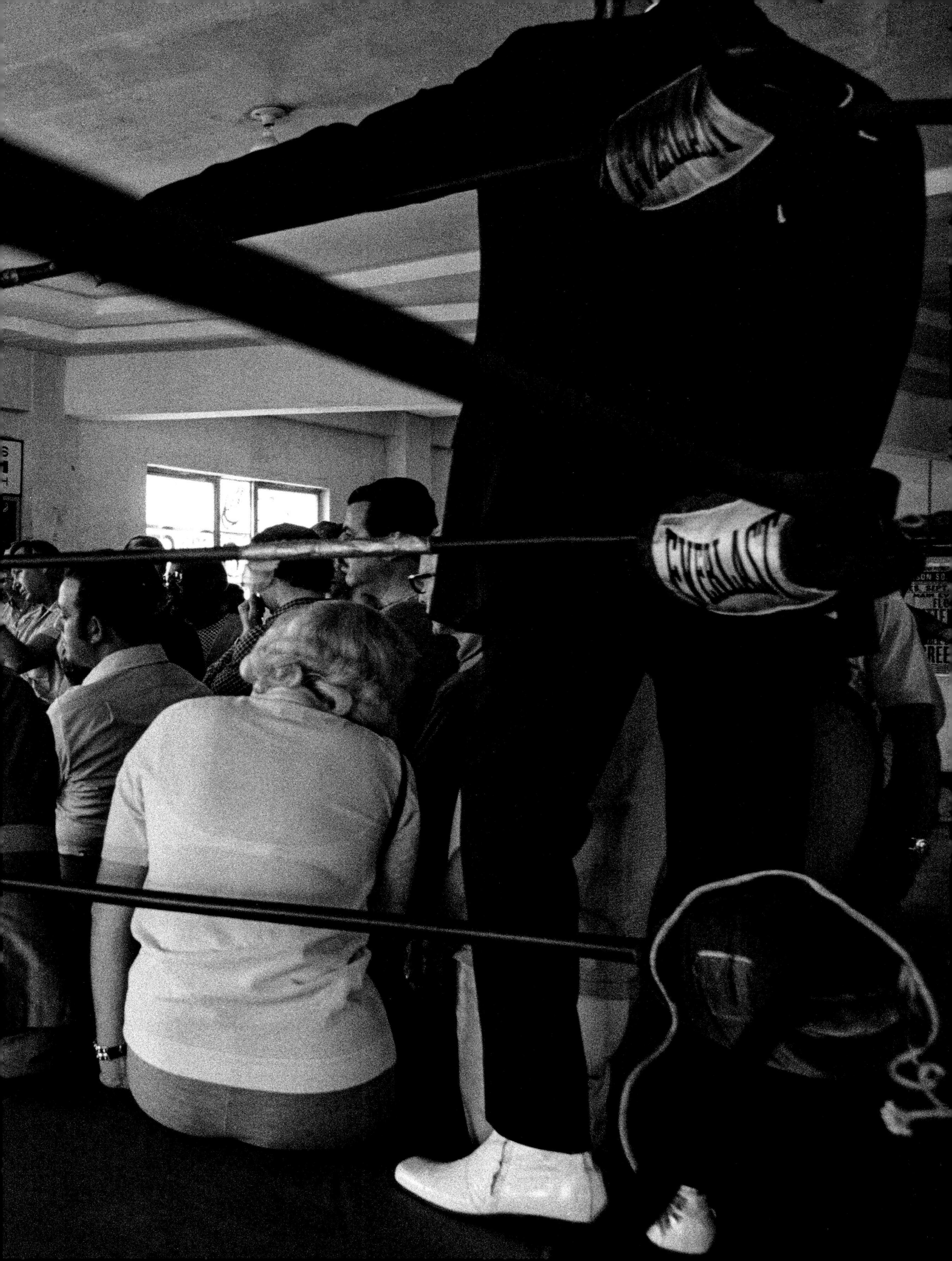

1 Larry Spitzer
Muhammad Ali rests on the ropes at the
5th Street Gym in Miami Beach.

February 1971

→ Larry Spitzer
Ali takes time to catch up on the news
while training in Miami Beach.

February 1971

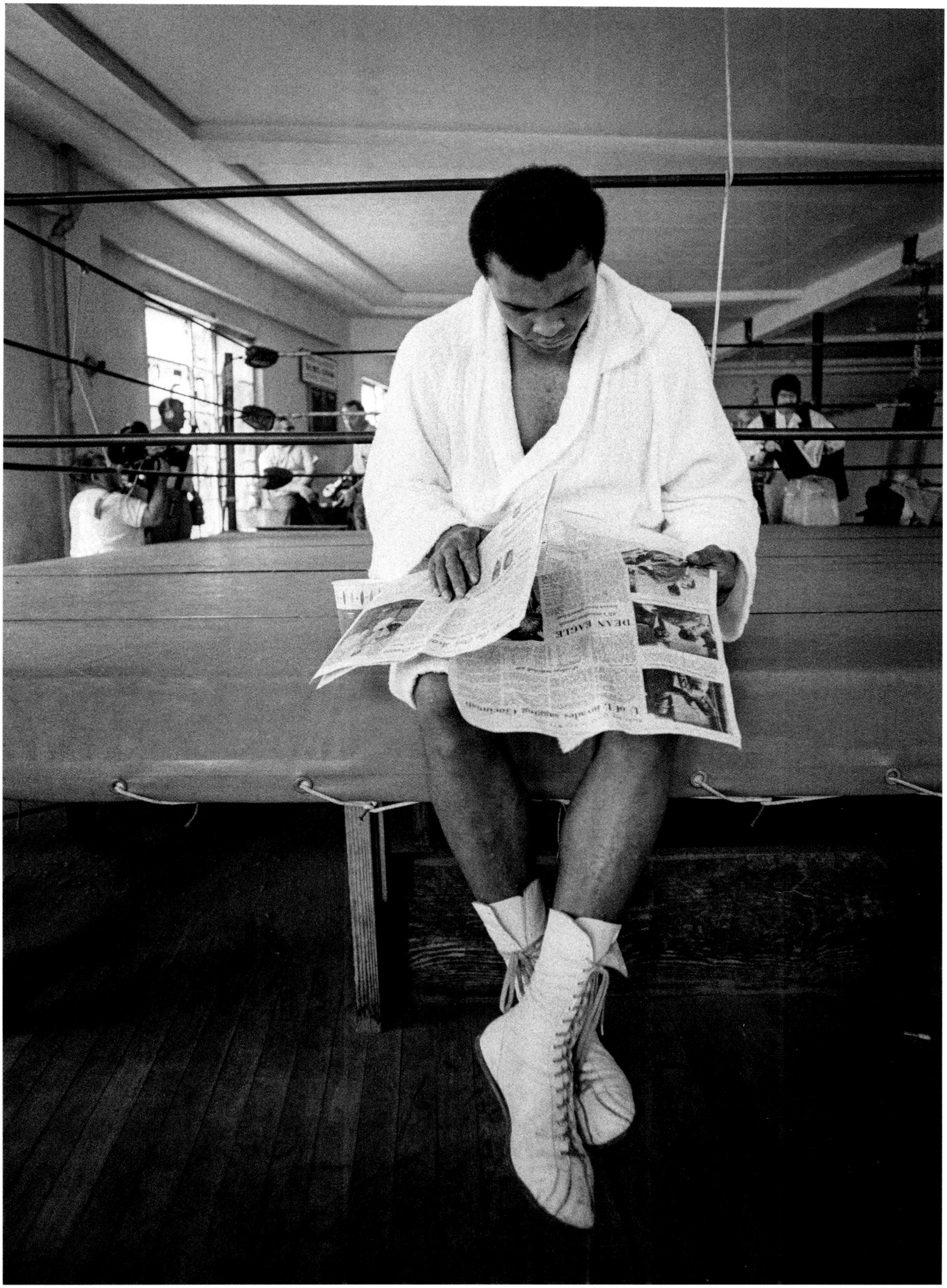

1 Larry Spitzer
Muhammad Ali runs through the streets
of Miami in the early morning.

February 1971

— 97

1 Larry Spitzer
Ali leaves Wolfie's all night deli while on
an early morning training run in Miami.

February 1971

1 Larry Spitzer
Muhammad Ali leaves Miami's legendary
Wolfie's restaurant following breakfast.

February 1971

1 Larry Spitzer
Ali, right, stops to talk with a man on the street corner in Miami while training for an upcoming fight against Joe Frazier.

February 1971

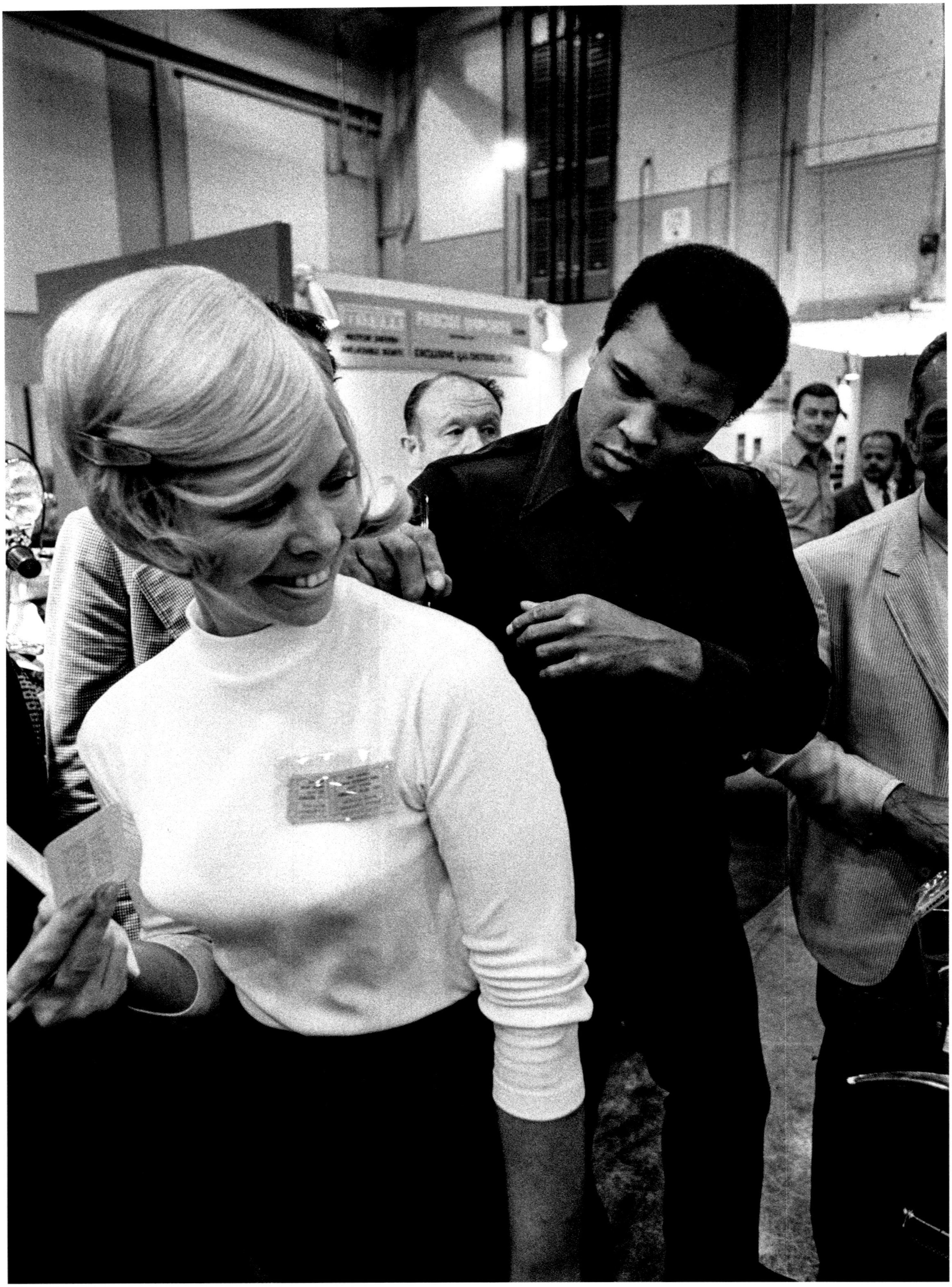

← Larry Spitzer
Muhammad Ali signs an autograph for a woman while attending the Miami Boat Show.

February 1971

↑ Larry Spitzer
Ali tries out a scooter at the Miami Boat Show.

February 1971

— 101

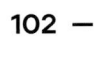

1 Larry Spitzer
Odessa Clay joins her son in his hotel room after a day of training.

February 1971

→ **Larry Spitzer**
Muhammad Ali has a rare quiet moment to read about boxing in a magazine in his hotel room in Miami.

February 1971

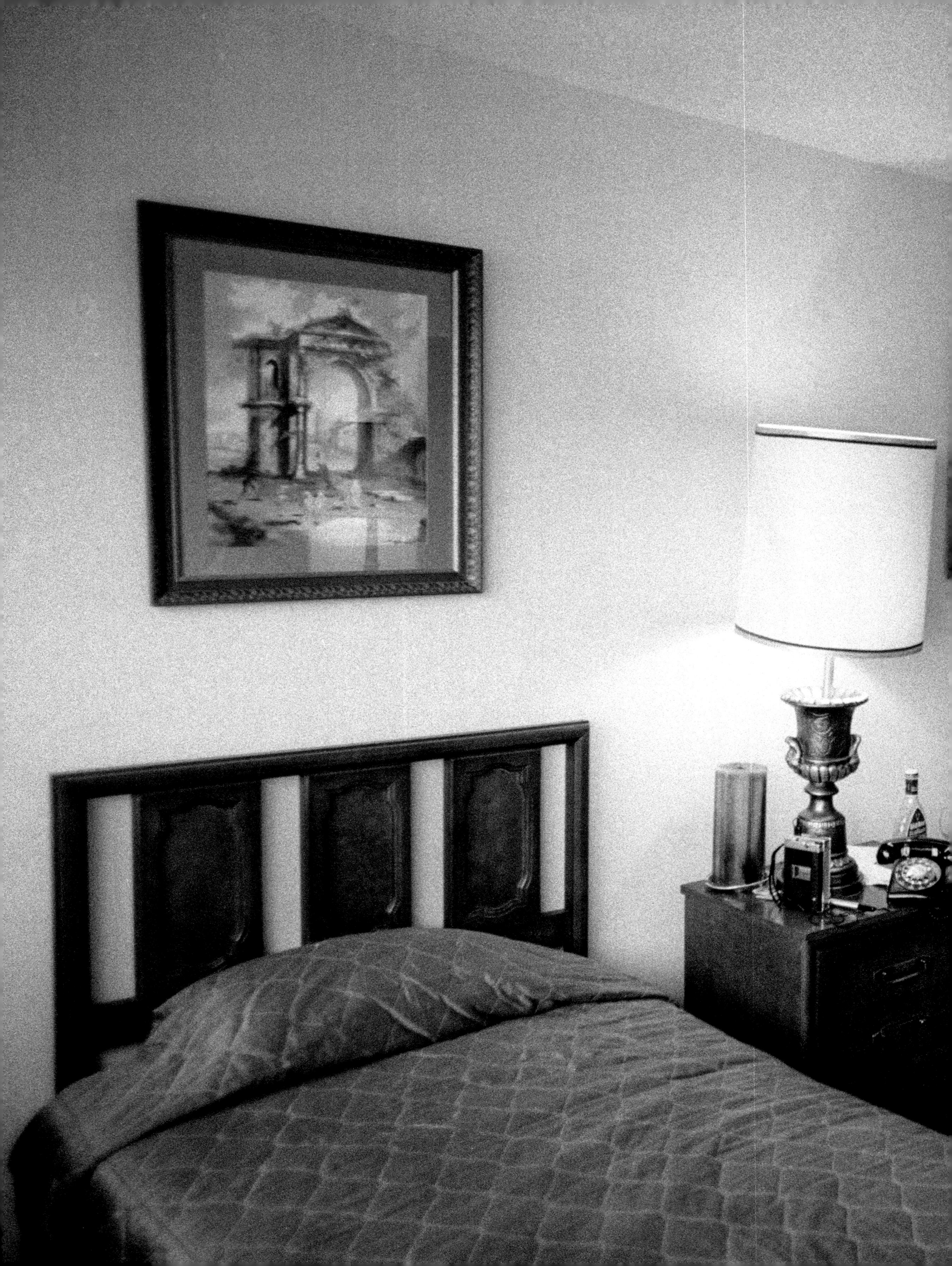

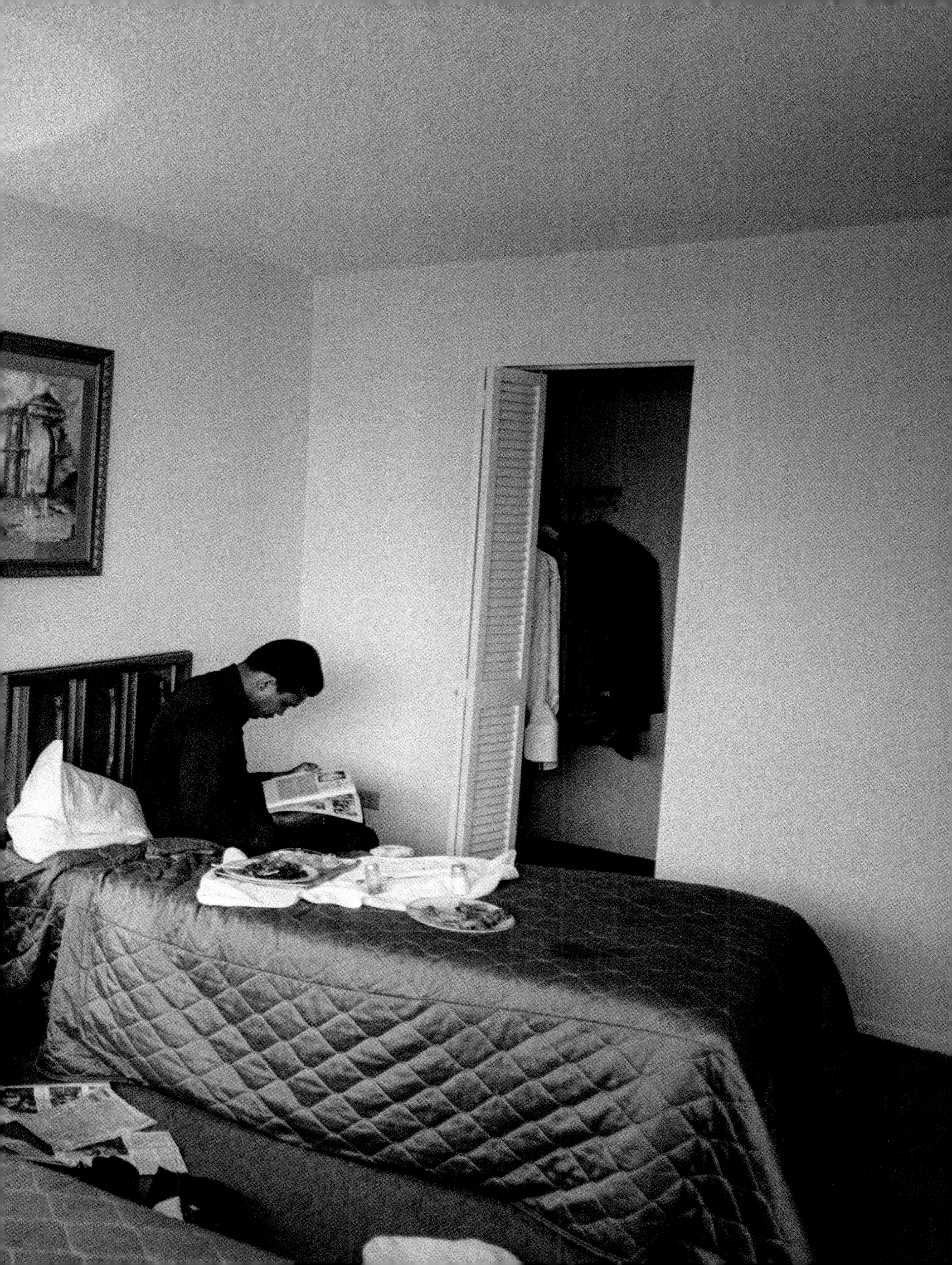

106 —

Home

— 107

1971
— 1976

"AT HOME I AM A NICE GUY: BUT I DON'T WANT THE WORLD TO KNOW. HUMBLE PEOPLE, I'VE FOUND, DON'T GET VERY FAR."

On the day after Muhammad Ali died, the government-sponsored Voice Of America declared him to be "the world's most famous person ever."

Considering the amount of territory and time that title takes in, it probably demands more documentation than has been presented to date. It certainly leaves some room for doubt.

Yet while Ali was unquestionably a global celebrity – rapidly recognized wherever he went – his deepest roots can be found a few blocks from the Ohio River, at 3302 Grand Ave.

"As you know, I'm from Louisville and I'm one who never forgets where he's from," Ali told a hometown crowd after reclaiming the heavyweight title against George Foreman in 1974.

The relationship was not always harmonious. In his 1975 autobiography, Ali claimed to have thrown his Olympic gold medal in the Ohio River after being refused service at a "whites-only" restaurant. Though that story has since been deemed apocryphal, it is consistent with Ali's long-running complaints about segregation in Louisville.

In registering as a conscientious objector and refusing Army induction in 1967, Ali cited racial attitudes in his hometown.

"Why should they ask me to put on a uniform and go 10,000 miles from home and drop bombs and bullets on brown people in Vietnam, while so-called Negro people in Louisville are treated like dogs and denied simple human rights?" he asked.

Ali grew up in the house on Grand Avenue, graduated from Louisville's Central High School in 1960, but he was an irregular resident of his hometown thereafter.

Upon returning from the Olympics, he moved first to Miami to train under Angelo Dundee, and later lived in Cherry Hill, N.J., Chicago, Los Angeles, Berrien Springs, Mich., and Paradise Valley, Ariz.

Though he would draw his last breaths in a hospital in Scottsdale, Ariz., his final resting place had been pre-determined: Louisville's Cave Hill Cemetery. Long before he became a citizen of the world, Muhammad Ali was a hometown guy who made good.

"He's left an impact on our city that will be with us for centuries," Louisville Mayor Greg Fischer said.

If he was not the most famous person ever, he was high on the list.

112

1 Bill Luster
A lady holds a sign welcoming
Muhammad Ali back to Louisville.

November 8, 1974

1 Bill Luster
Ali speaks at the entrance to Central High
School during a return visit to Louisville.

November 8, 1974

1 Bill Luster
Muhammad Ali shares a moment with a friend at Central High School during a return visit to Louisville.

November 8, 1974

— 115

1 Bill Luster
Ali makes a point while addressing the crowd at a welcome home event in Louisville.

November 8, 1974

116

1 Bill Luster
Muhammad Ali receives a hero's
welcome on a return trip to Louisville.

November 8, 1974

— 117

→ **Larry Spitzer**
The Belvedere is packed with fans as
Louisville native Ali is welcomed home.

November 8, 1974

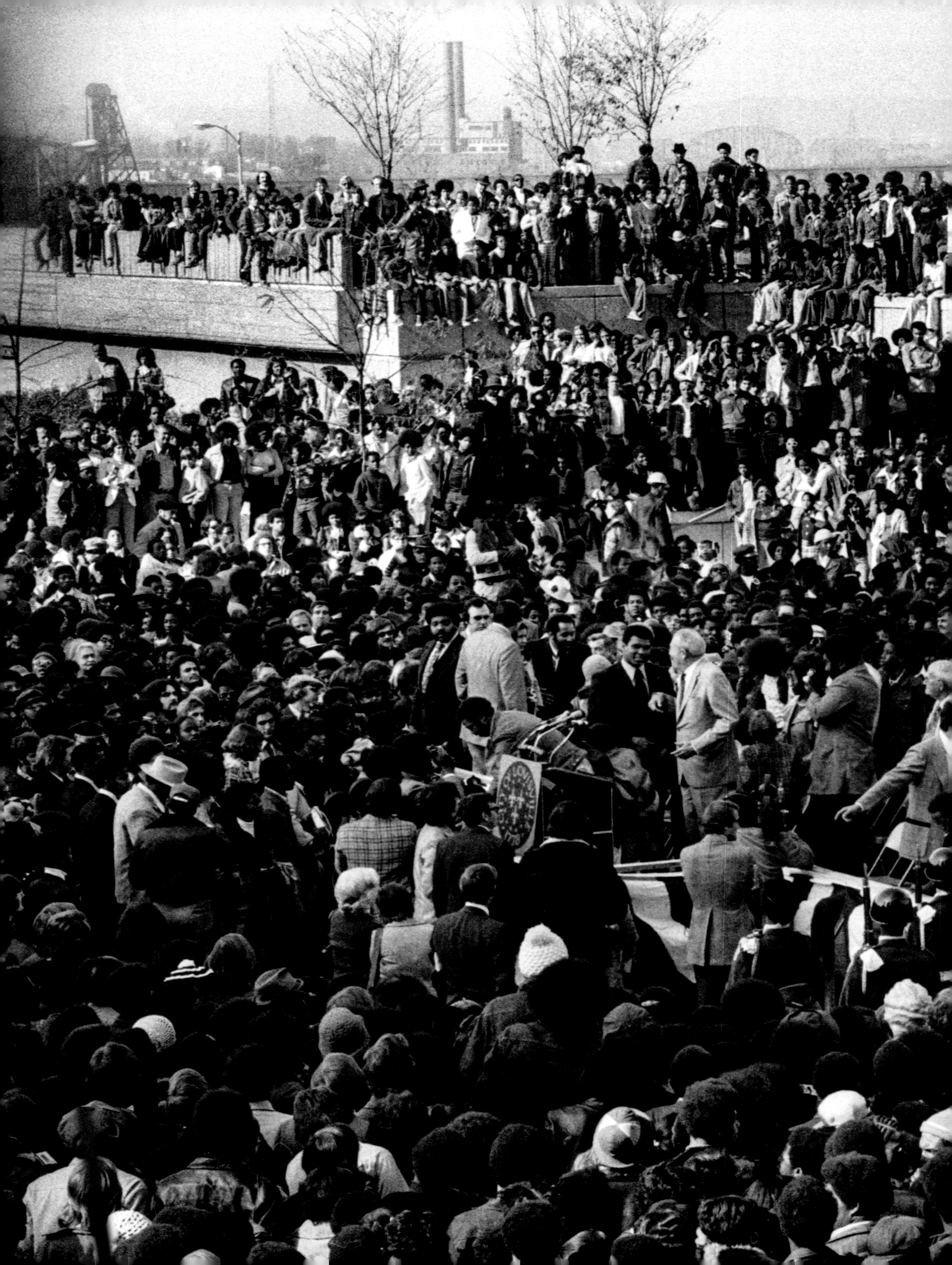

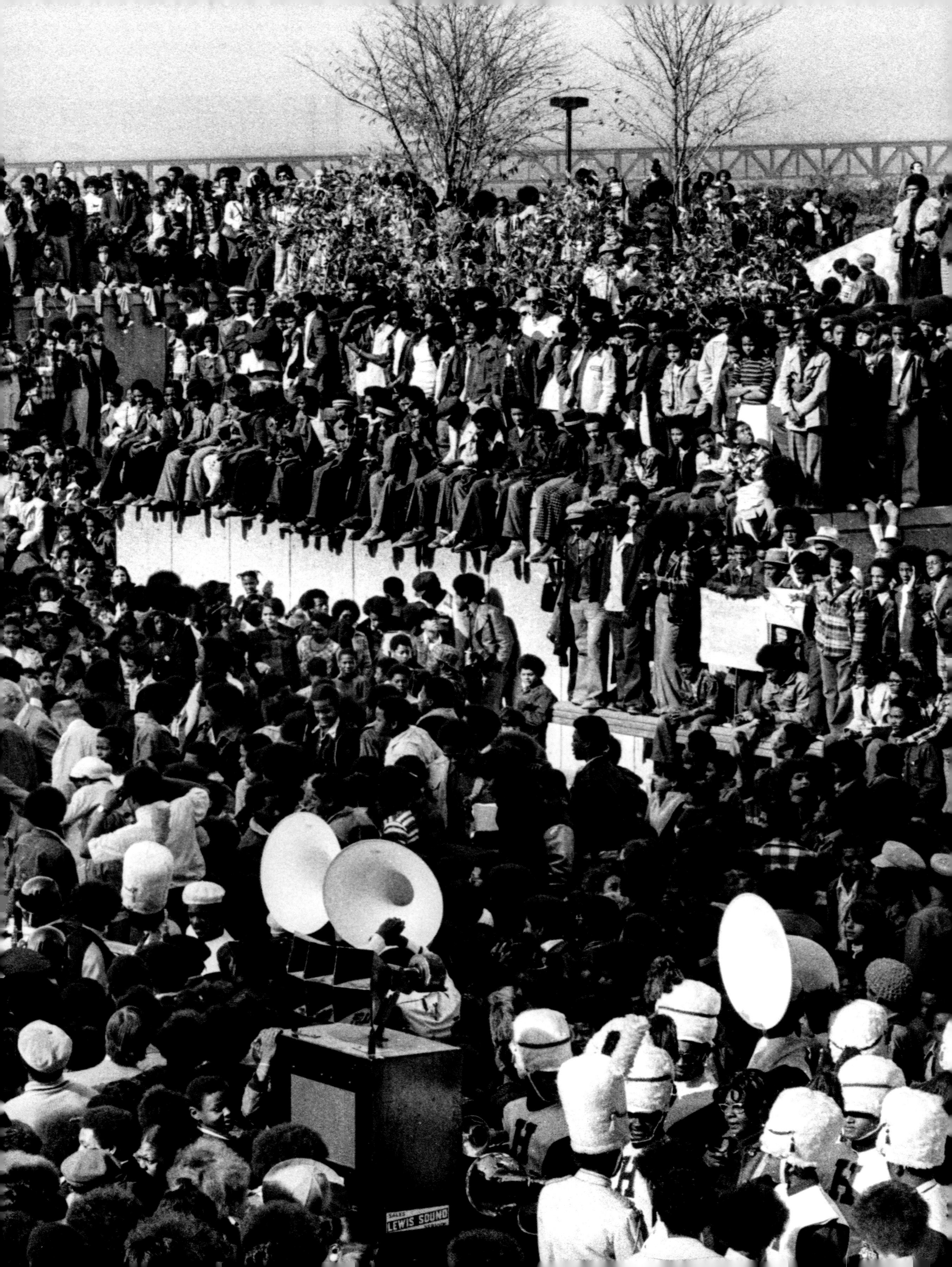
LEWIS SOUND

1 Bill Luster
Scenes from Muhammad Ali's return trip to Louisville.

November 8, 1974

→ **Bill Luster**
Ali addresses a huge crowd of people who came out to welcome him home to Louisville.

November 8, 1974

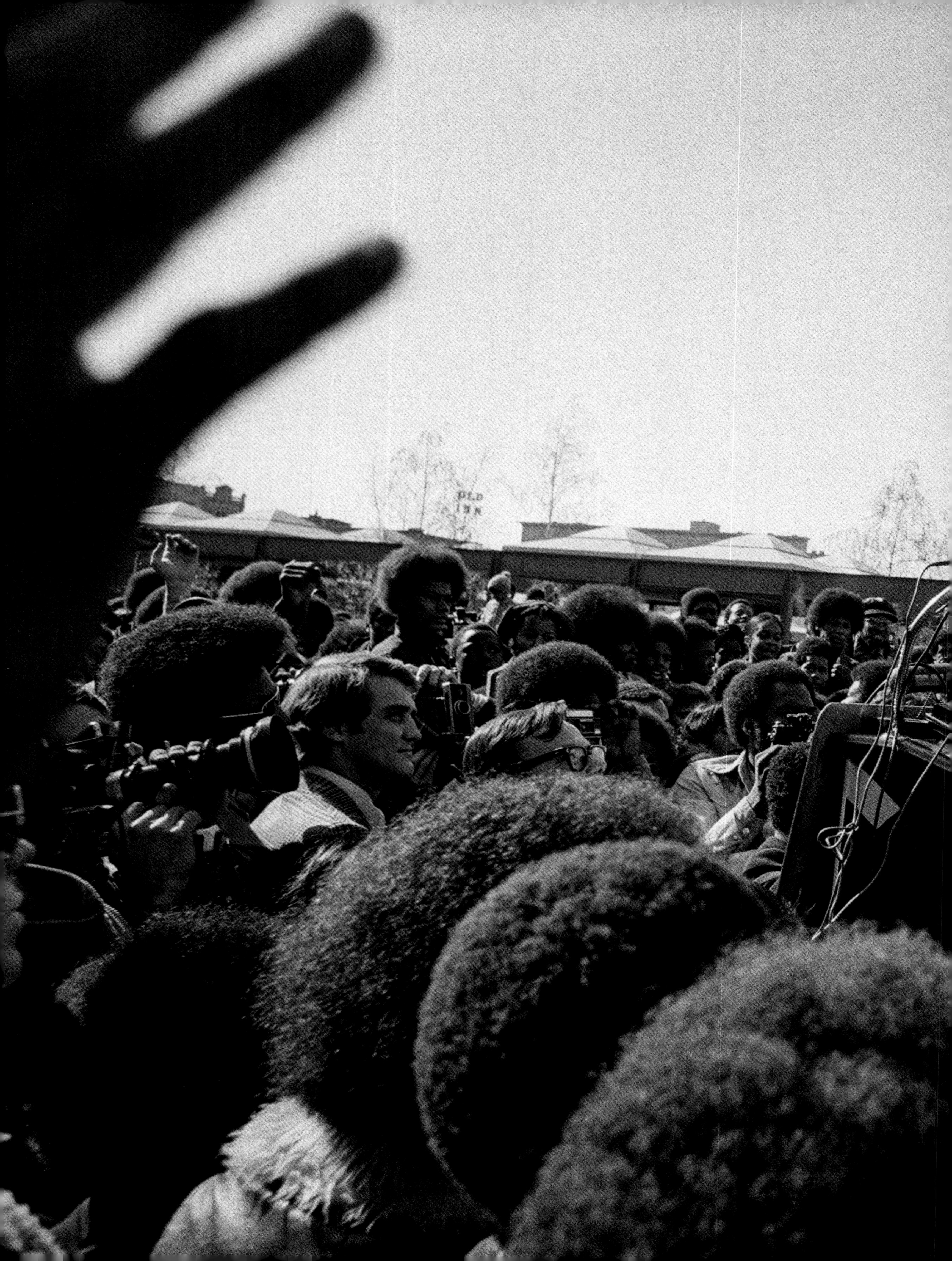

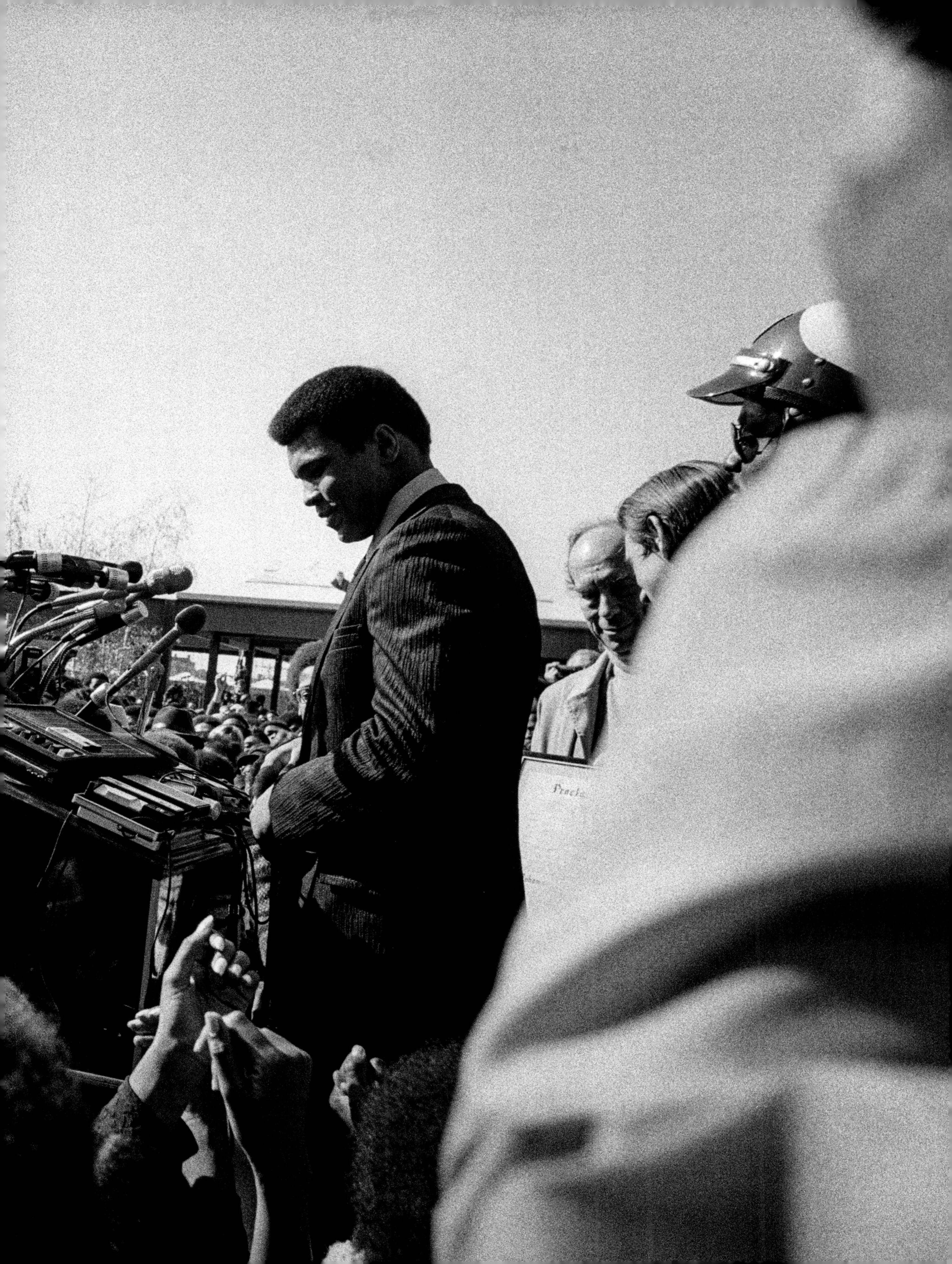

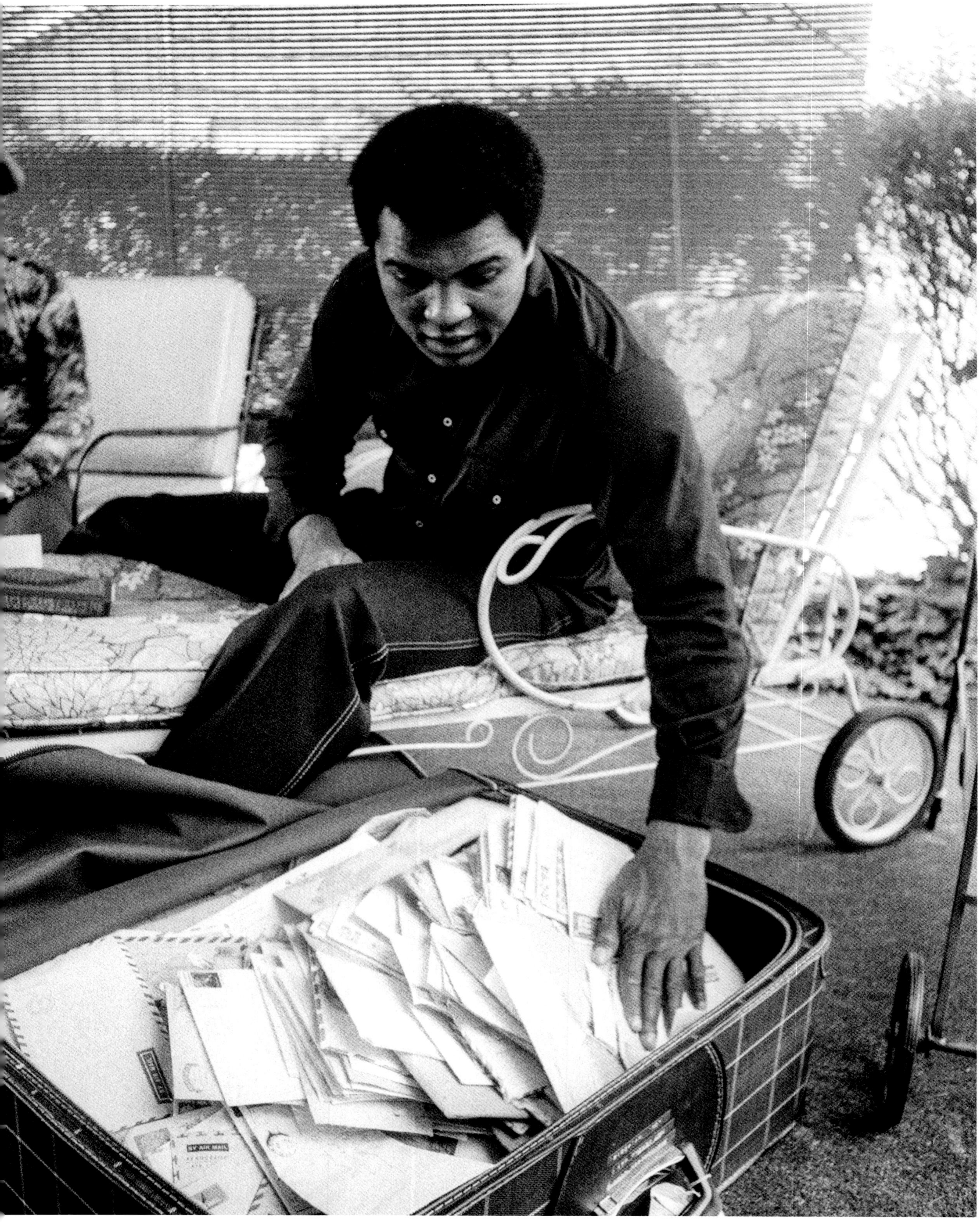

← Bud Kamenish
Muhammad Ali sorts through fan mail at his parent's home in Louisville.

July 26, 1975

↑ Bud Kamenish
Ali hugs his mother Odessa Clay on a trip home to Louisville. A niece of Mrs. Clay once said, "she went into every greasy little gym she could to see him fight."

July 26, 1975

1 Keith Williams
West Louisville residents give heavyweight boxing champion Muhammad Ali a warm reception while riding in a motorcade through the city.

October 16, 1975

— 127

1 Robert Steinau
Ali is greeted by Ben Montgomery while giving a tour of west Louisville.

May 31, 1975

1 Bill Luster
Muhammad Ali gives a bear hug to Howard Cosell of ABC Sports while attending a Kentucky Derby party at the home of John Y. Brown.

May 2, 1975

1 Bill Luster
Cosell, center, puts up his dukes against Ali, right, during a Kentucky Derby party at the home of John Y. Brown.

May 2, 1975

1 Dan Dry
Muhammad Ali picks up Bayinah Pasha, the 18-month-old daughter of a friend, prior to an exhibition bout in Louisville.

December 10, 1976

— 131

1 Dan Dry
Ali tapes his hands in a restroom at Trinity High School before fighting an exhibition match there. Several amateur matches were also on the card for a Golden Gloves benefit show.

December 10, 1976

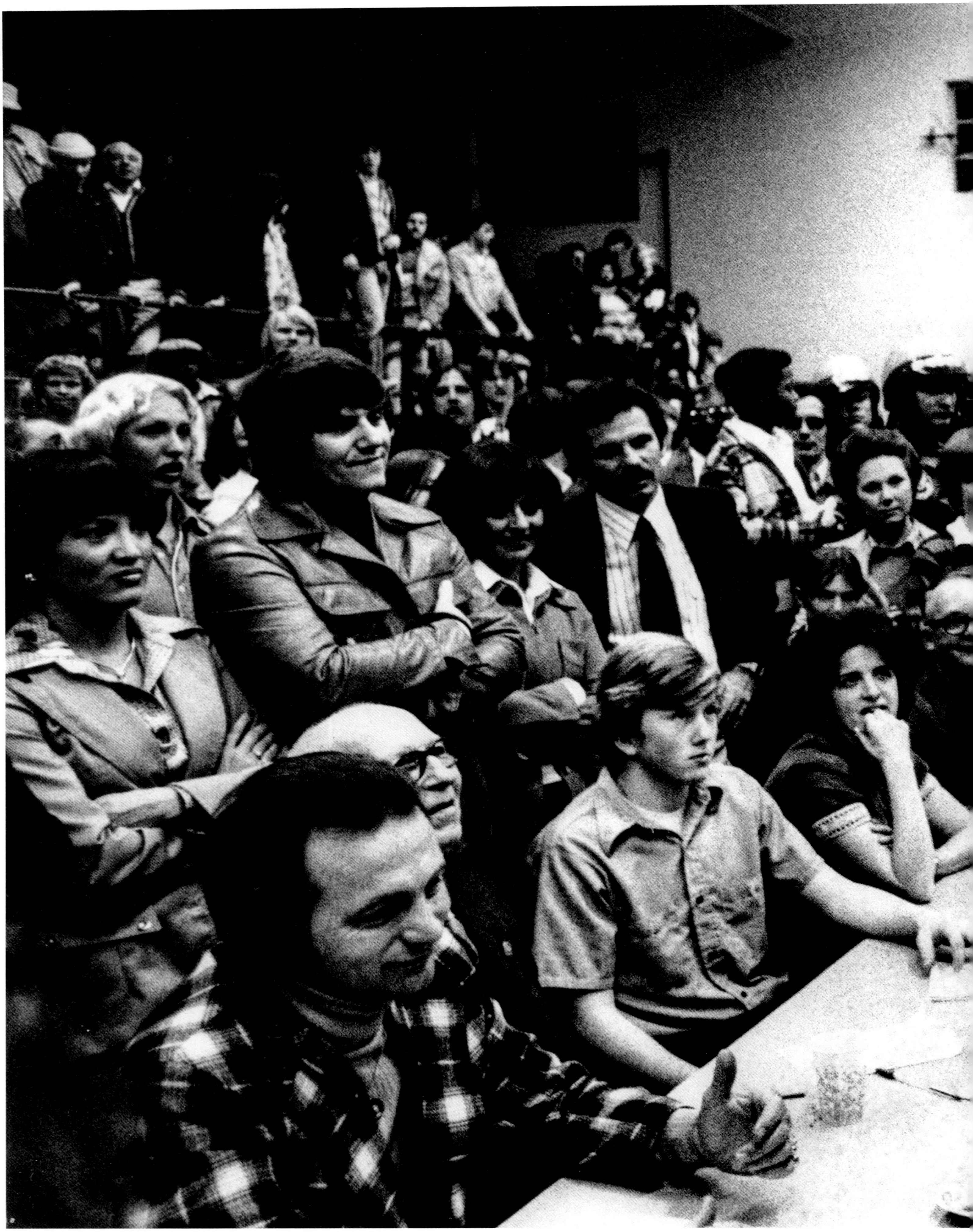

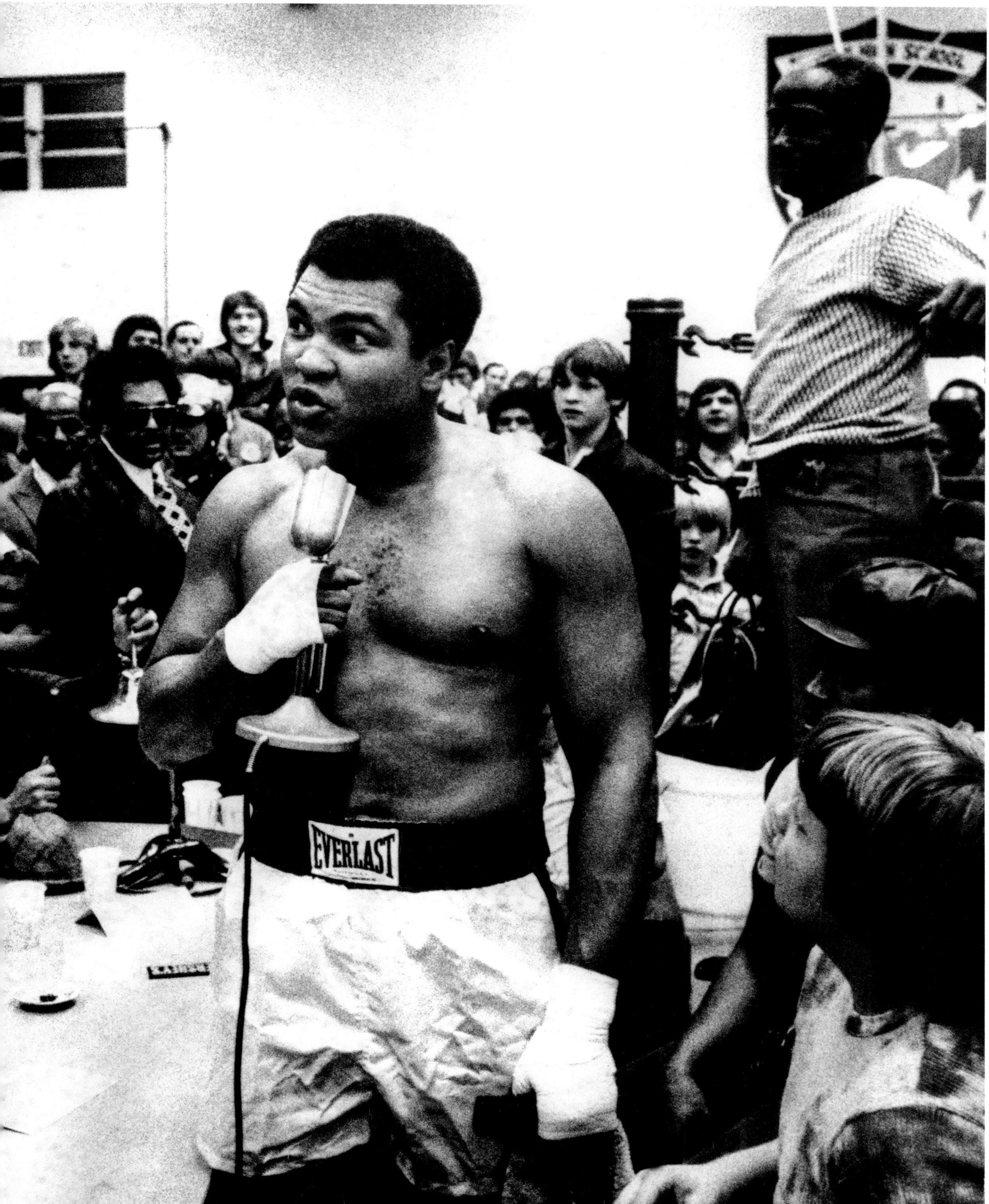
EVERLAST

— Dan Dry
Muhammad Ali speaks at an exhibition bout at Trinity High School to raise money for the local Golden Gloves boxing program. A crowd of about 1,200 people watched Ali spar against life-long friend Jimmy Ellis. He was in the ring for the first time since his controversial decision over Ken Norton.

December 10, 1976

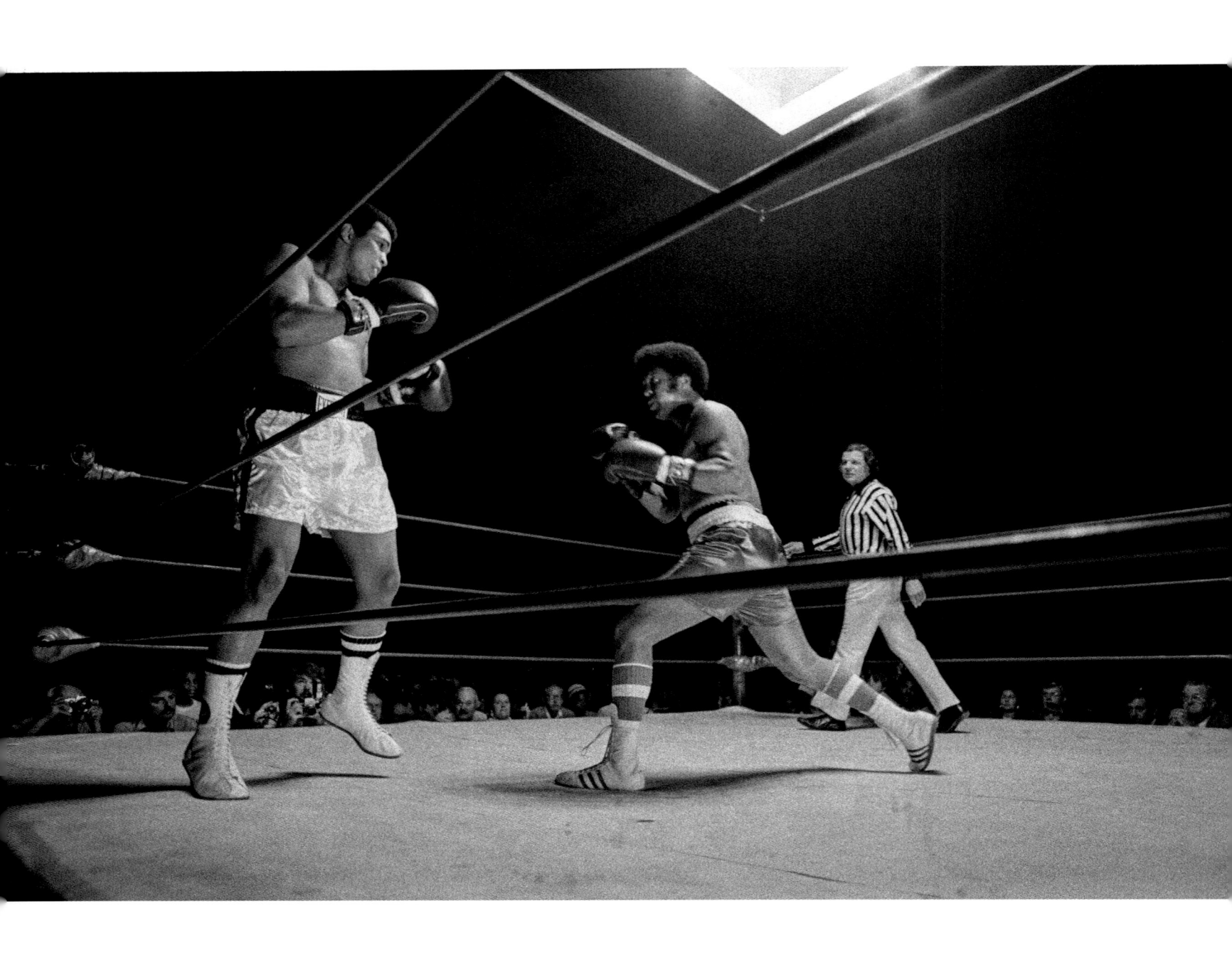

← **Dan Dry**
Ali, left, has his guard up against Jimmy Ellis during an exhibition match at Trinity High School.

December 10, 1976

↑ **Bill Luster**
Ali looks out from the ring during an exhibition match with fellow Louisville boxer Jimmy Ellis at Trinity High School.

December 10, 1976

"It's hard to be humble when you're as great as I am."

— Bill Luster
Muhammad Ali sits in the hallway near his dressing room at the Louisville Gardens before an exhibition match.

1978

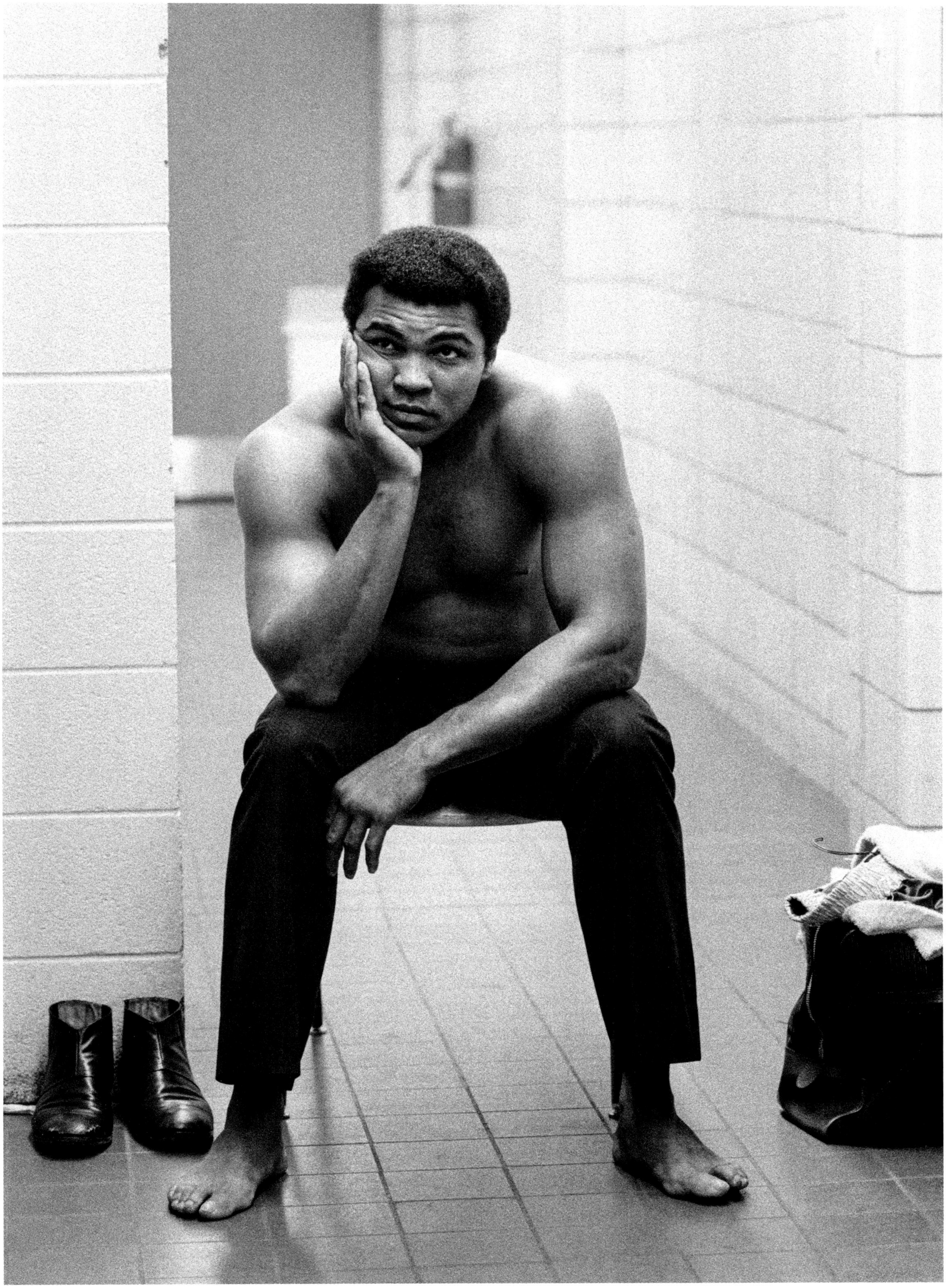

Deer Lake

— 139

1974
— 1978

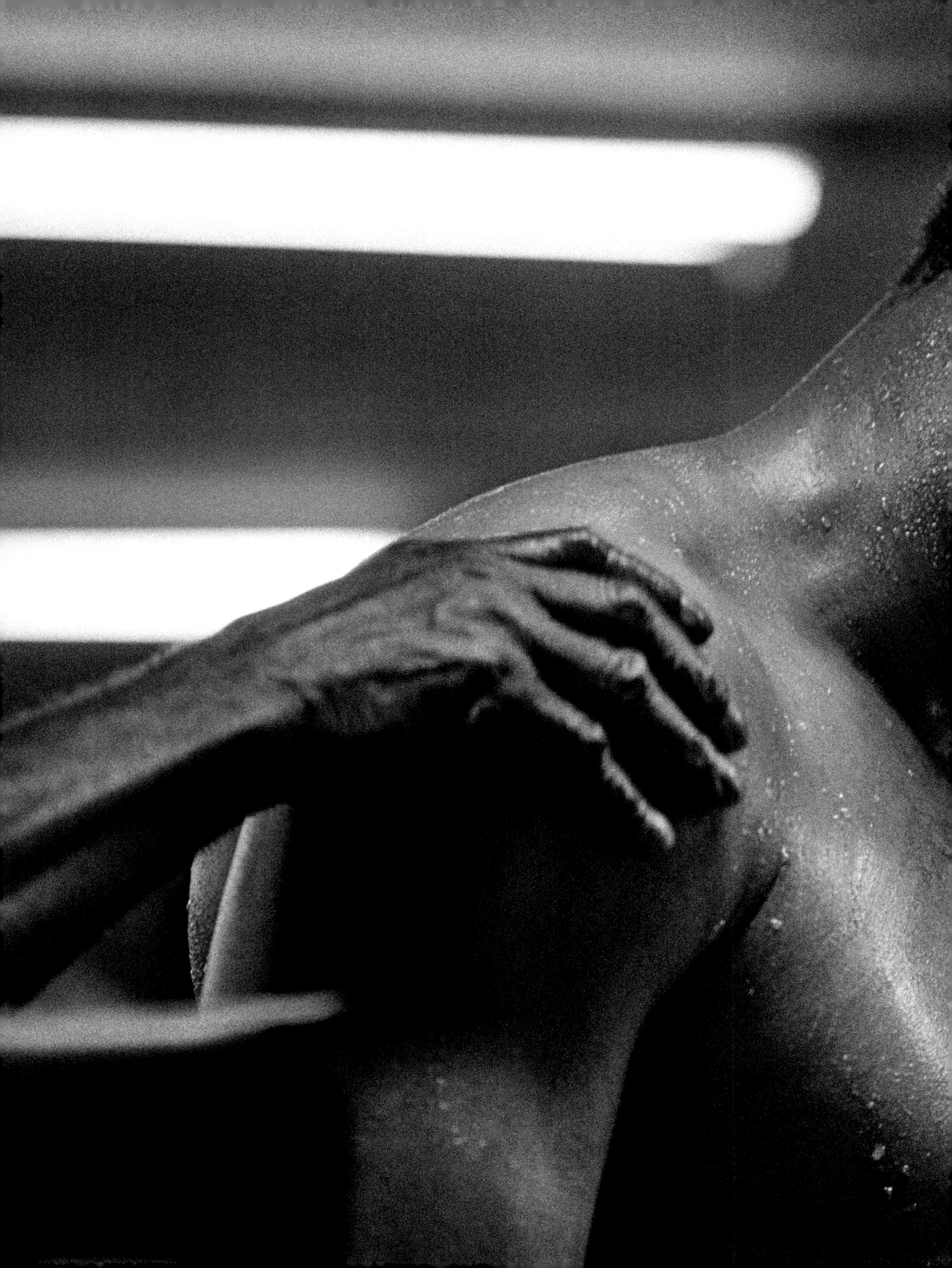

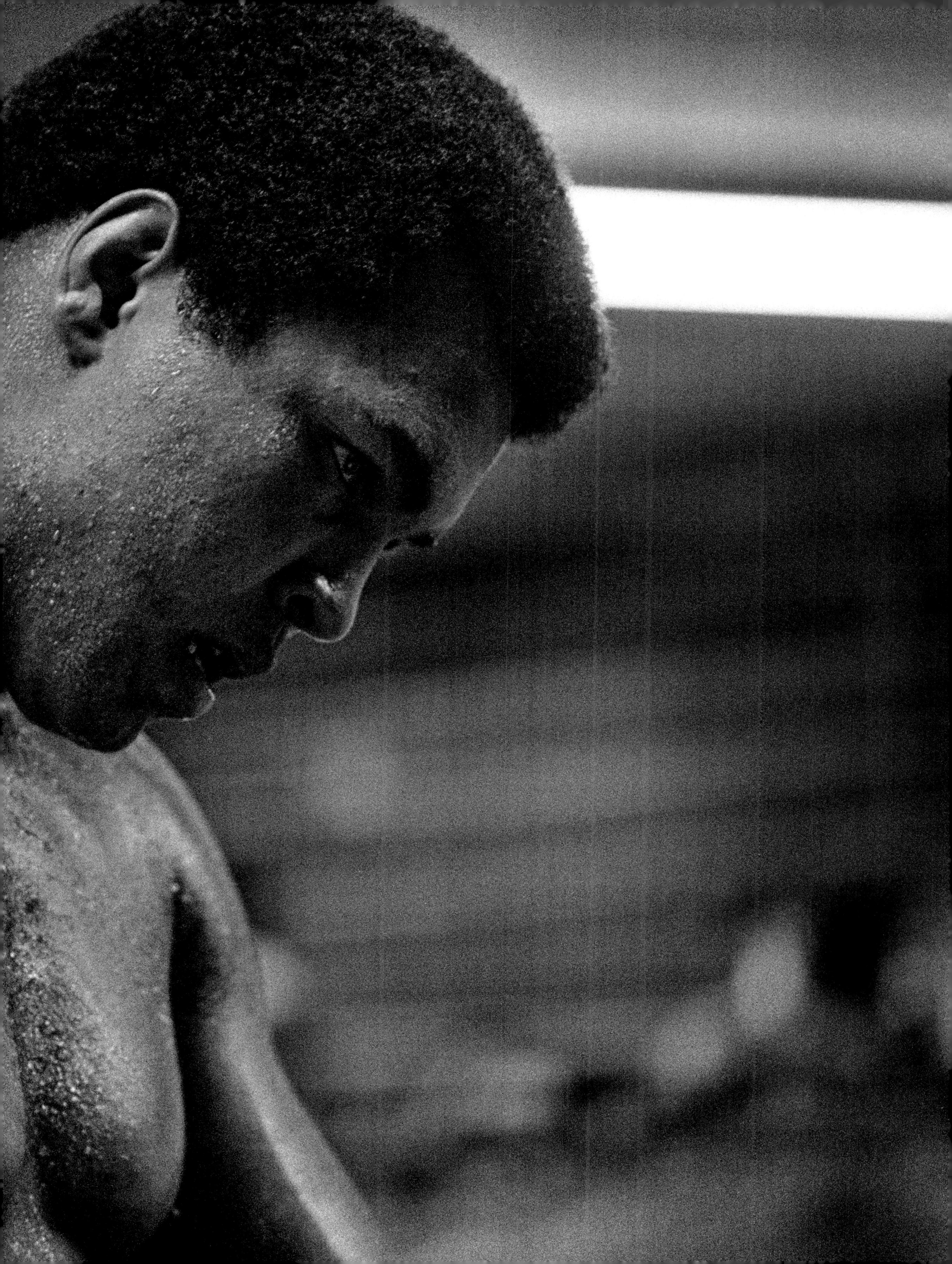

"IF YOU EVEN DREAM OF BEATING ME YOU'D BETTER WAKE UP AND APOLOGIZE."

144 —

If ever a town evoked a single individual and a singular purpose, it was Deer Lake, Pa.

To see that dateline on the sports page was to know Muhammad Ali was back in training and that the countdown to his next fight could commence.

Ali purchased six acres of the small borough north of Reading, Pa. — population 687 as of the 2010 census — and trained there from 1972 through 1980. That period included his two bouts with Joe Frazier and his "Rumble in the Jungle" with George Foreman.

Built at the crest of Sculps Hill Rd., Ali's low-frills camp consisted mainly of log cabins, some of the timber felled by the champ himself, with a gym, a dining hall, a mosque and a barn for his horses and donkey. Water came from a well.

"I'm more at home here than I am in my Cherry Hill (N.J.) house," Ali told talk show host Dick Cavett. "I'm living like the slaves did, like Jack Johnson did."

Ali commissioned his father to paint boulders on the property with the names of famous fighters such as Johnson (and himself), but he remained remarkably accessible to those fans who took the pains to make the pilgrimage.

"Here I am, the best-known man in all the world, and anyone can walk in here," Ali told New Orleans columnist Peter Finney. "You can't do that with John Wayne. You can't do that with Robert Redford. You can do it with Muhammad Ali."

Subsequent owners have tried to capitalize on Ali's connection to the property. For a time, it was known as the Butterfly & Bee Bed and Breakfast. Mike Madden, son of NFL Hall of Fame coach John Madden, bought the place following Ali's 2016 death with the intent of turning it into a museum.

"My challenge now is figuring out a way to get people up there and through the place," Madden told the Philadelphia Inquirer. "It tells a great story about an important historical figure. I just wonder if these kids who walk around with their noses in their phones all day will get it."

→ C. Thomas Hardin
Muhammad Ali throws a punch at sparring partner Fred Reed while training at his Deer Lake compound.

1978

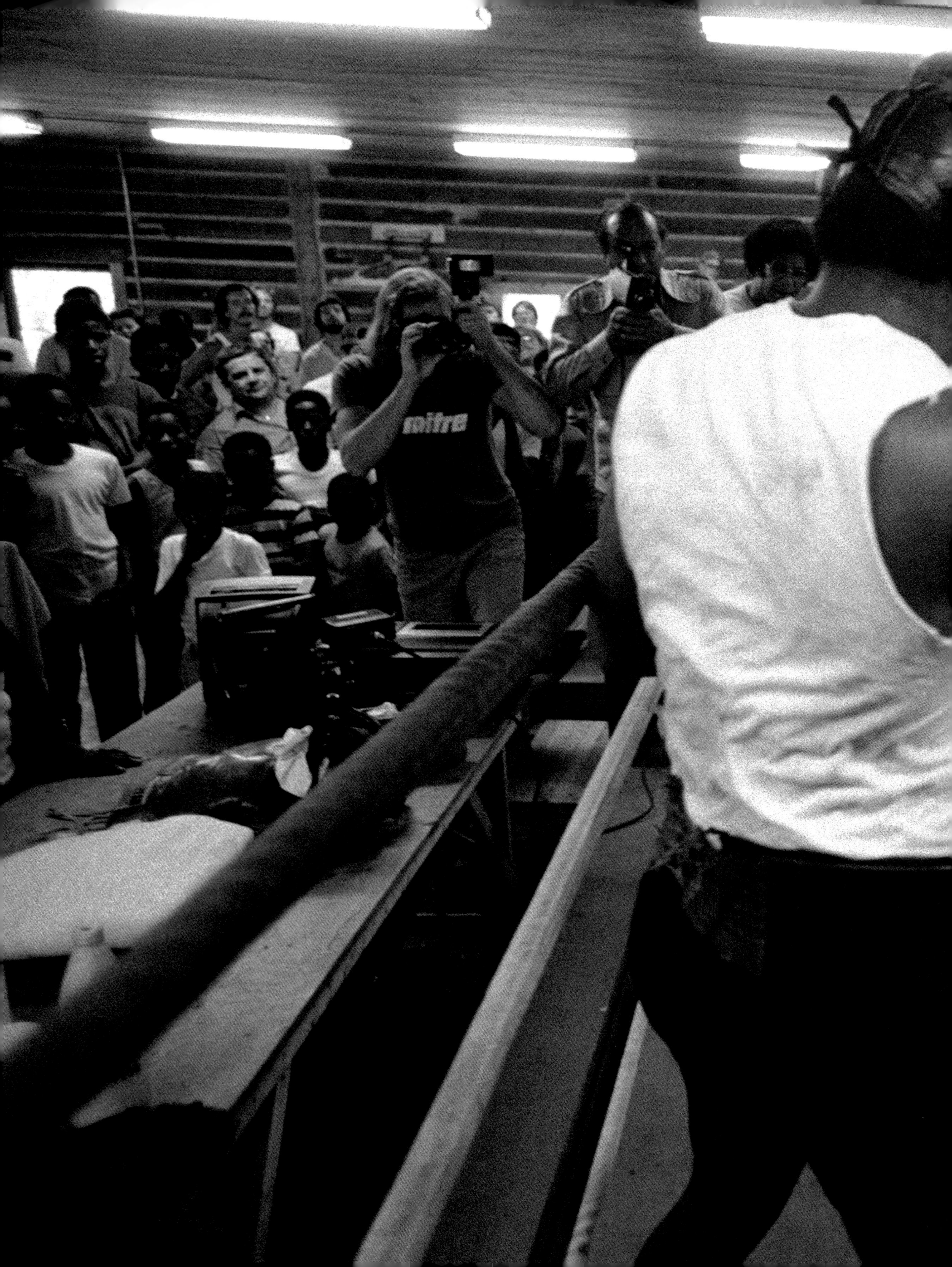
mitre

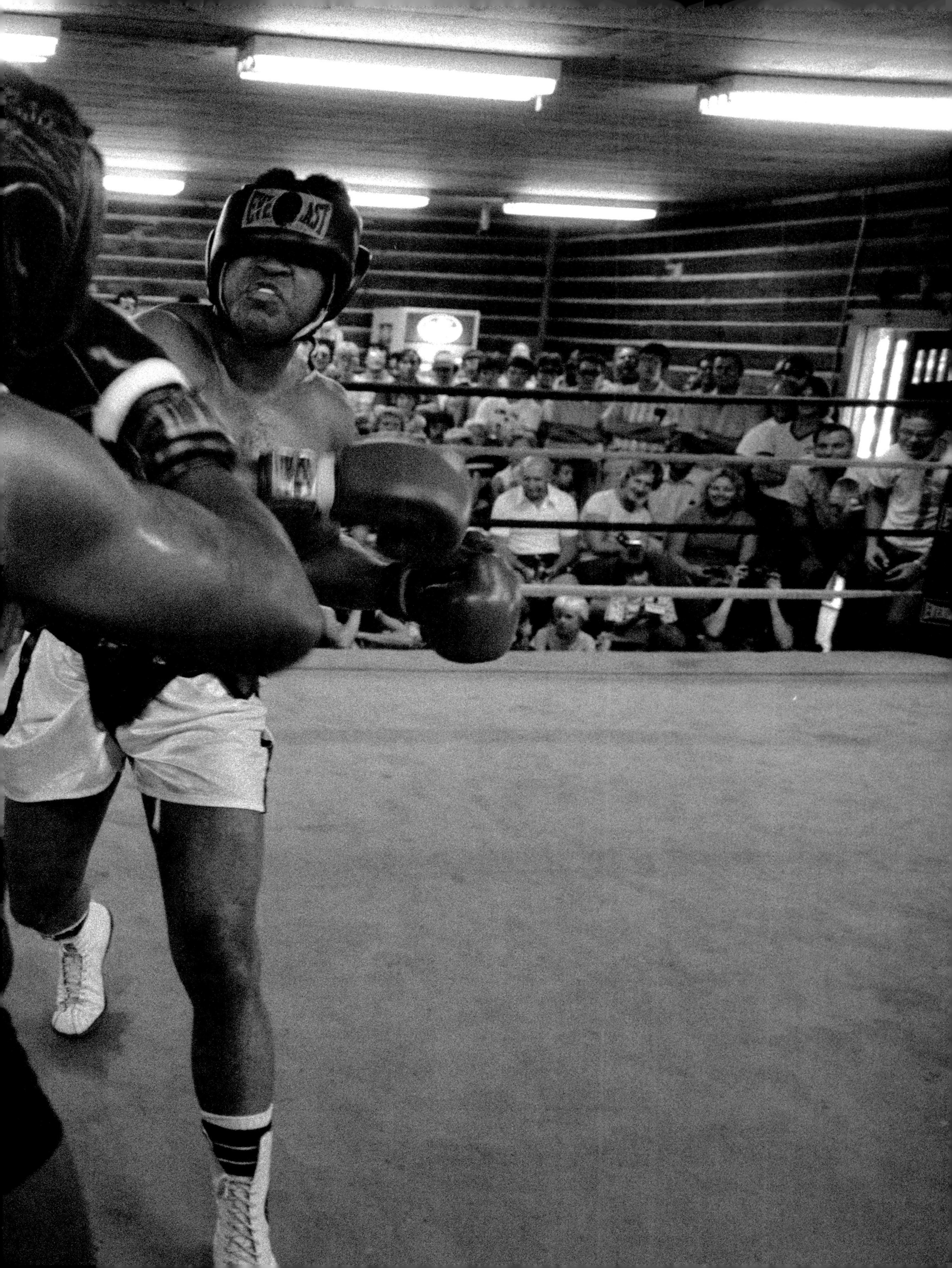

1 Keith Williams
Muhammad Ali sits in front of a small mosque at the Deer Lake training center before heading off on a morning run.

August 1978

1 Keith Williams
Shrouded in early morning fog, Ali takes his daily three-mile run along a Pennsylvania country road.

August 1978

1 C. Thomas Hardin
Ali prefers company for his morning run.
With wife Veronica, he jogs in the mist of
the Pennsylvania countryside.

1978

→ **Keith Williams**
Ali stares out from the ring while training
to fight Leon Spinks for the second time.

August 1978

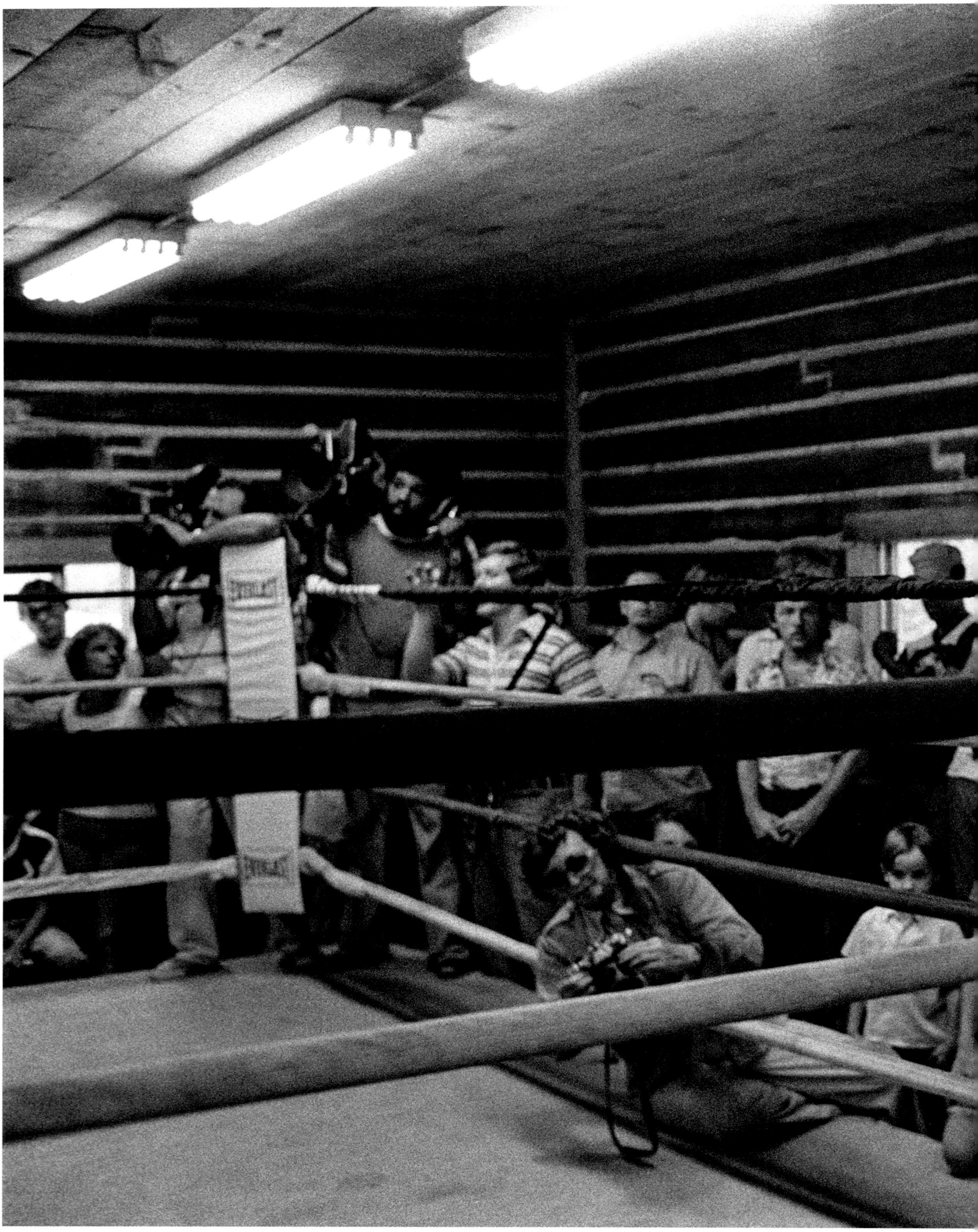

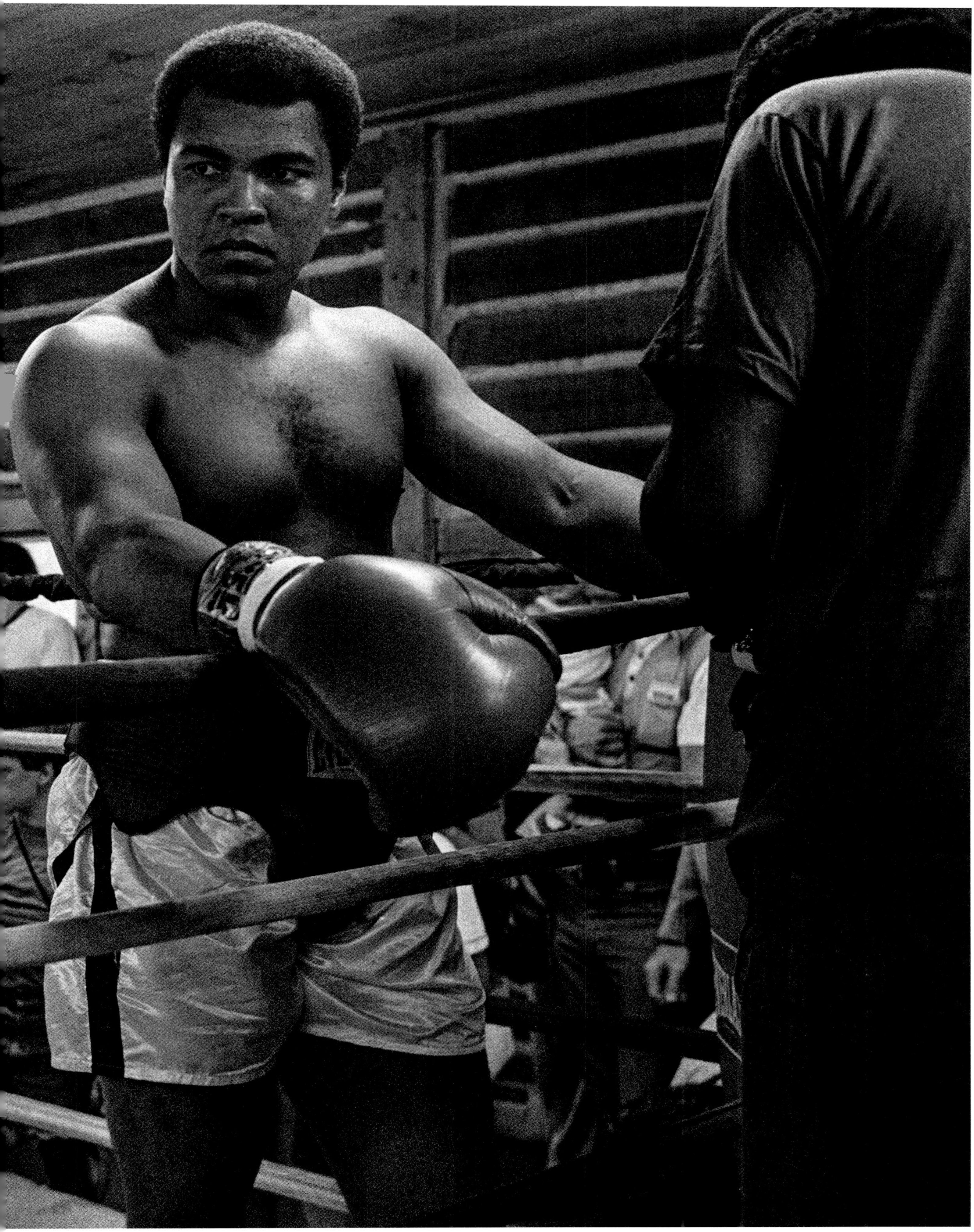

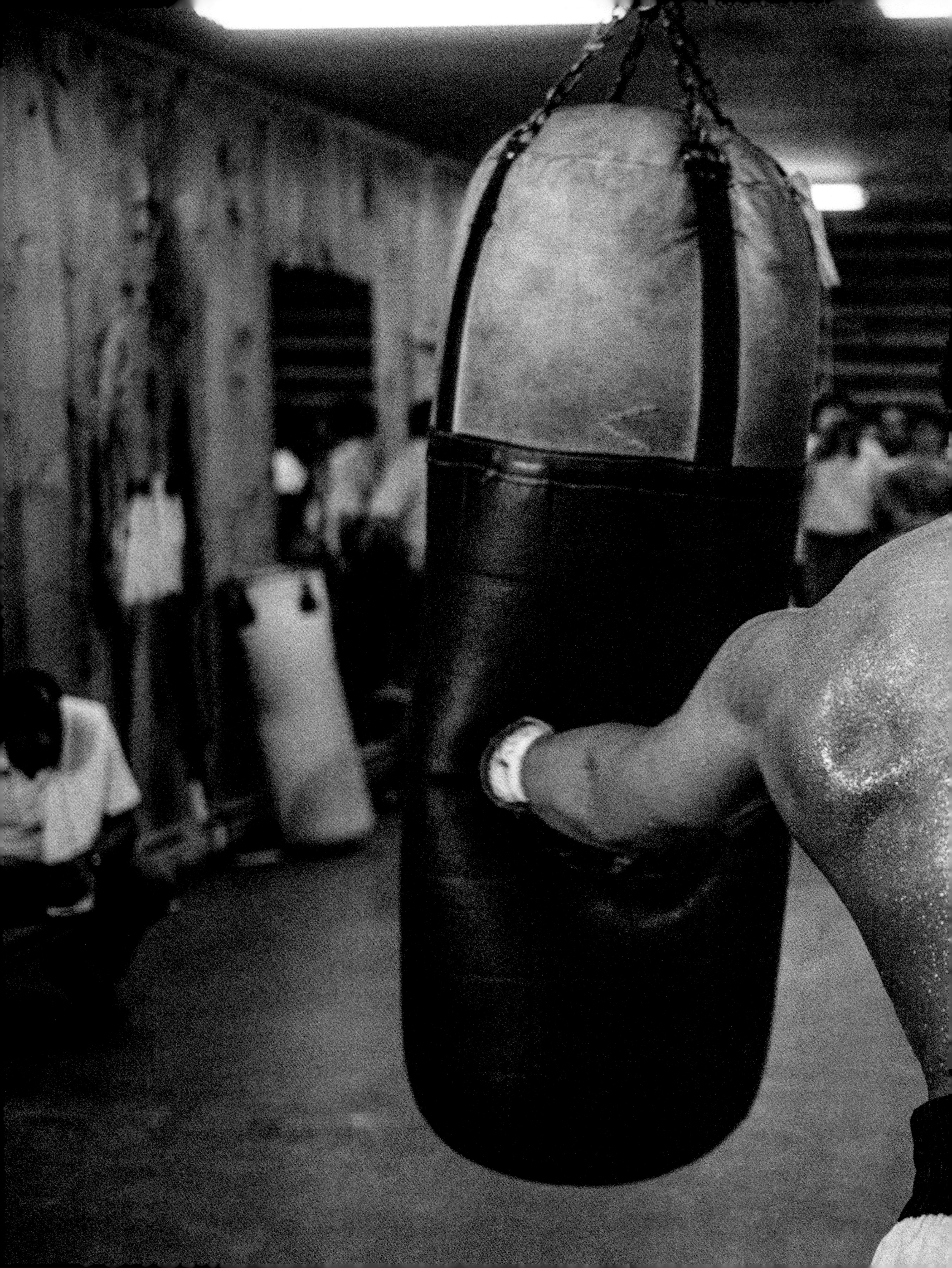

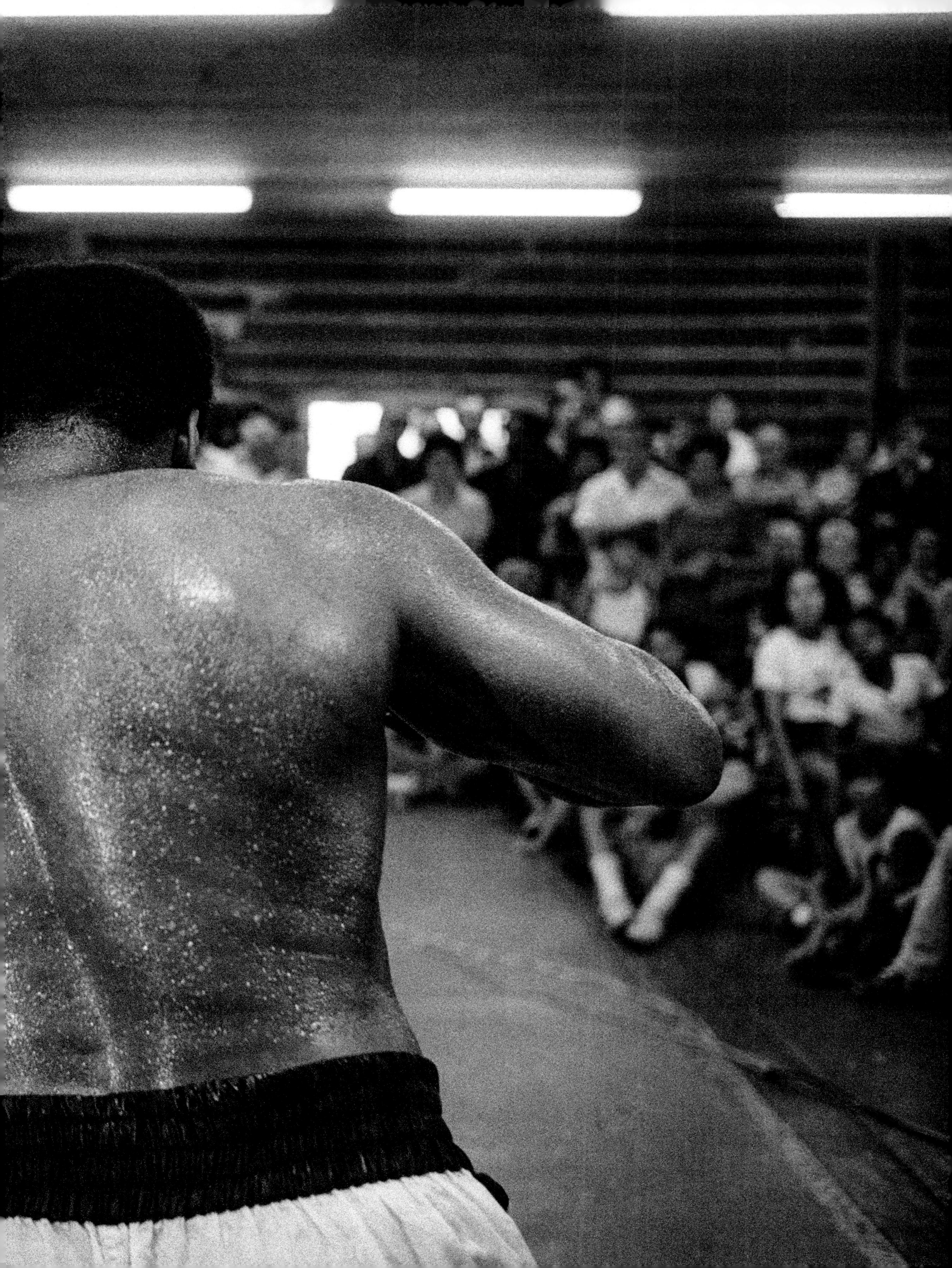

← C. Thomas Hardin
Muhammad Ali trains on a punching bag while preparing for his second fight against Leon Spinks.

1978

↑ C. Thomas Hardin
Ali is flanked by a painting of himself by the artist Leroy Neiman at his Deer Lake training camp.

1978

1 C. Thomas Hardin
Ali shadow boxes in front of a mirror that is on a wall next to cutouts of himself.

→ Keith Williams
Spectators watch every move that Muhammad Ali makes while in the ring against a sparring partner. The crowds are good for his ego and his attitude, he says. With people watching he can't cheat on his training.

1978

August 1978

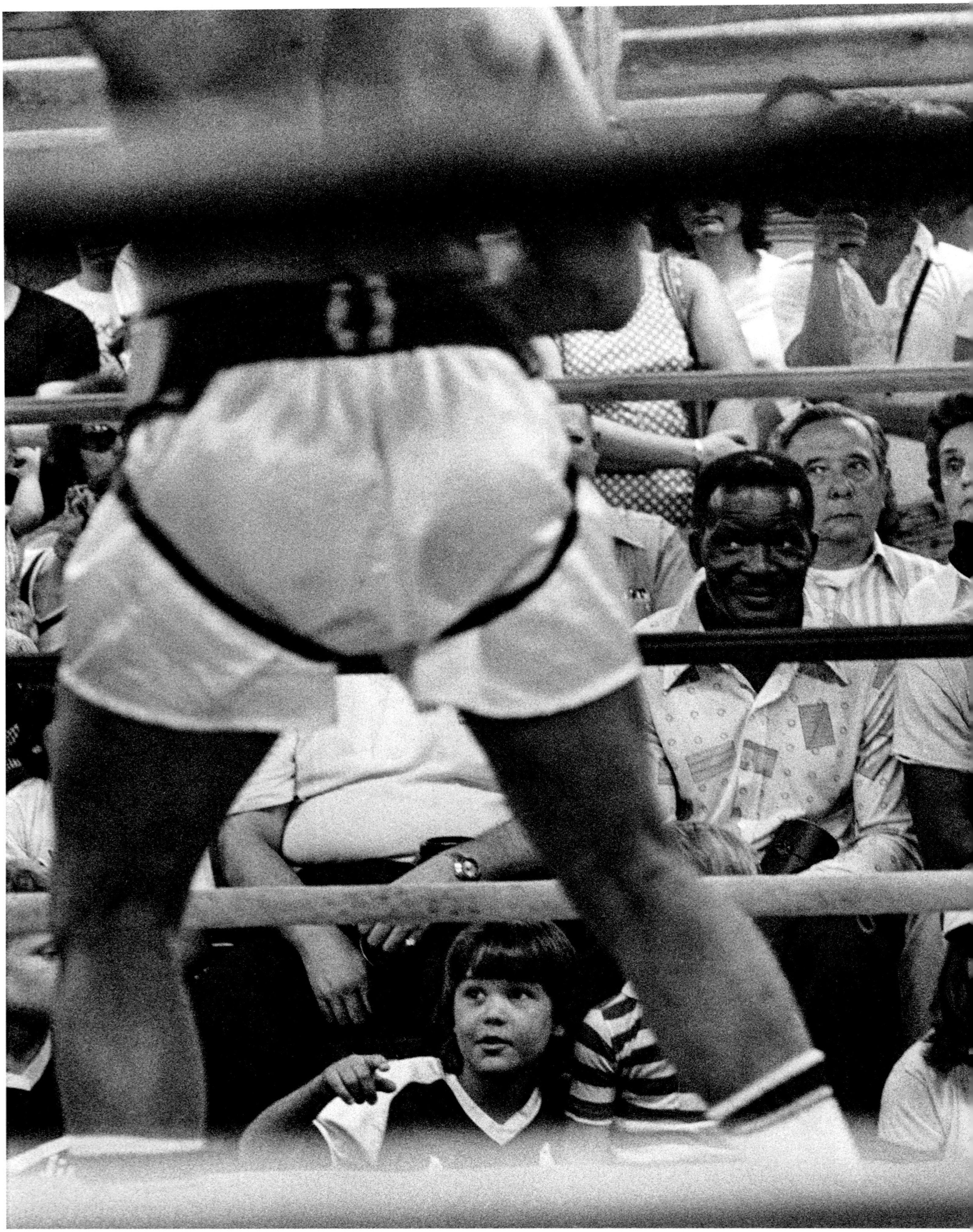

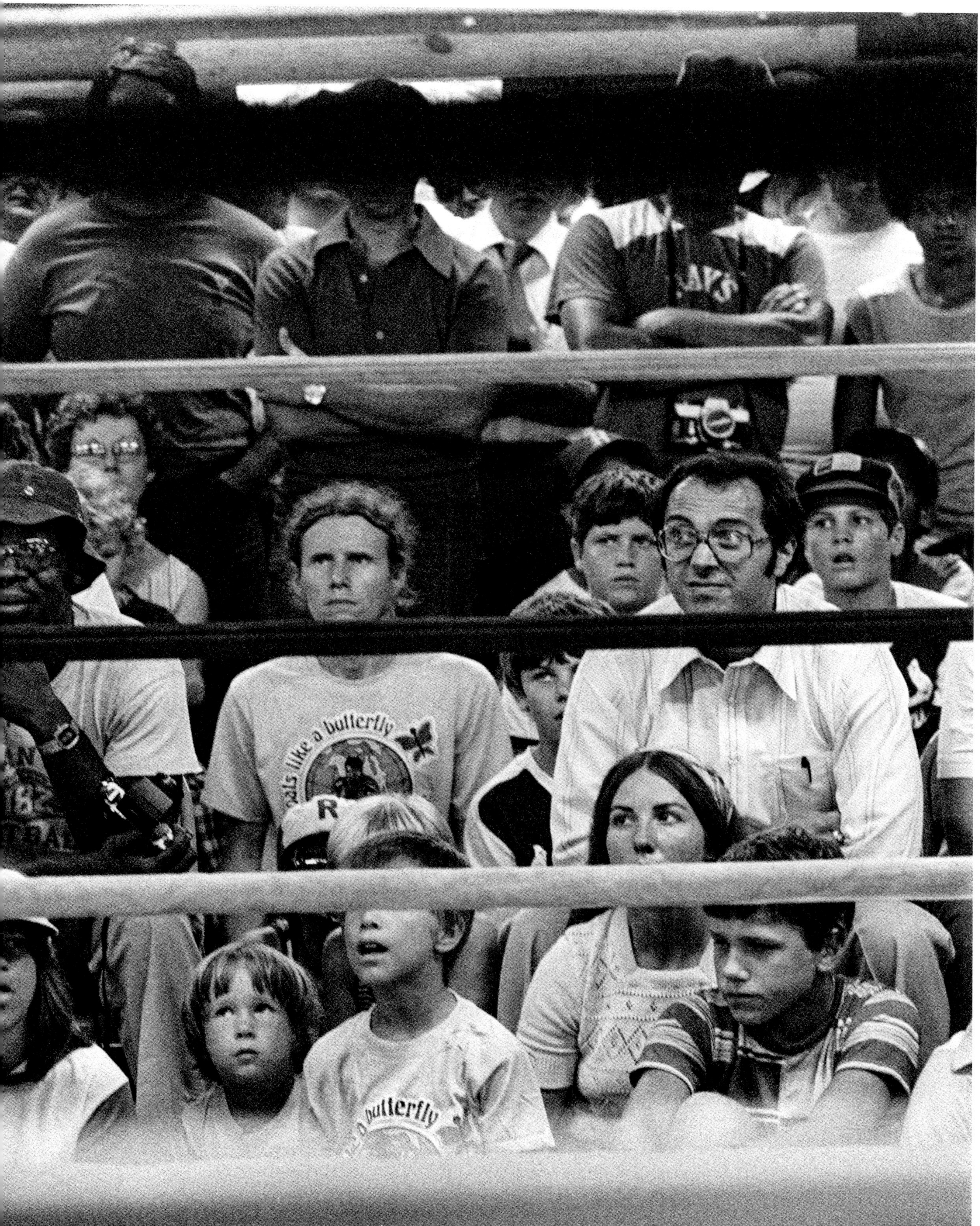
like a butterfly
butterfly

"How tall are you? So I can know in advance how far to step back when you fall down!"

1 Keith Williams
Sweat pours from Ali as he trains for a rematch with Leon Spinks.

August 1978

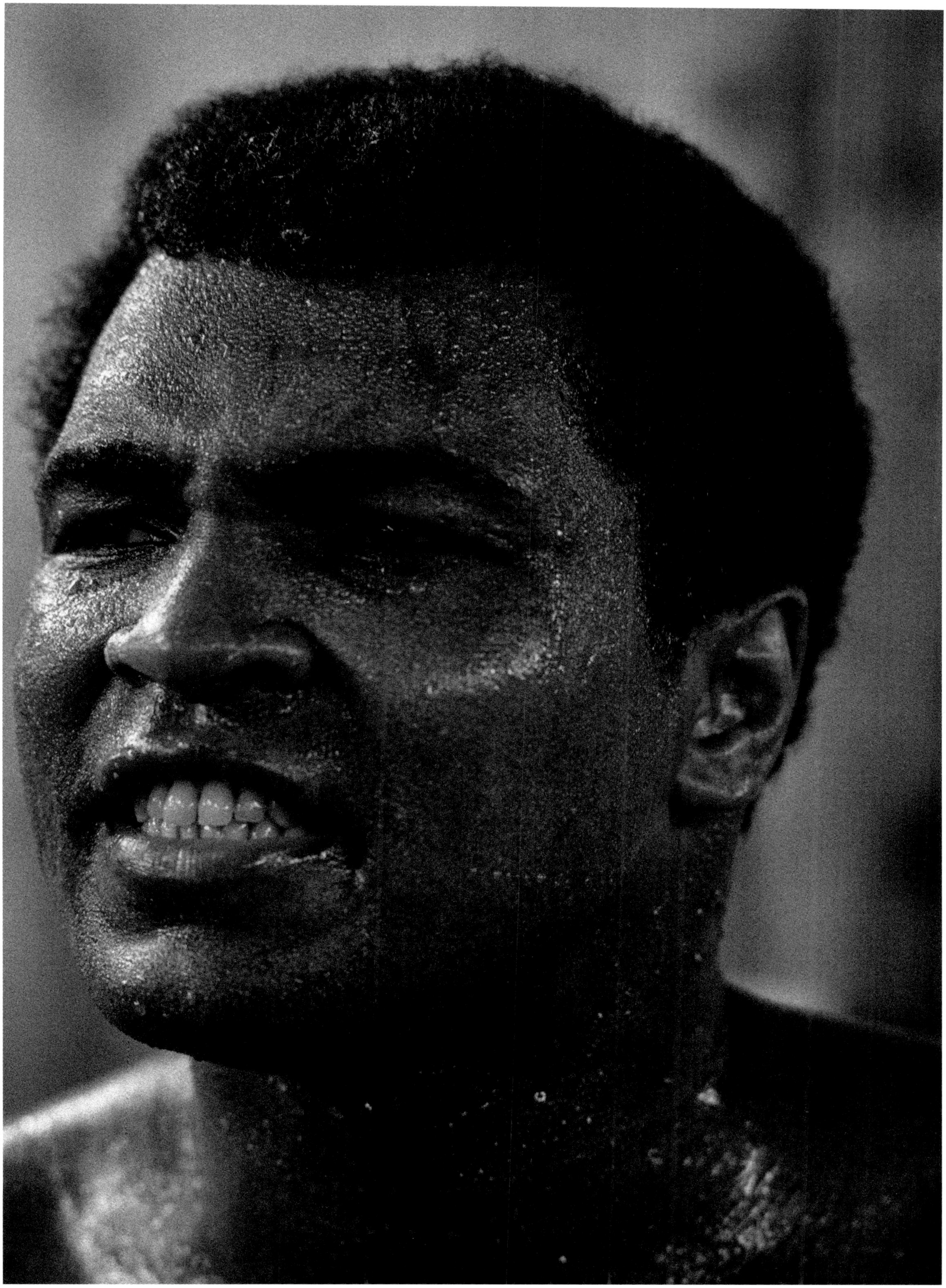

1 C. Thomas Hardin
Luis Sarria prepares Muhammad Ali's face for a workout. It is a face Ali praises. "Look at that face. Twenty-four years of boxing, and I'm still pretty." Sarria served as Ali's "cut man" for many years.

1978

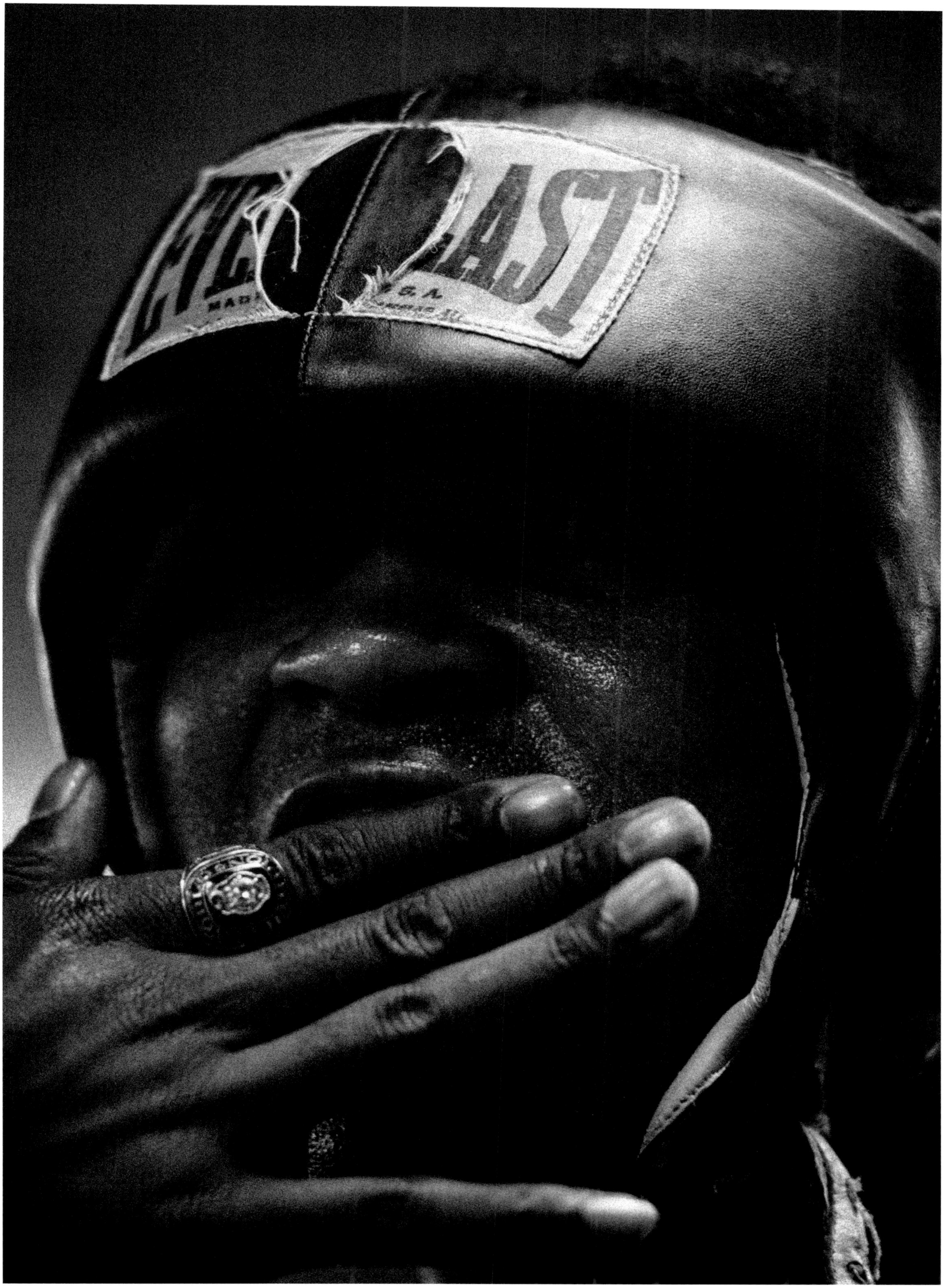

164 —

1 C. Thomas Hardin
Lloyd Wells, left, and Luis Sarria, right, study Ali after he completed 300 situps, part of his daily routine of exercises. "I'm suffering, this is slavery," Muhammad Ali says of the sit-ups.

1978

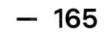

1 C. Thomas Hardin
Ali works through a routine of leg crunches while at his training camp in Pennsylvania.

1978

166 —

1 C. Thomas Hardin
A wall contains Muhammad Ali's poems and inspirational literature at his training camp.

1978

— 167

1 C. Thomas Hardin
Muhammad Ali writes poems on a wall at his camp.

1978

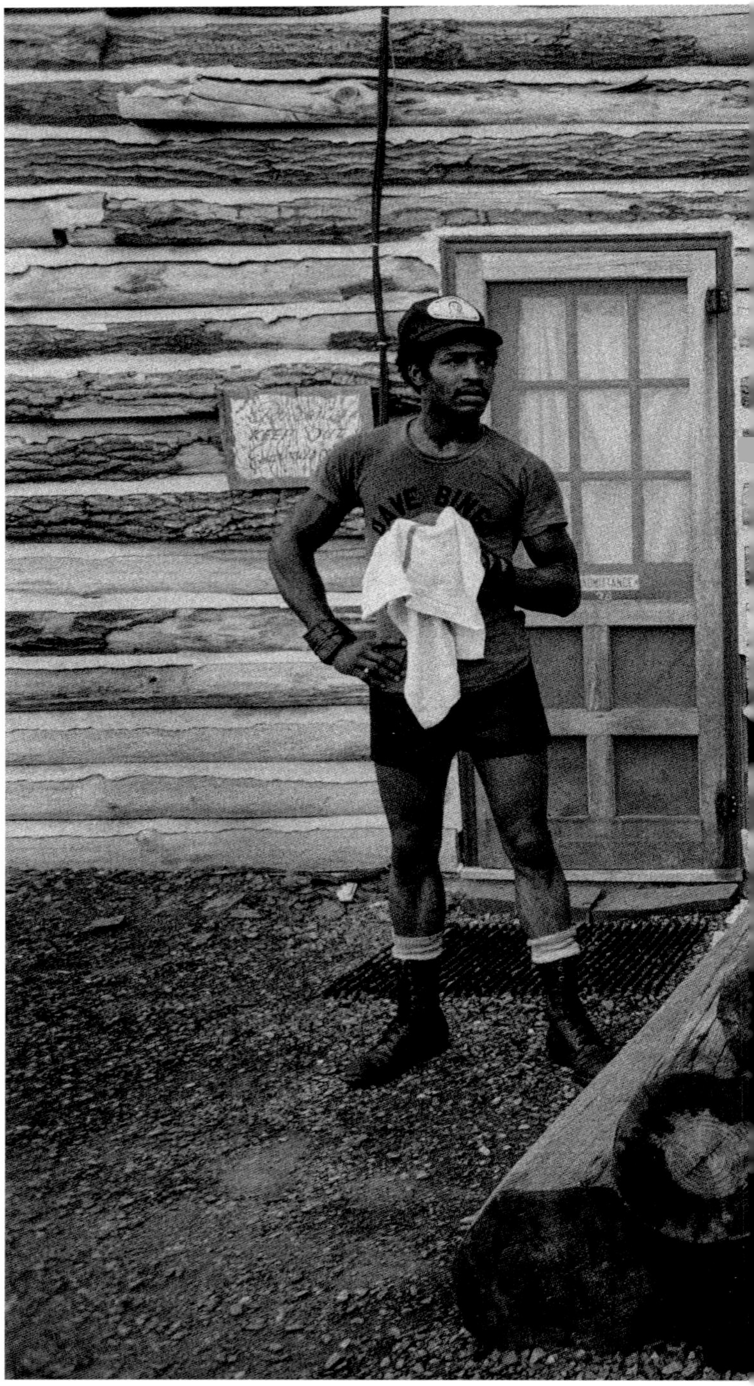

— 169

1 C. Thomas Hardin
Muhammad Ali talks with a training partner prior to his morning run.

1974

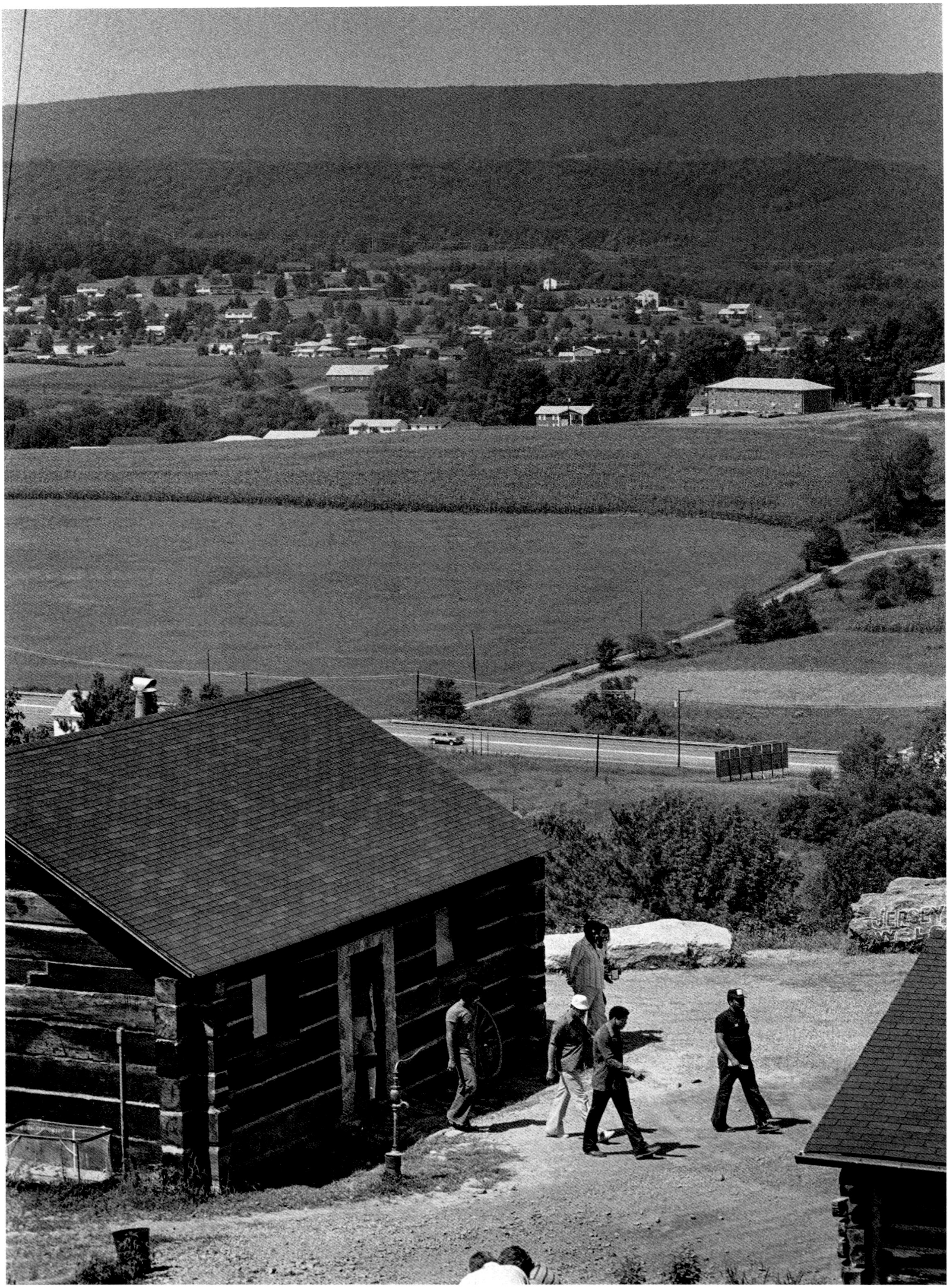

← **Keith Williams.**
Muhammad Ali walks through his training complex in Pennsylvania.

August 1978

↑ **C. Thomas Hardin**
Ali shadow boxes on a road above the Pennsylvania countryside that runs through his training camp.

1978

172

"Impossible is just a big word thrown around by small men who find it easier to live in the world they've been given than to explore the power they have to change it. Impossible is not a fact. It's an opinion. Impossible is not a declaration. It's a dare. Impossible is potential. Impossible is temporary. Impossible is nothing."

1 C. Thomas Hardin
A crowd gathers around Muhammad Ali as he performs magic tricks at his camp.

1978

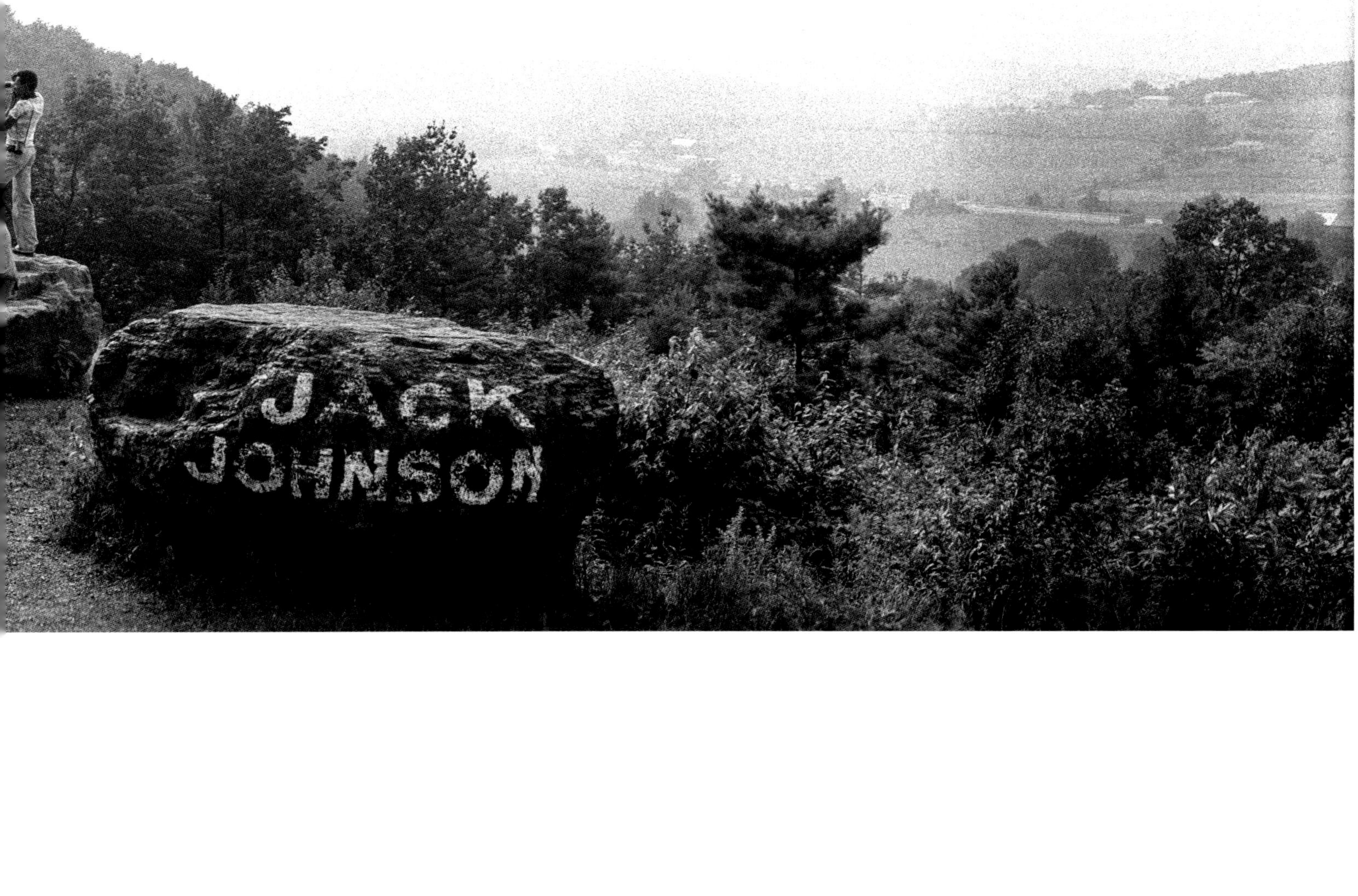
JACK
JOHNSON

1 C. Thomas Hardin
Muhammad Ali was disappointed by his idol Sugar Ray Robinson, but refuses to disappoint now that he himself is an idol as he comforts a girl who was knocked to the ground.

1978

"Service to others
is the rent you pay
for your room
here on earth."

1 C. Thomas Hardin
Muhammad Ali holds court as fans gather around the legendary boxer at his training camp.

1978

— 179

1 C. Thomas Hardin
Ali sports a boxing glove while engaging a crowd at his training camp.

1978

↑ C. Thomas Hardin
Muhammad Ali playfully spars with a visitor while a young boy tries to hold back his arm.

1978

→ C. Thomas Hardin
Children gather around Ali as he takes a break from training for a rematch with Leon Spinks.

1978

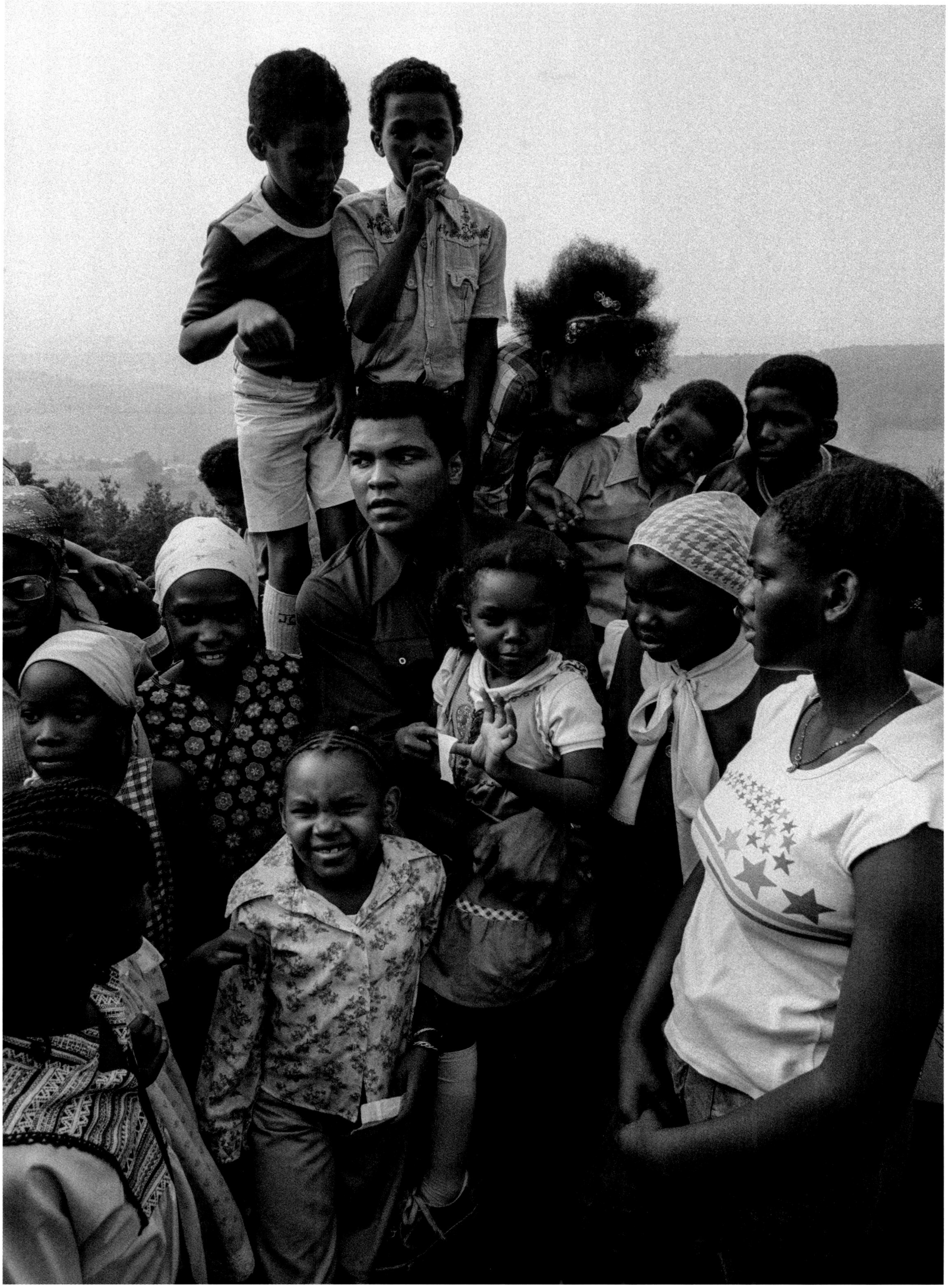

1 Keith Williams
A robe belonging to Muhammad Ali hangs from a gutter of a building at the Deer Lake training center.

August 1978

1 C. Thomas Hardin
Ali temporarily leaves his magic in the ring for newly-learned magic at the card table.

1978

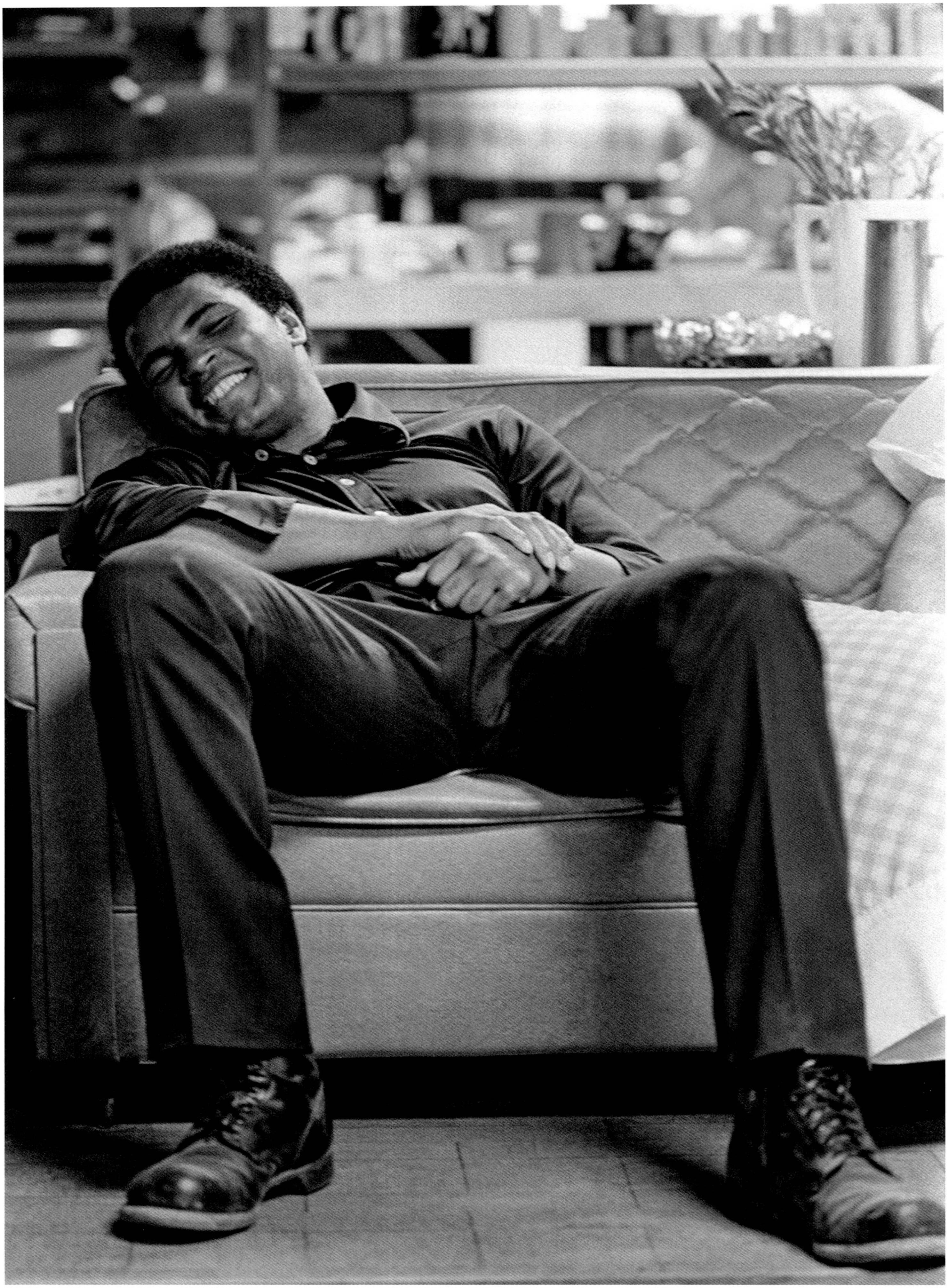

1 C. Thomas Hardin
Muhammad Ali relaxes in a rustic cabin at his training camp in Pennsylvania.

1974

186

1 Keith Williams
Muhammad Ali plays with his daughter Hana while at his training camp in Pennsylvania.

August 1978

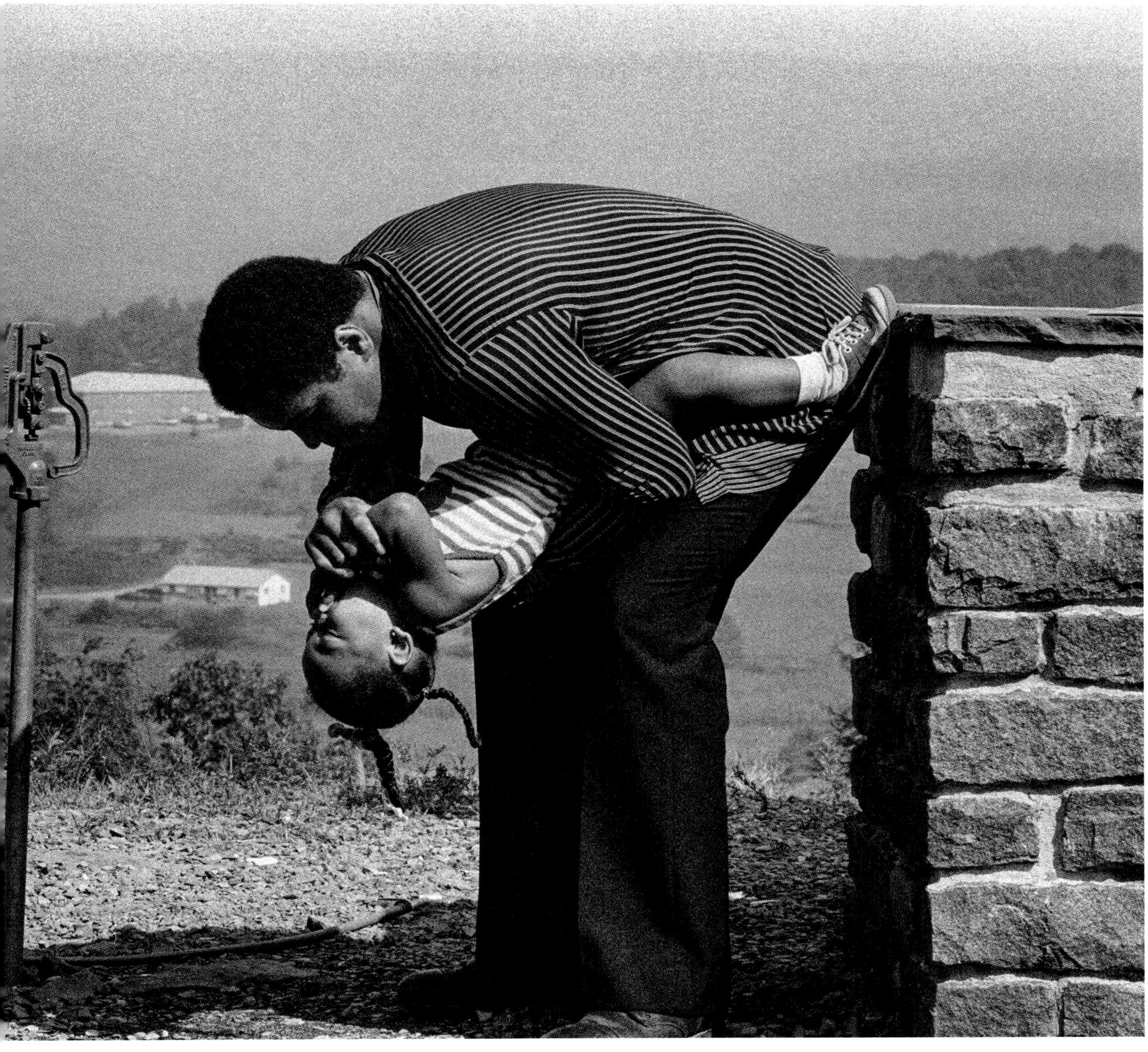

1 Keith Williams
Muhammad Ali lays on a couch with his daughter Hana after a day of training.

August 1978

1 Keith Williams
Ali walks past his car, a Stutz Bearcat, while carrying his daughter Hana. In the background is one of the rocks his father painted with the names of legendary boxers.

August 1978

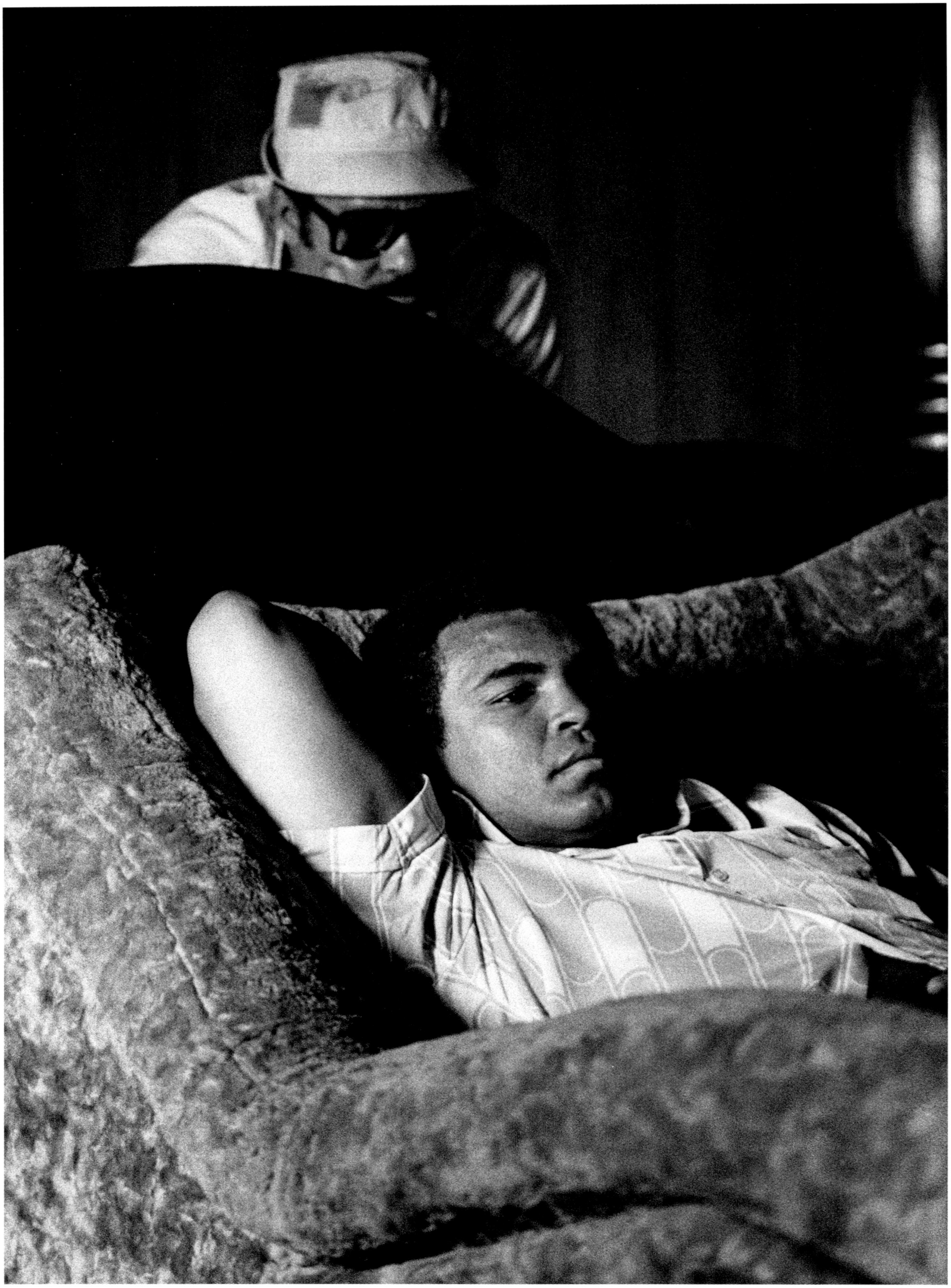

1 Keith Williams
Muhammad Ali relaxes while in training in Pennsylvania.

August 1978

192

↑ C. Thomas Hardin
Muhammad Ali prays before his early morning run.

1978

→ C. Thomas Hardin
Ali begins each day with prayer at his mosque. "How you gonna beat a man that God's with," the champ says.

1978

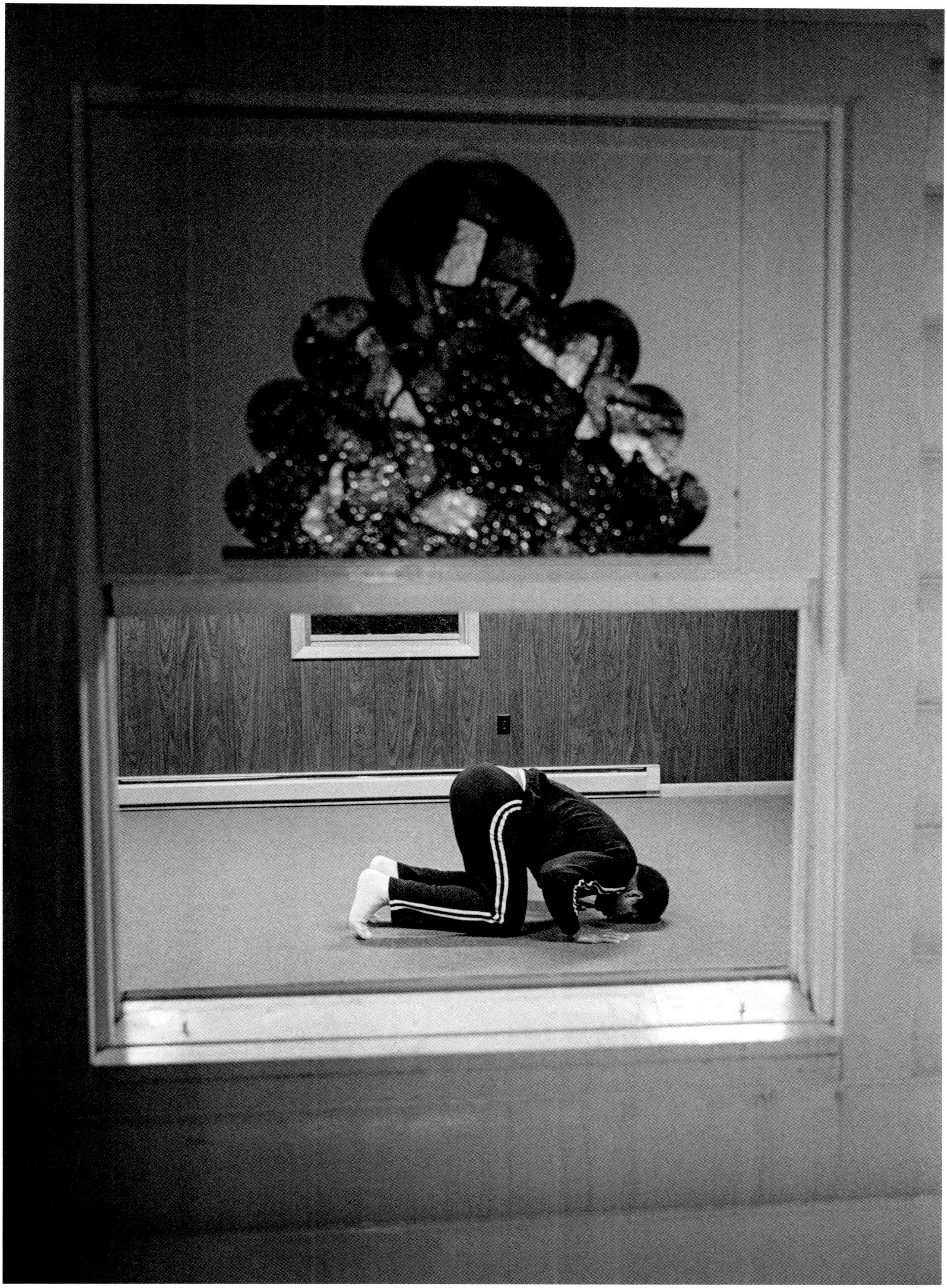

vs. Spinks

1978

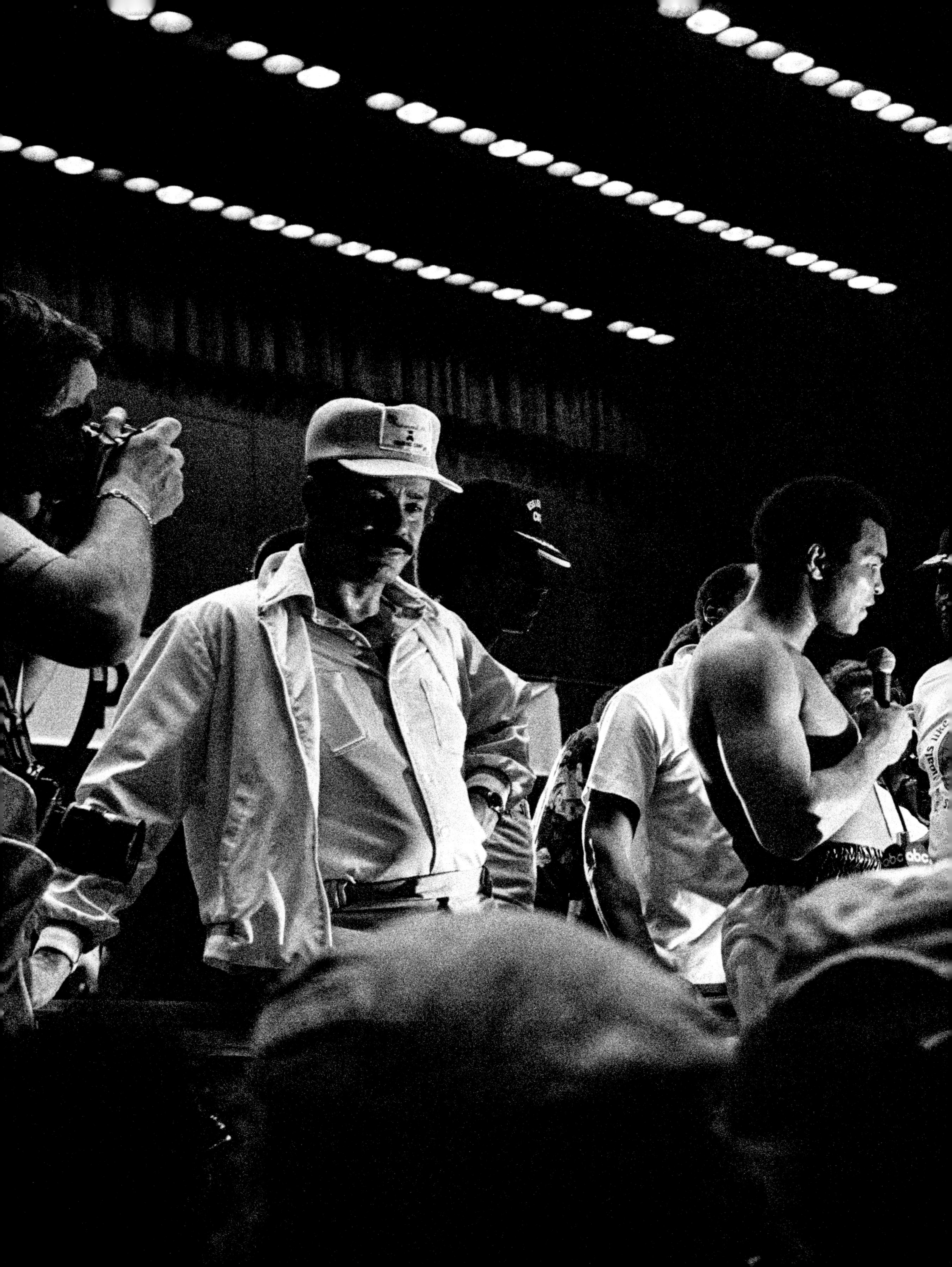
abc

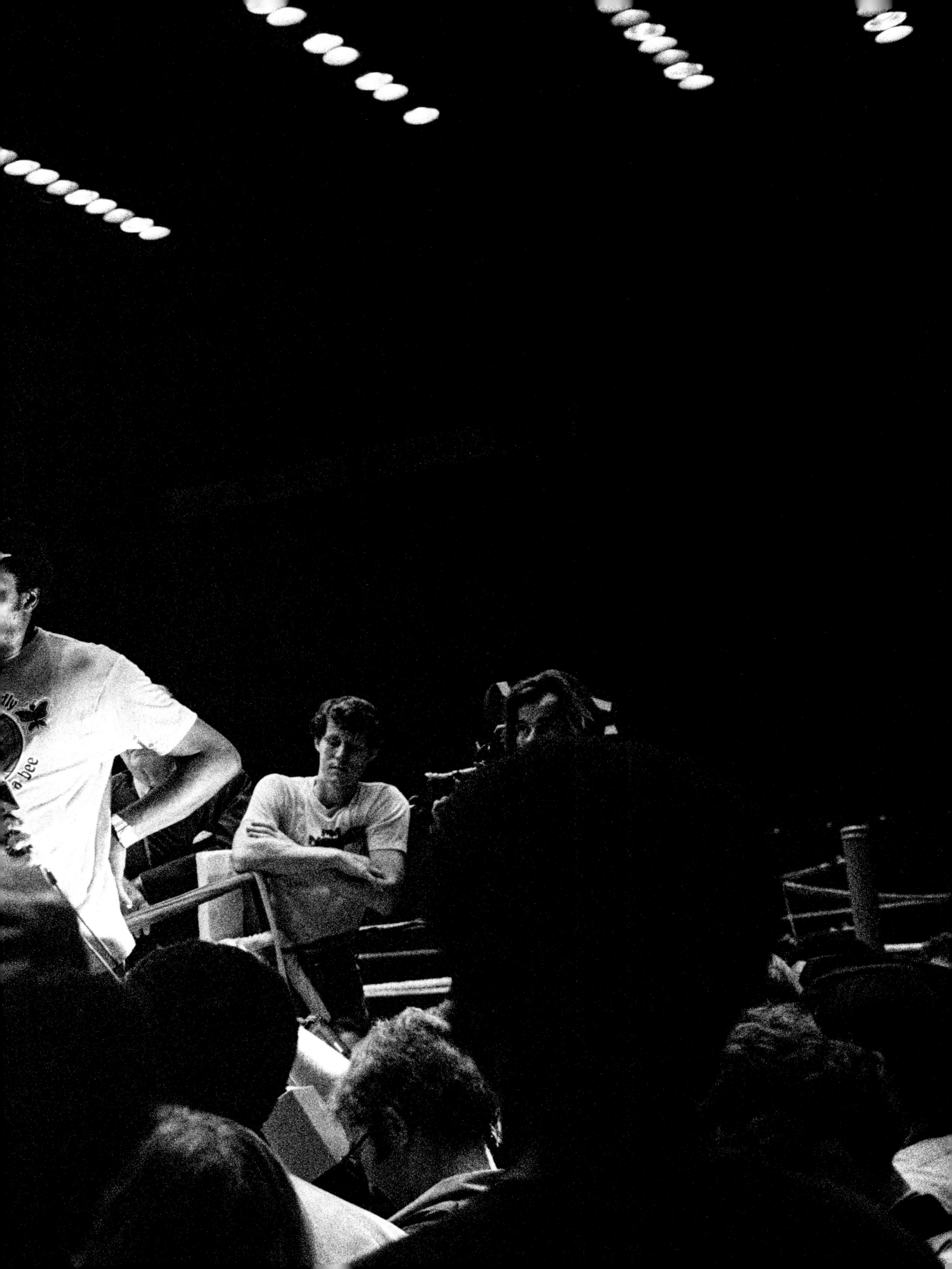

"I SHOULD BE A POSTAGE STAMP. THAT'S THE ONLY WAY I'LL EVER GET LICKED."

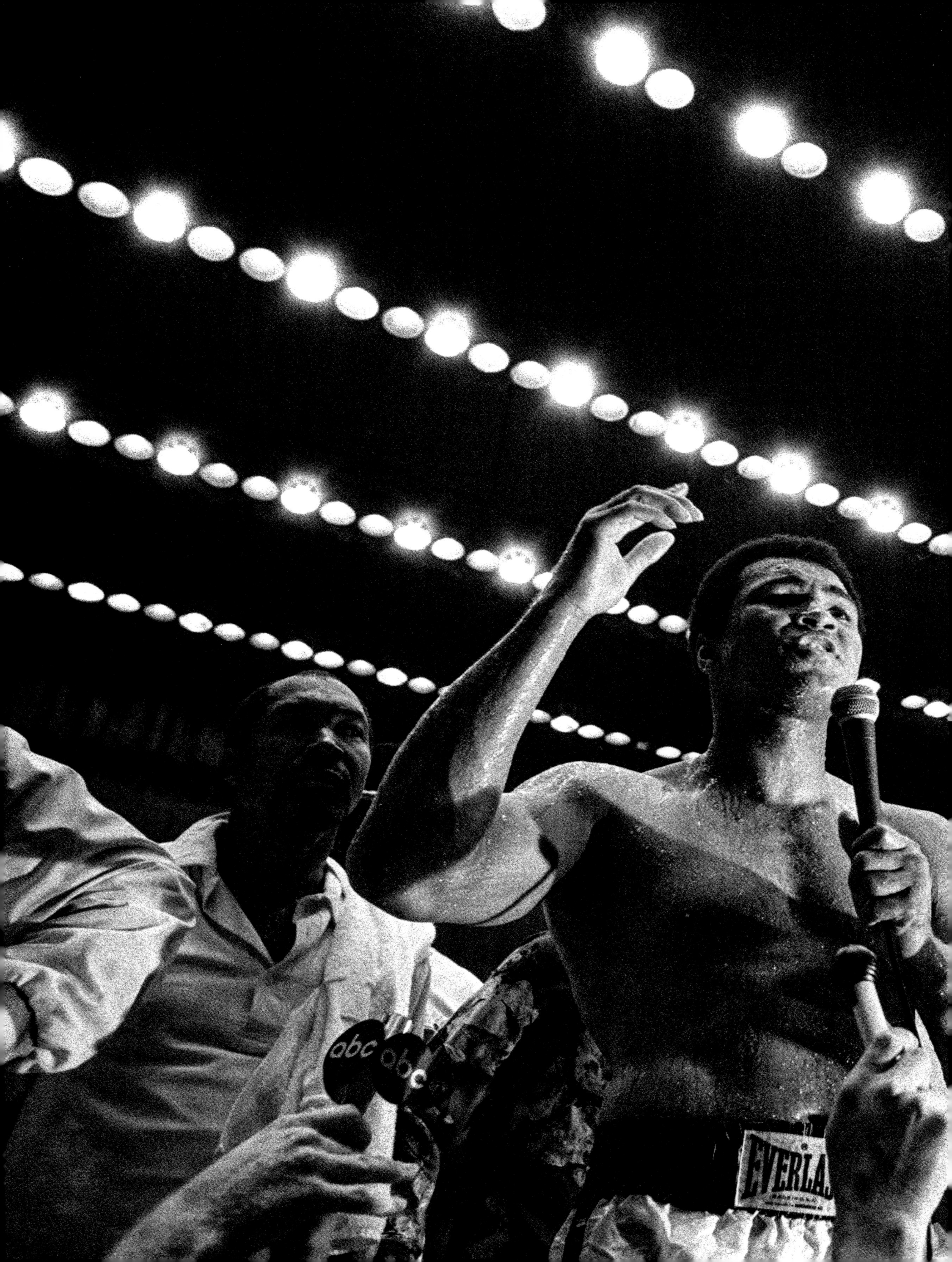
abc
abc
EVERLA

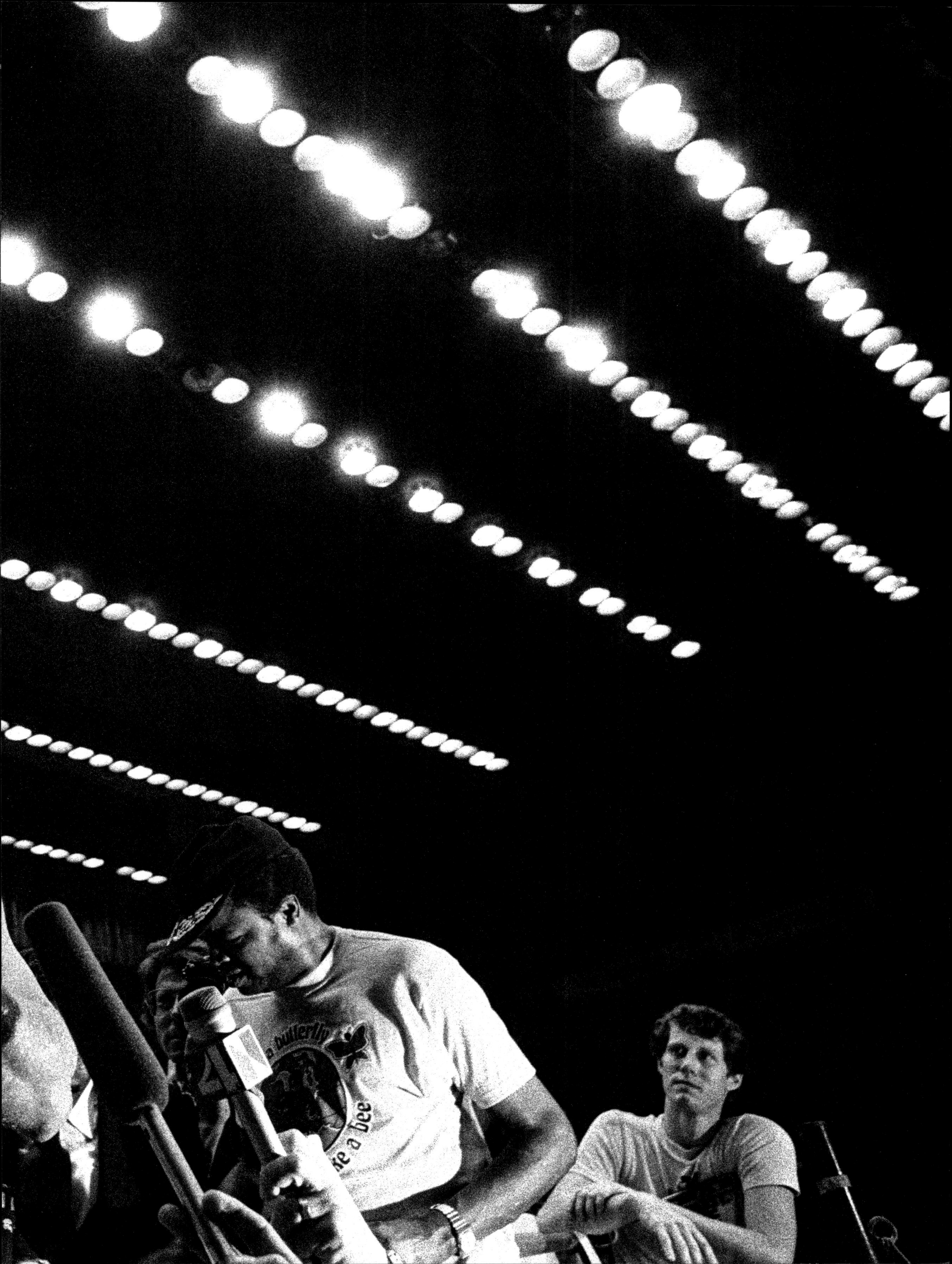

← C. Thomas Hardin
Muhammad Ali speaks to the media prior to his rematch with Leon Spinks in New Orleans.

September 1978

In reclaiming his title from Leon Spinks, Muhammad Ali became heavyweight boxing's first three-time champion. It was the final glimpse of his greatness as a fighter and the last time he would have the last word against an opponent who had previously defeated him.

Ali had won 14 straight fights over a span of nearly five years when Spinks took his title in Las Vegas in February, 1978. Ali later said he had taken Spinks too lightly, trusting the same rope-a-dope strategy that had exhausted George Foreman in Zaire four years earlier.

But though the inexperienced Spinks was a conspicuously raw talent – he entered the ring having fought only 31 rounds as a professional — he did not wear down as Foreman had. When Ali finally got going in the later rounds, Spinks kept coming.

"It was embarrassing that someone with so little fighting skills could beat me," Ali told biographer Thomas Hauser. "I didn't train right. I gave away the first six rounds figuring he'd tire out, and then it turned out it was me that got tired."

Resolved to atone, Ali pressed Spinks for a prompt rematch. And though his skills had diminished, his starpower remained intact. He was still the strongest attraction in the sport.

Spinks would be stripped of his WBC title for failing to face its No. 1 ranked contender, Ken Norton, but fighting Ali attracted an announced crowd of 63,350 to the Louisiana Superdome on Sept. 15, 1978. At the time, this was the largest crowd to watch boxing indoors. The TV rating was a robust 46.7.

Pre-fight visitors to Ali's camp at Deer Lake, Pa., found the former champion up by 5 a.m., running at dawn, sparring more than he had in years, committed to peak condition for what he said would be his last fight.

Spinks, meanwhile, struggled with motivation and self-discipline. Seemingly determined to sabotage his career, Spinks was evicted, arrested and caught with cocaine within three months of winning the title. Prone to aggressive partying, he would stop training without notice and at least once eluded his bodyguard, the pre-fame Mr. T.

The result was what Howard Cosell would later call it a "terrible fight," with Ali docked the fifth round for holding. But after Ali established his superiority over Spinks en route to a unanimous decision, Cosell was moved to quote from Bob Dylan's "Forever Young" in his ringside commentary:

"May your hands always be busy.
May your feet always be swift.
May you have a strong foundation
When the winds of changes shift."

Wishing, however, would not make it so. Muhammad Ali would not win another fight.

↑ C. Thomas Hardin
Muhammad Ali addresses the media from the ring in New Orleans.

September 1978

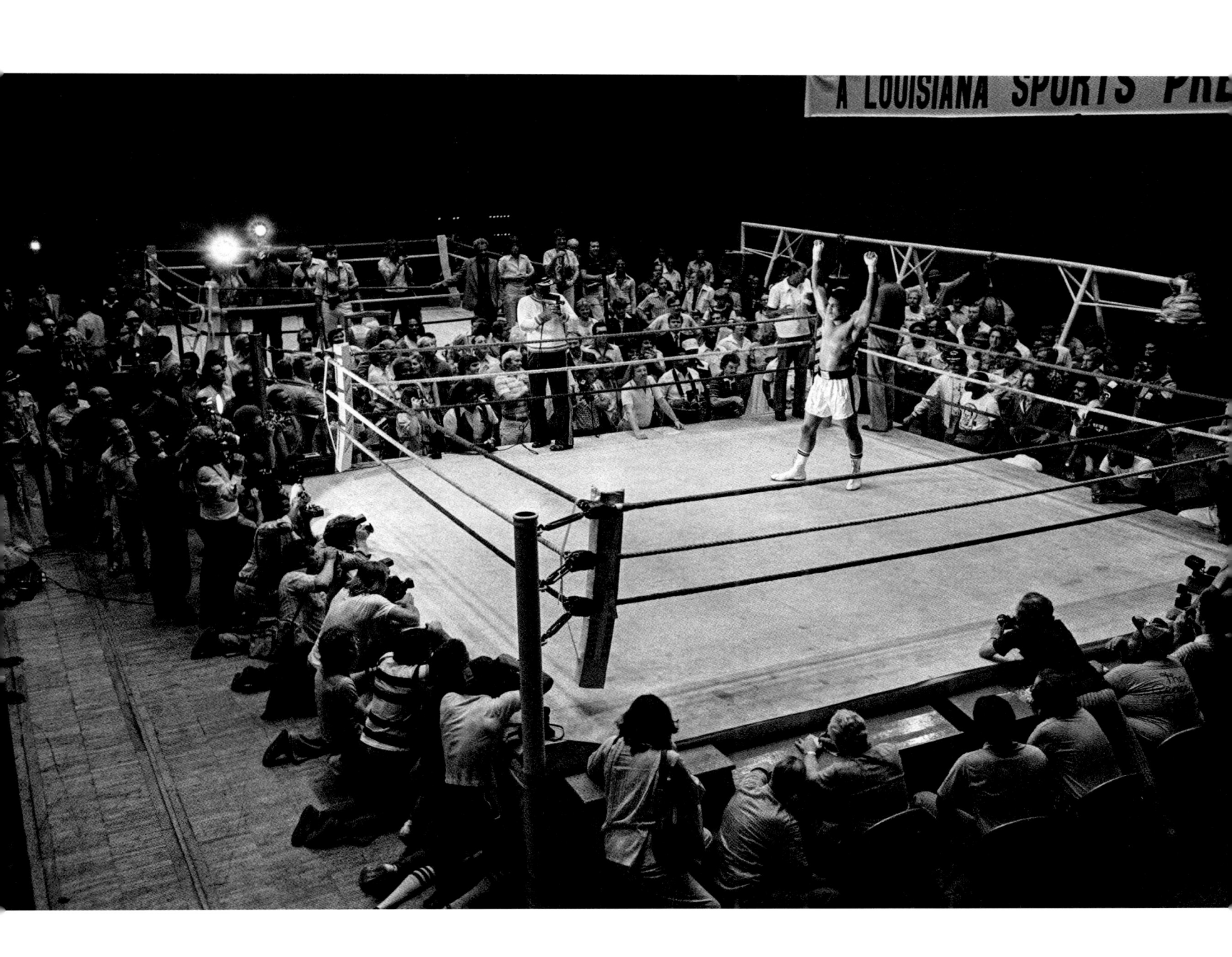

1 C. Thomas Hardin
Photographers kneel at the side of the ring for a photo of Ali.

September 1978

206 —

1 Keith Williams
Muhammad Ali reads the newspaper after completing his morning workout regimen before sunrise in New Orleans.

September 1978

1 C. Thomas Hardin
Ali discusses his upcoming fight with his advisors.

September 1978

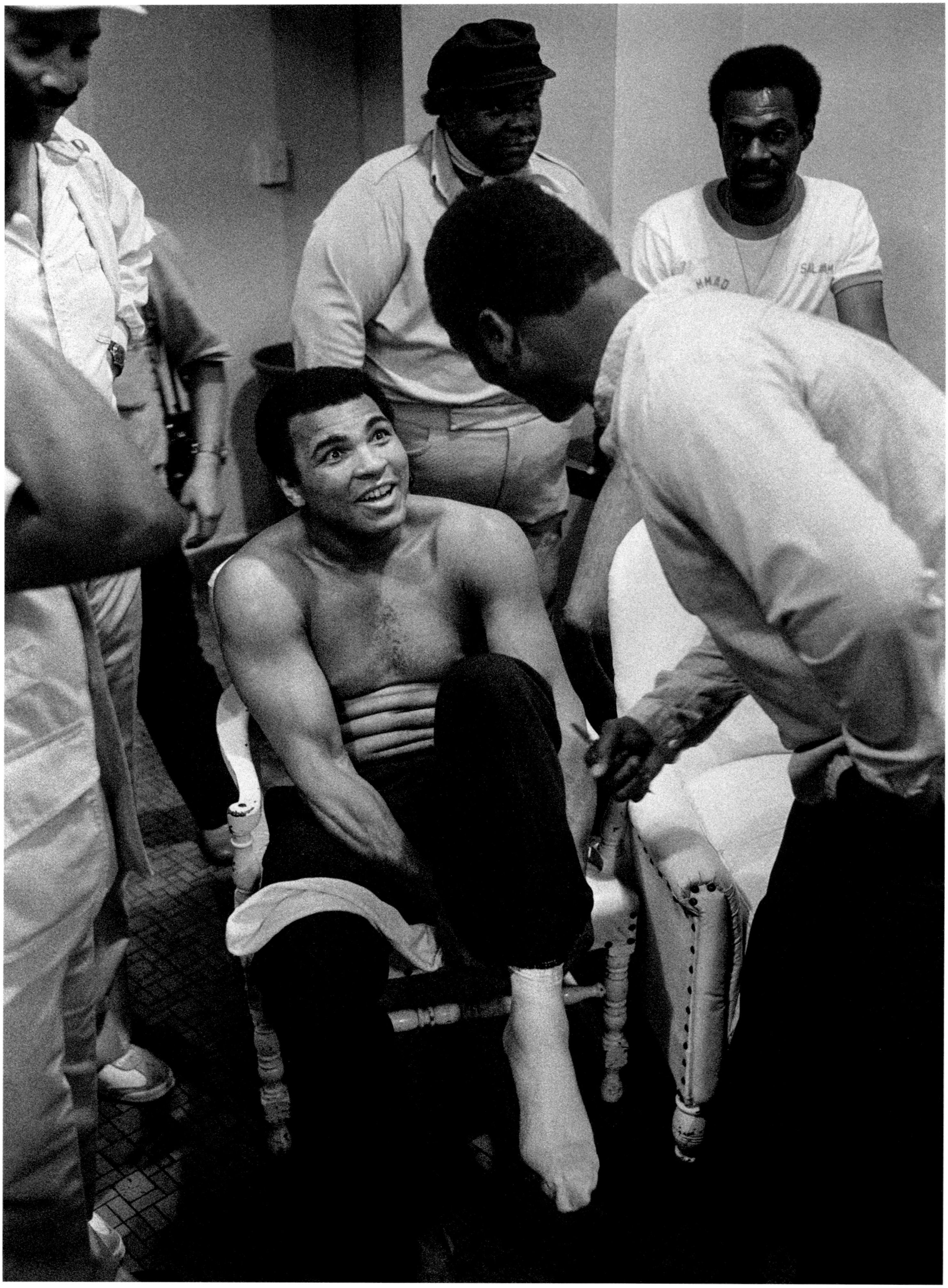

"Joe Frazier is so ugly that when he cries, the tears turn around and go down the back of his head."

1 Keith Williams
Former heavyweight boxing champion Joe Frazier, right, visits with Muhammad Ali prior to his rematch with Leon Spinks.

September 13, 1978

210 —

1 C. Thomas Hardin
Muhammad Ali is surrounded as he makes his way to the ring.

September 15, 1978

↑ Keith Williams
Fans cheer as Ali makes his way to the ring.

September 15, 1978

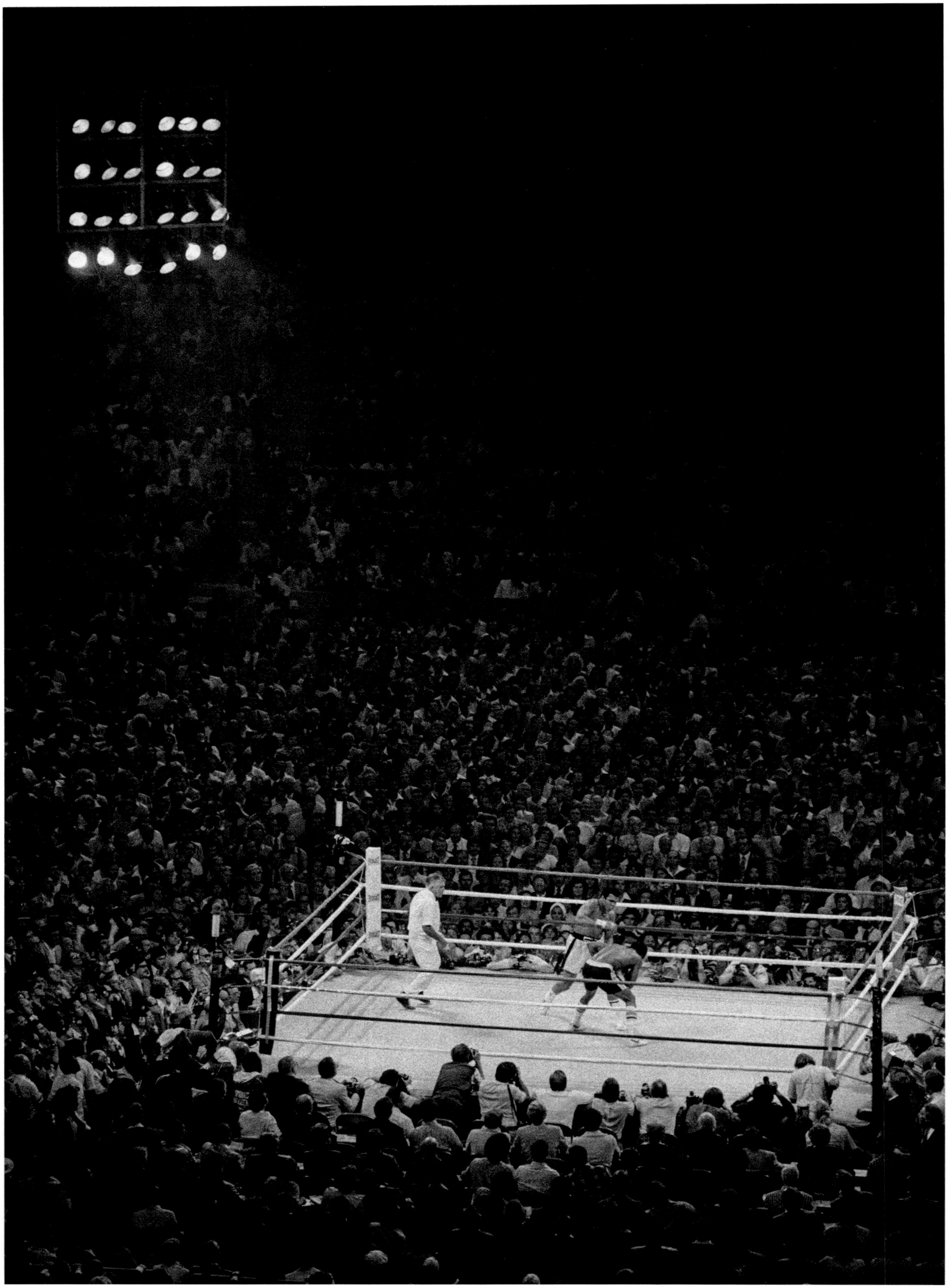

1 C. Thomas Hardin
Muhammad Ali and Leo Spinks square off for the second time.

September 15, 1978

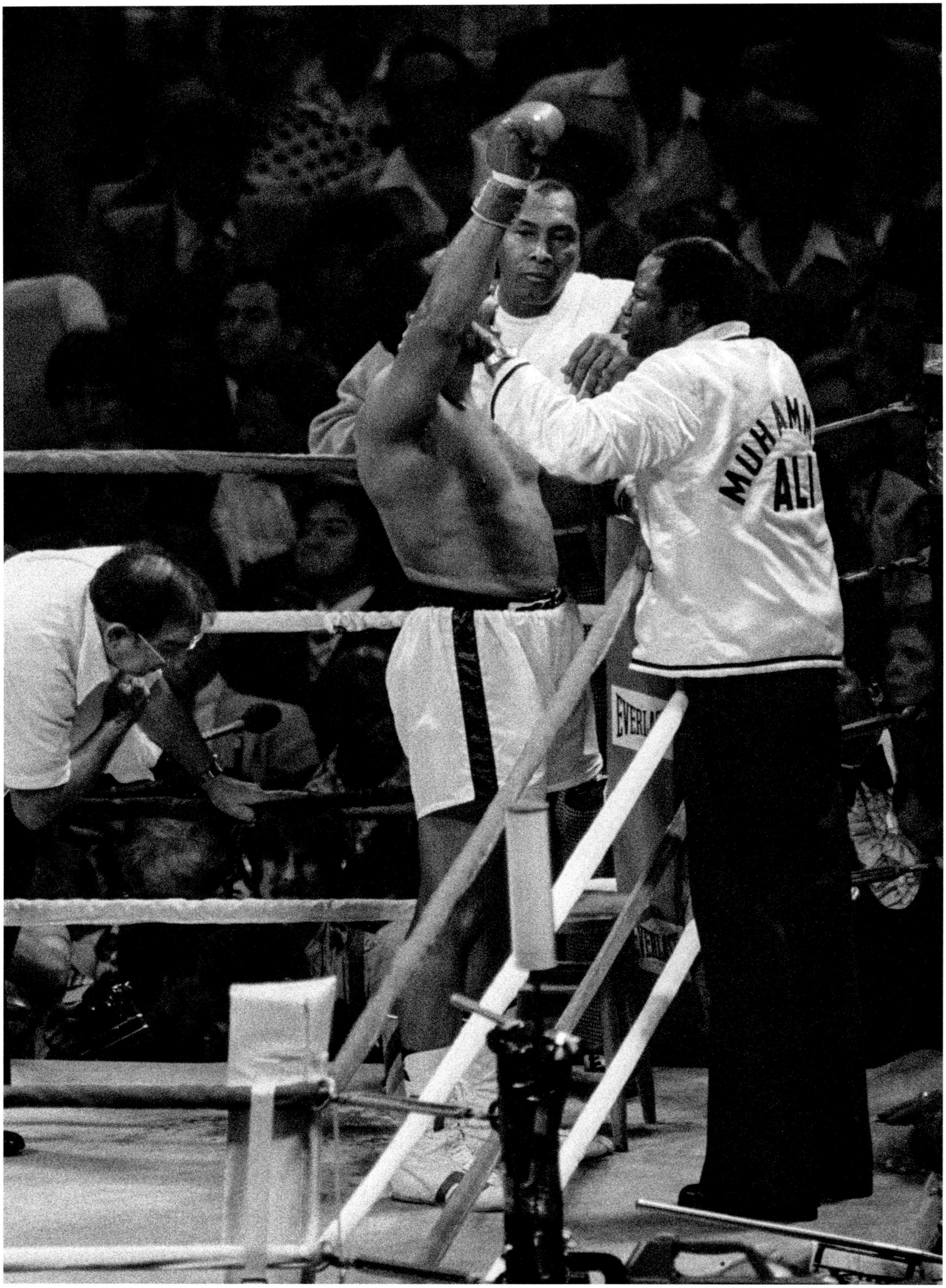
ALI

← C. Thomas Hardin
Cornerman Drew "Bundini" Brown checks
Muhammad Ali's mouth during his
rematch with Leon Spinks.

September 15, 1978

↑ Keith Williams
After defeating Spinks in a 15-round
decision, Ali addresses the crowd.

September 15, 1978

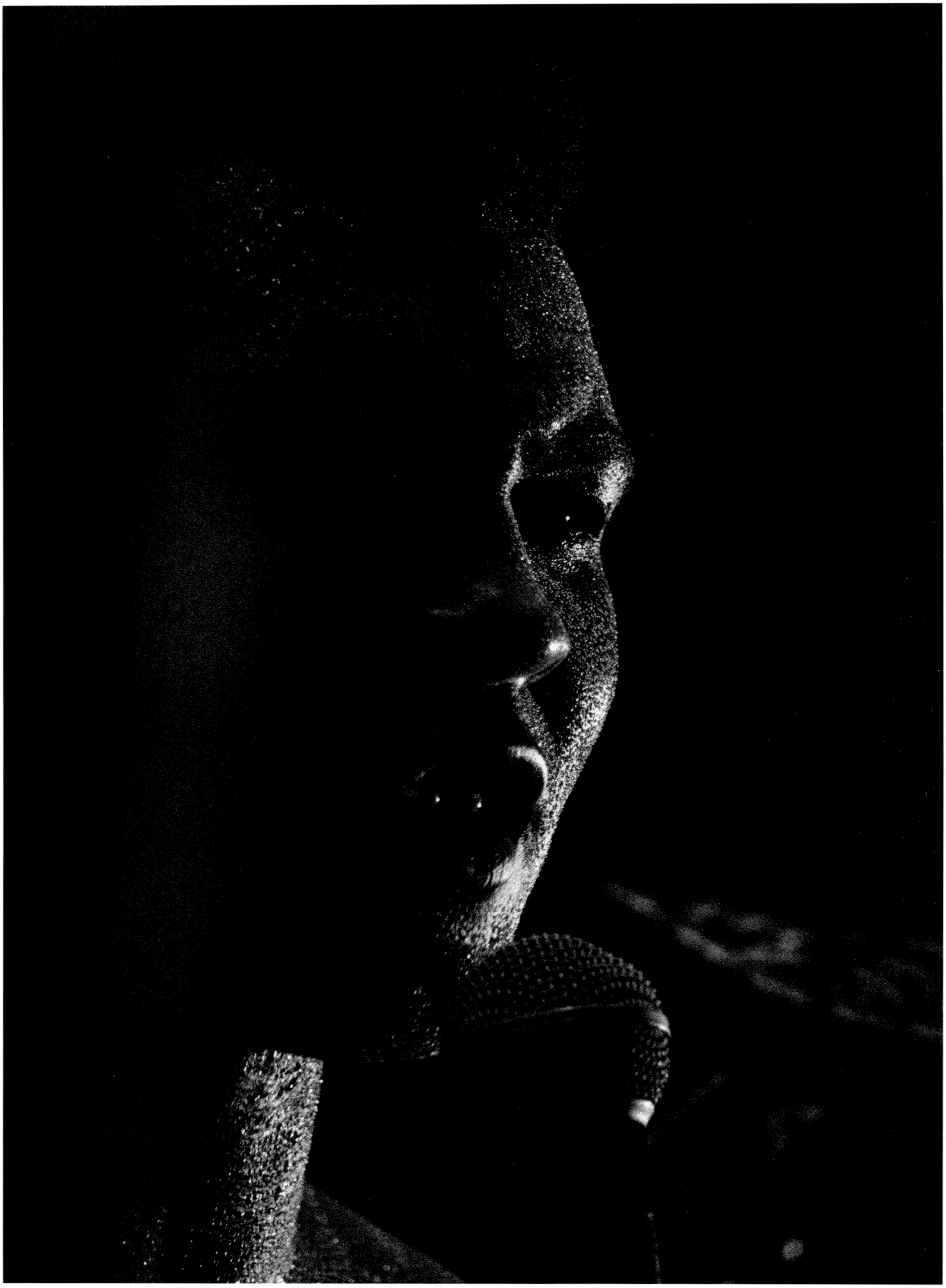

→ **Keith Williams**
Muhammad Ali relaxes with family and staff in his hotel room following the fight.

September 15, 1978

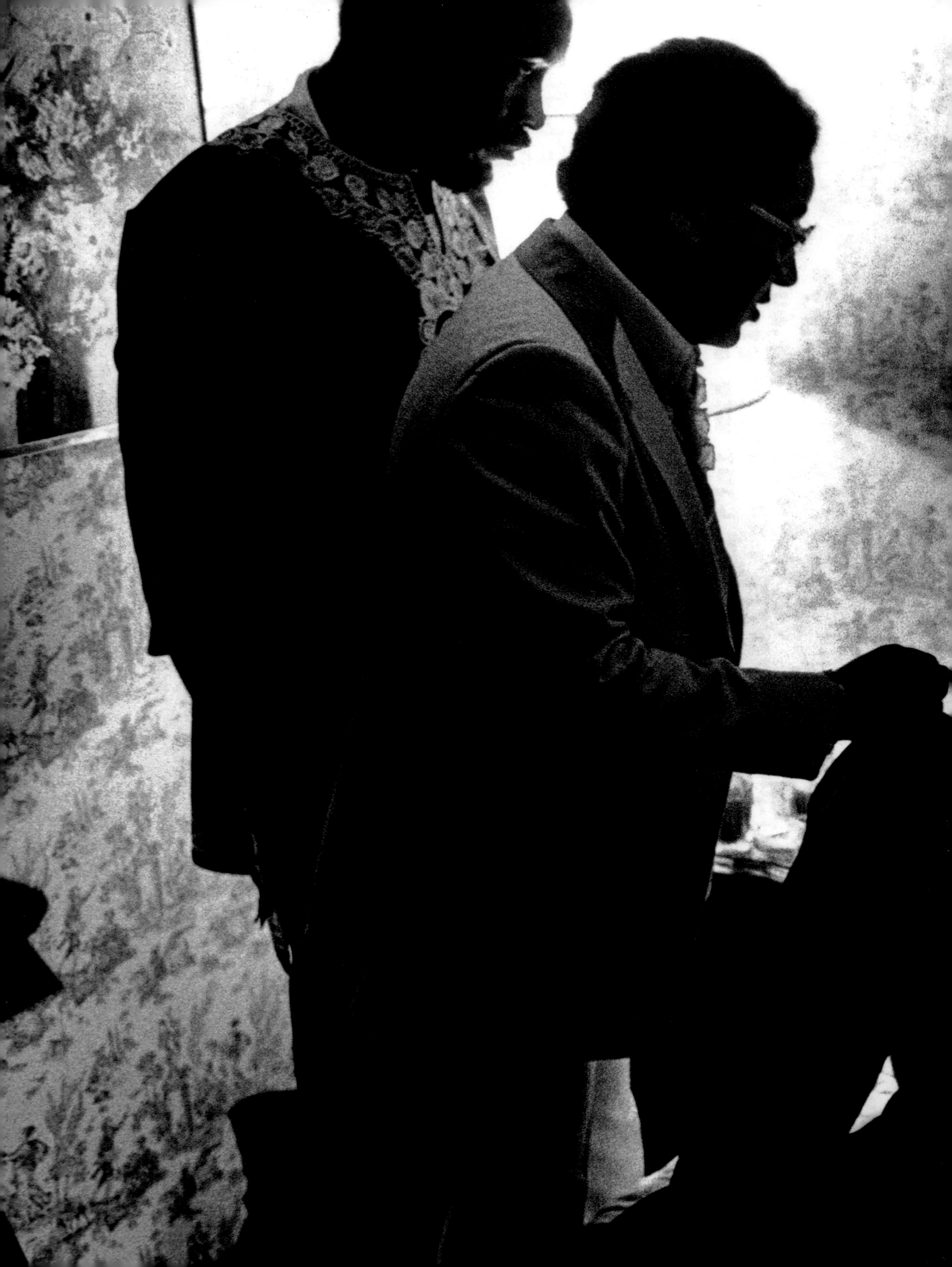

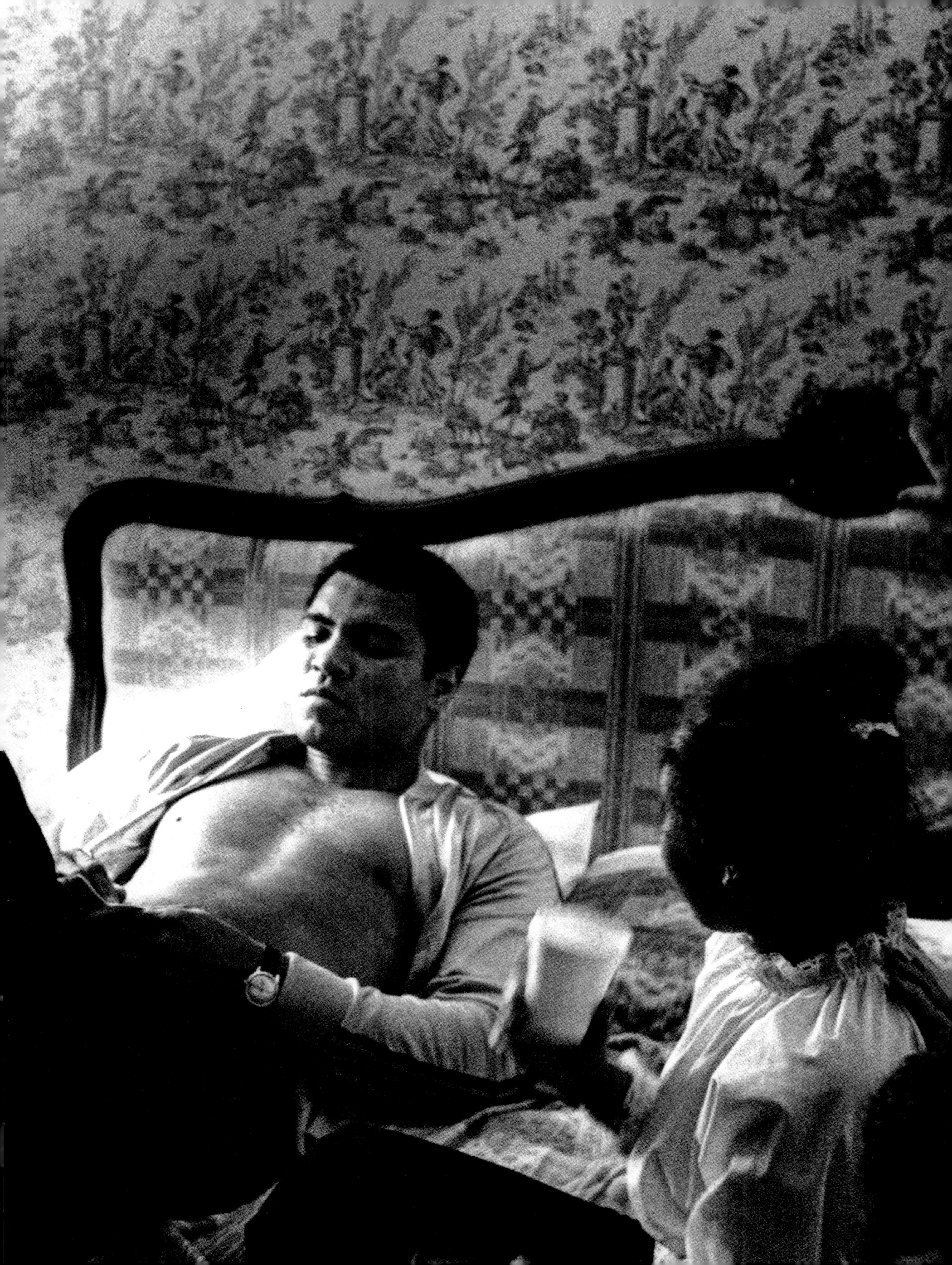

220 —

Retirement

1978
— 1980

"I'M NOT THE GREATEST, I'M THE DOUBLE GREATEST!"

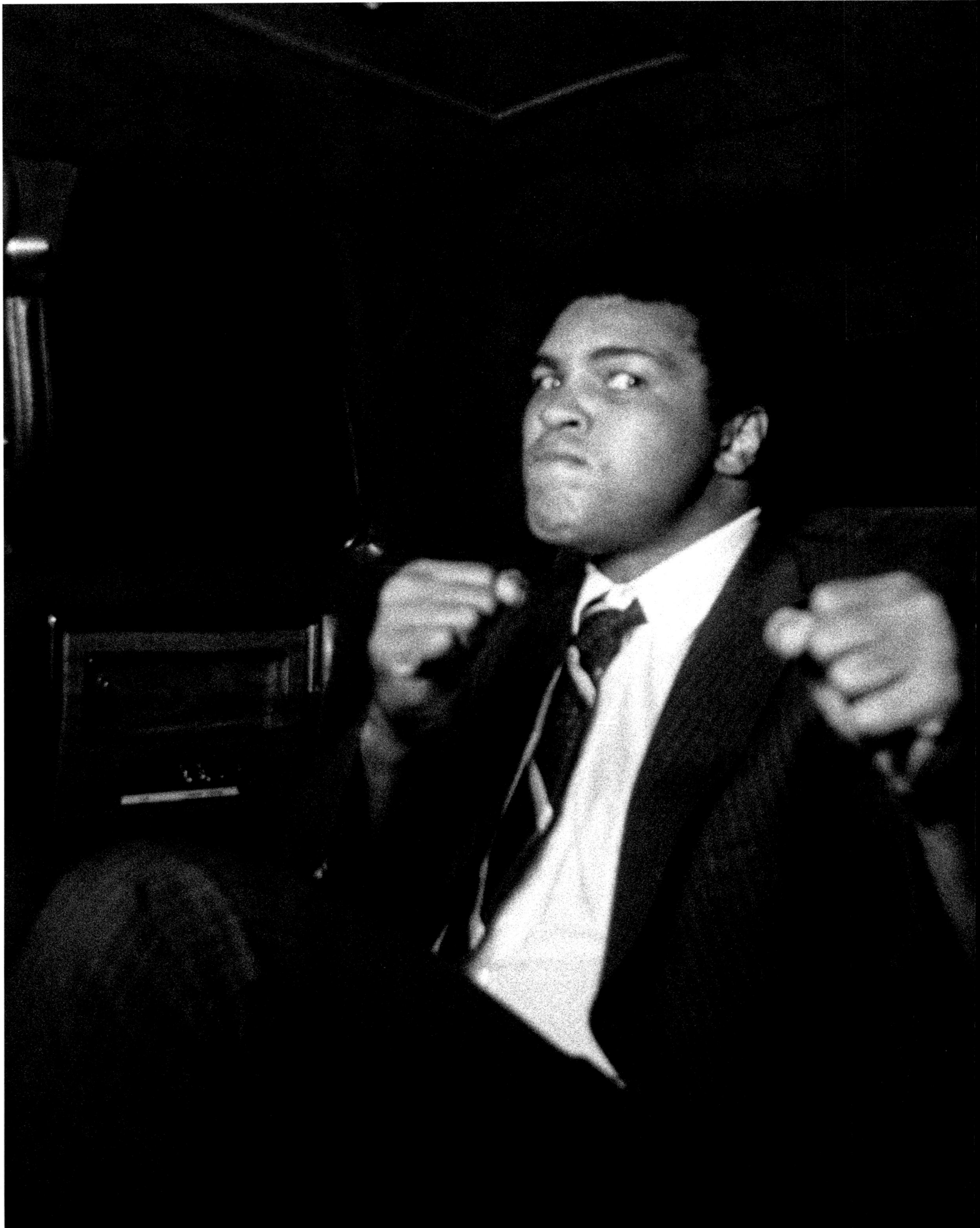

← **Dan Dry**
Ali boxes with Courier Journal photographer Dan Dry in the back of Ali's limo on the way to a welcome home event in Louisville.

October 29, 1980

Fighters are not to be trusted with their own welfare. They get paid to take punishment, and the transactions invariably look more lopsided as they grow older.

Had Muhammad Ali stuck with his original plan, and retired after winning the heavyweight title for the third time against Leon Spinks in 1978, he could have spared himself the damage inflicted by Larry Holmes and the sad spectacle of his last bout against Trevor Berbick.

But as much as Ali talked, he was not so good a listener. Overruling the advice of his inner circle and his own admissions that it was time to stop, Ali rationalized a return to the ring in 1980, and fought again the following year in the Bahamas when no state except South Carolina would grant him a license.

"It's time to get out, time for a change," Ali told the Courier Journal's Billy Reed before he changed his mind to fight Holmes. "I'm tired, my reflexes are slow, it's so hard to get in shape ...

"Now, nobody can hit me, nobody can get my title, nobody can hurt me. A lot of people, racists, wanted to see me flat on my back. Now, they never will. I'm so glad to go out a winner."

Holmes would not succeed in knocking Ali down, but he so dominated him that all three judges awarded him every round until trainer Angelo Dundee stopped the fight after the 10th.

Actor Sylvester Stallone, who rose to fame as Rocky Balboa, compared the 10th round to watching an autopsy on a living person.

Whether the Holmes bout hastened the onset of Ali's Parkinson's disease is unclear, but a study of voice recordings shows Ali's speech slowed by 26 percent between 1970 and 1980.

"He absorbed way more blows than the average fighter because, as he got older and slower, part of his strategy was to allow his opponents to hit him," author Jonarhan Eig concluded. "He thought he could wear down his opponents by letting them punch him in the head, then wait until the late rounds when they're tired and beat them."

This was the celebrated "rope-a-dope" strategy Ali used to beat George Foreman and reclaim his title in 1974. But it carried a cost.

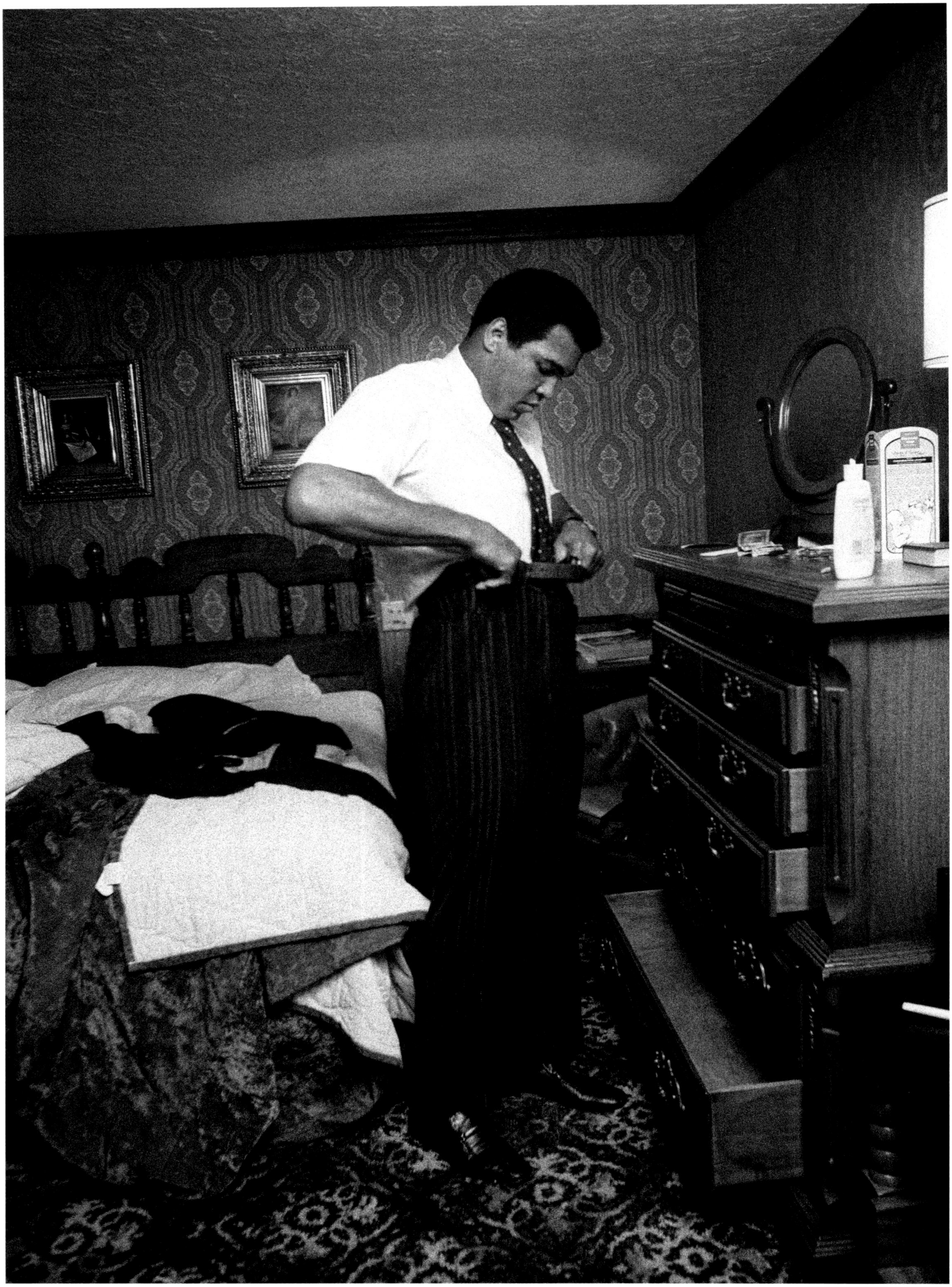

← Keith Williams
Muhammad Ali dresses for a public appearance in Louisville as the city welcomes him home.

September 21, 1978

↑ Keith Williams
Ali conducts business from his hotel bed while visiting Louisville.

September 21, 1978

230 —

1 Keith Williams
Muhammad Ali enjoys the company of friends and family.

September 21, 1978

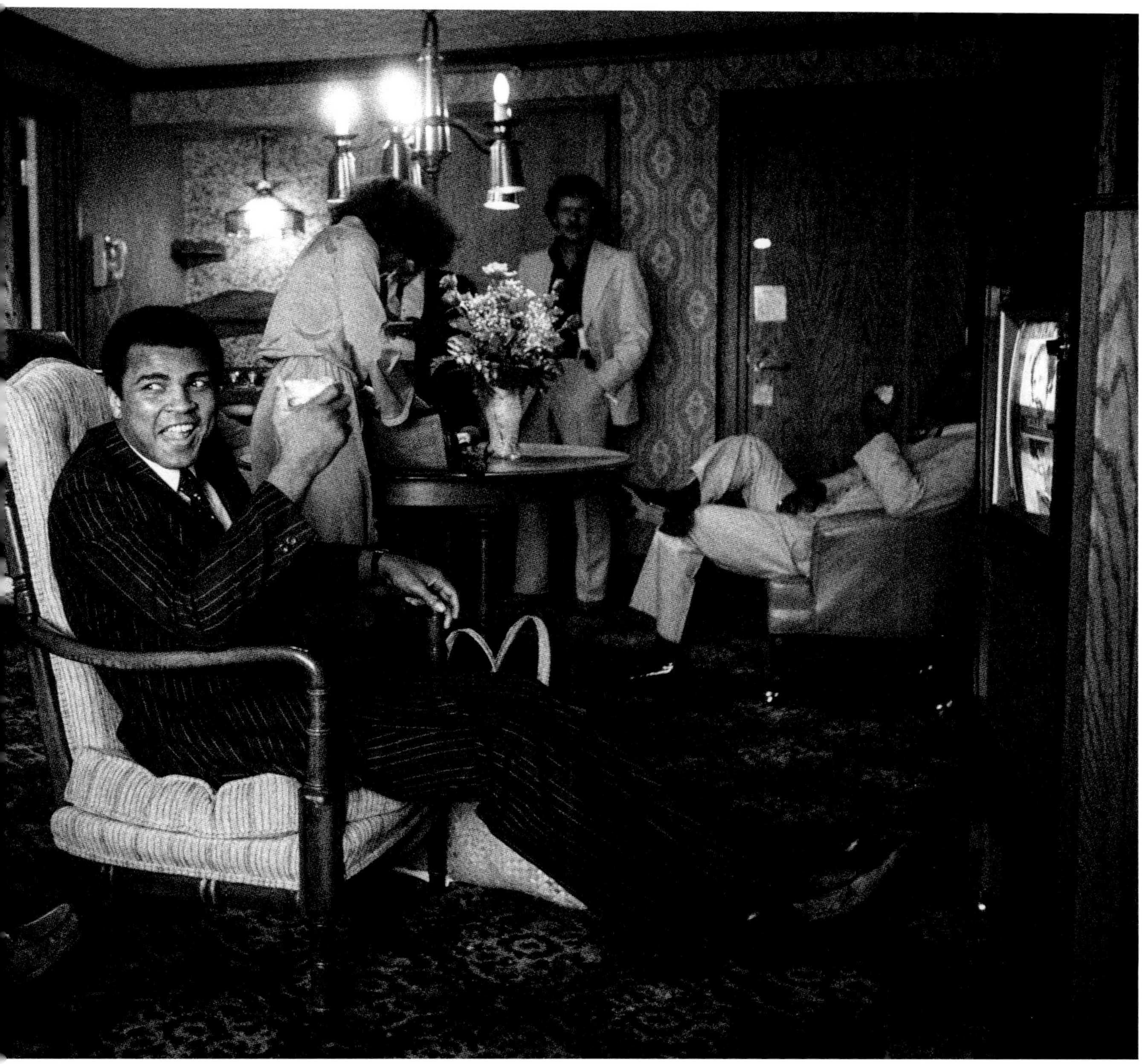

1 Keith Williams
Muhammad Ali rgets dressed at his hotel in Louisville prior to a public appearance at Fairgrounds Stadium.

September 21, 1978

— 233

1 Keith Williams
Ali rolls into Fairgrounds Stadium in a limousine for a welcome home event in Louisville.

September 21, 1978

1 Keith Williams
After winning back the heavyweight championship title in 1978, Muhammad Ali gave the credit to his father, Cassius Marcellus Clay Sr., during a celebration at the state fairgrounds in Louisville.

September 21, 1978

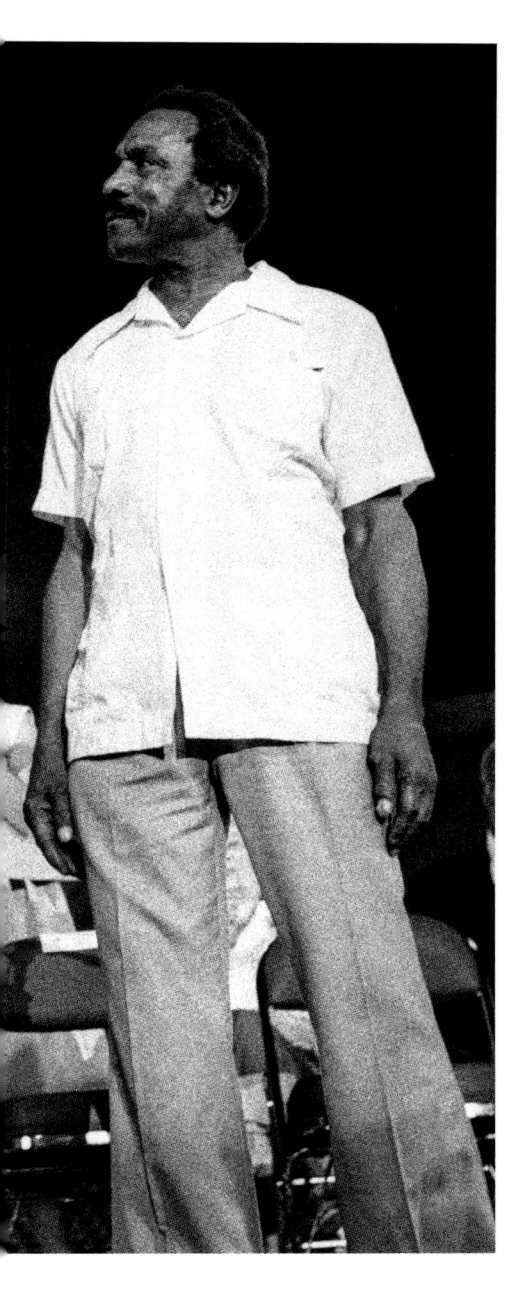

→ **Pam Spaulding**
In retirement Ali found more time for personal interests such as attending the Kentucky Derby with his wife Veronica.

1980

236 —

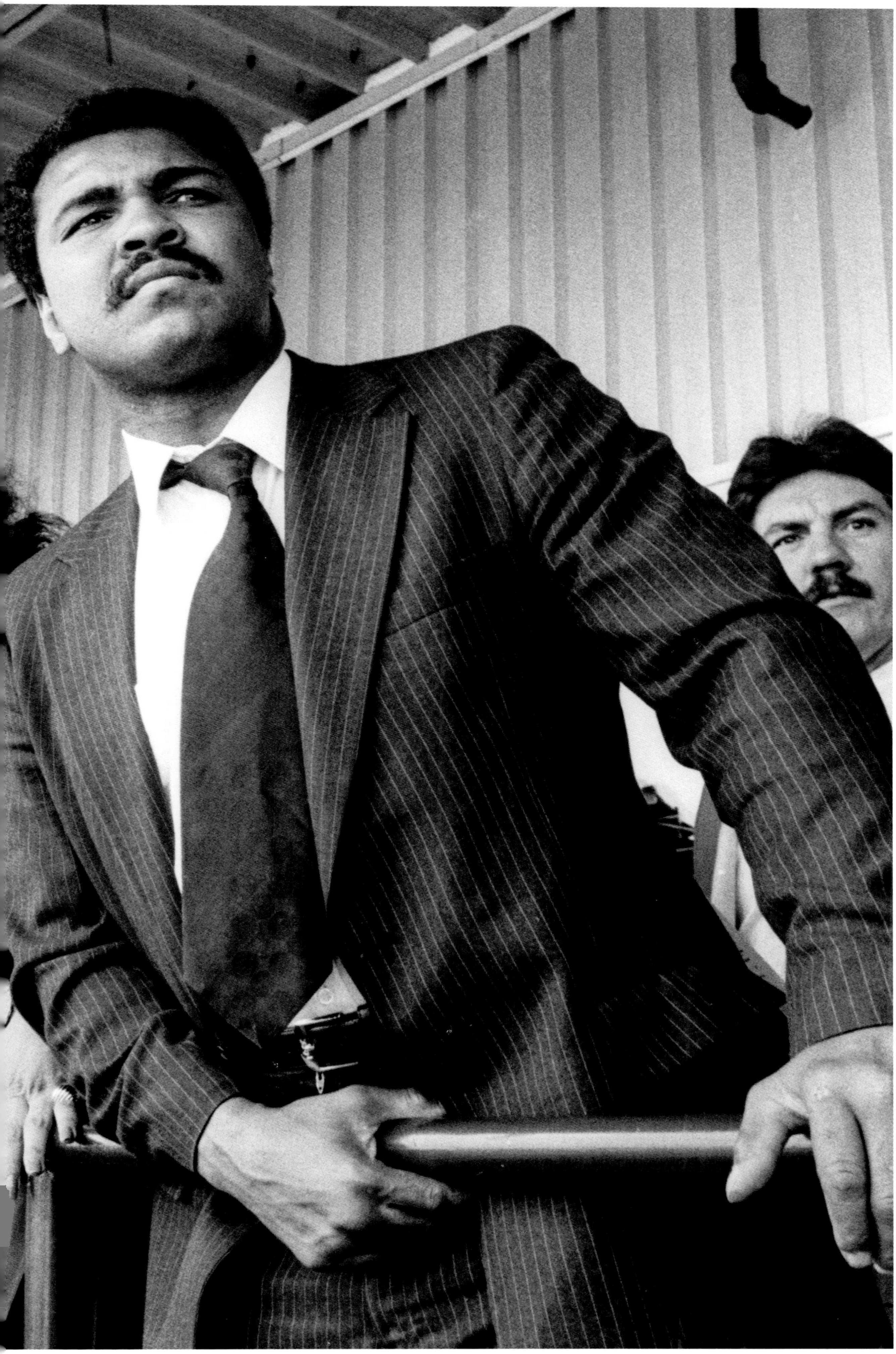

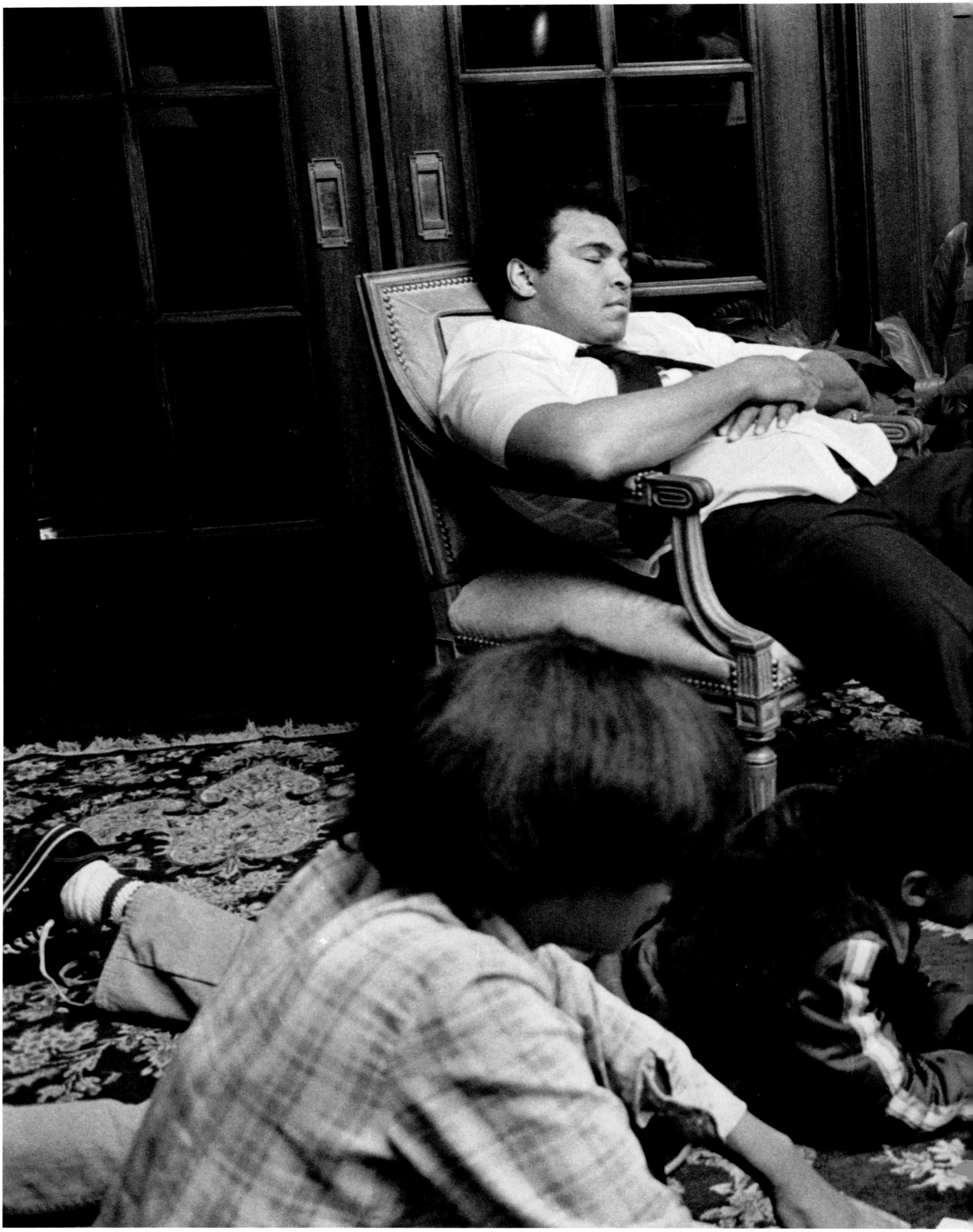

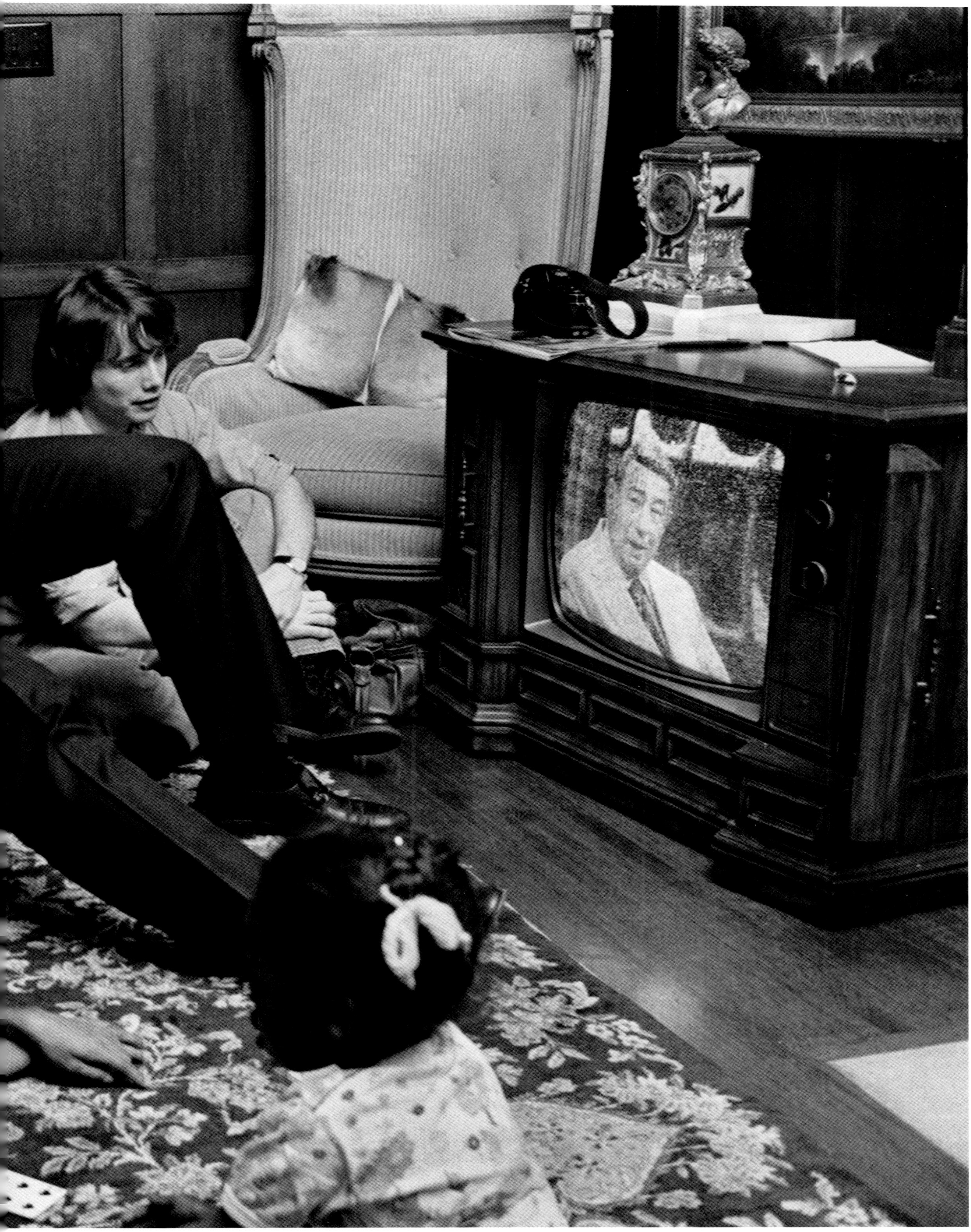

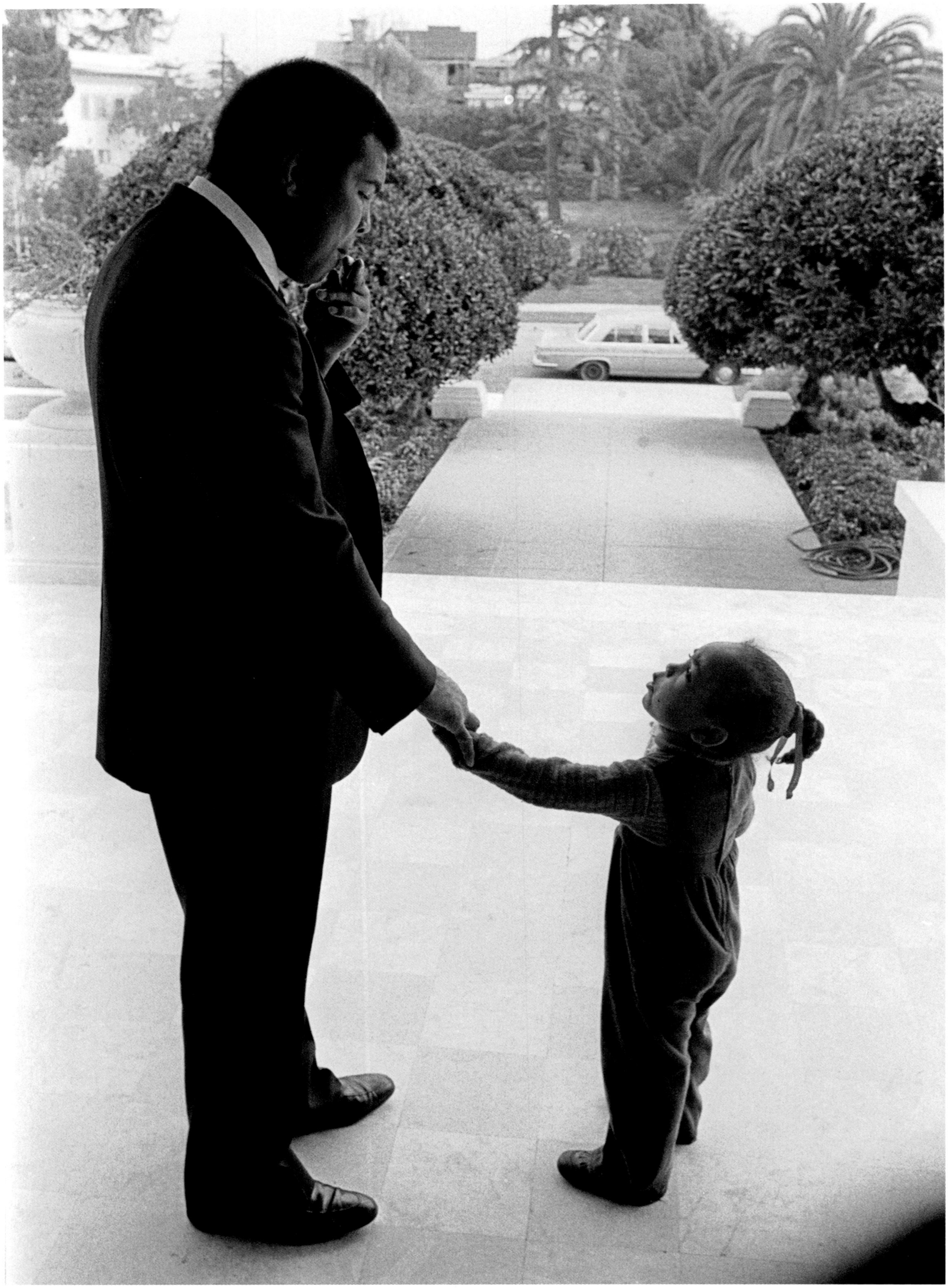

— 241

← **Keith Williams**
Muhammad Ali teases his daughter Hana while living in retirement in Los Angeles, California.

January 1980

Page 238–239

Keith William
Ali falls asleep in his Los Angeles home while watching his friend Howard Cosell on television. Ali and Cosell would often verbally spar while discussing his fights.

January 1980

↑ **Keith Williams**
Ali kisses his daughter Laila while his wife, Veronica, holds his daughter Hana while living in Los Angeles during his brief retirement.

January 1980

242 —

1 Keith Williams
Muhammad Ali enjoys a snack in the
kitchen of his Los Angeles home.

January 1980

↑ Keith Williams
Ali enjoys a Popsicle with his daughter Hana during his first retirement in Los Angeles.

January 1980

→ Keith Williams
Ali playfully spars with a young man on the streets of San Pedro, California.

January 1980

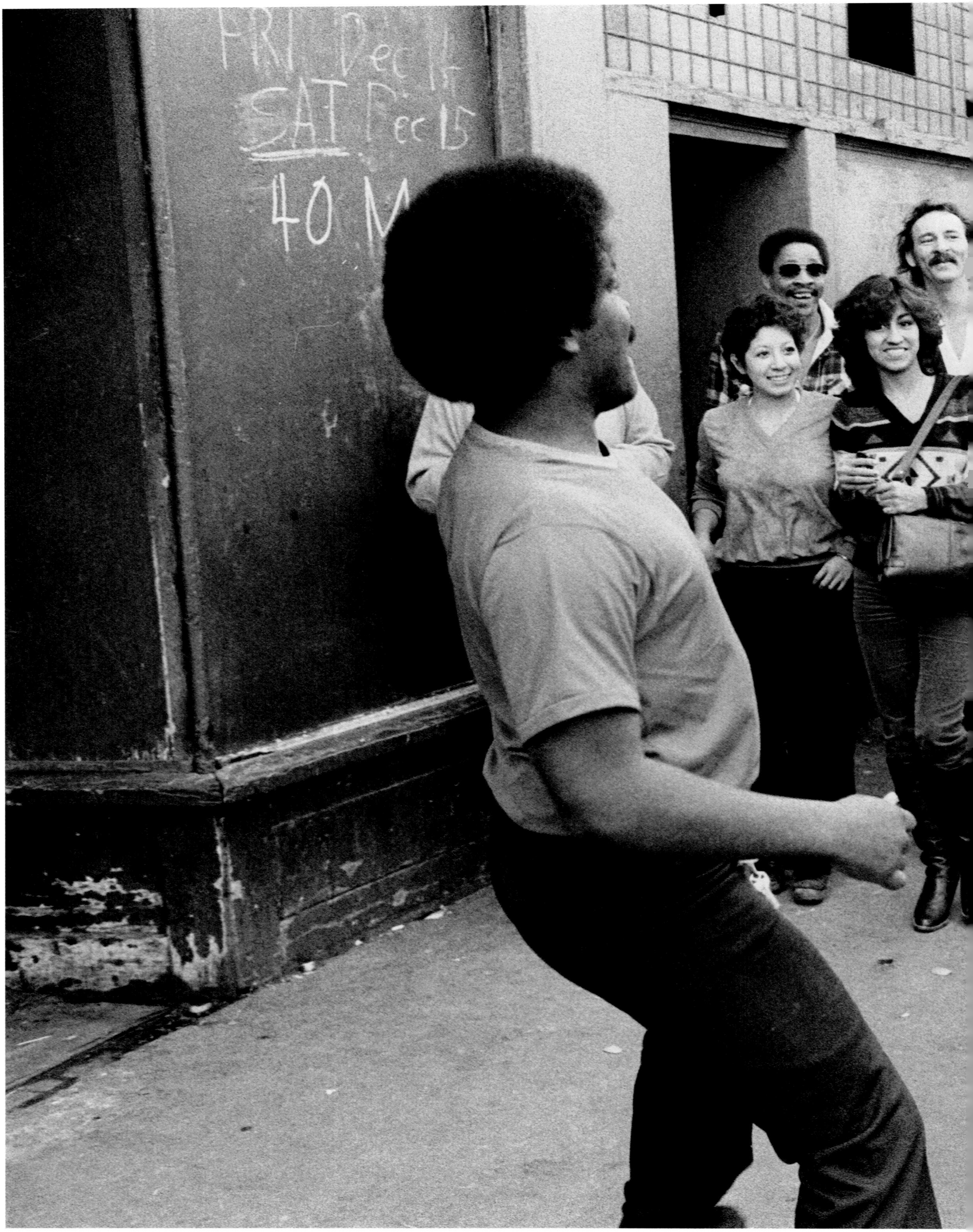
SAT Dec 15
40 M

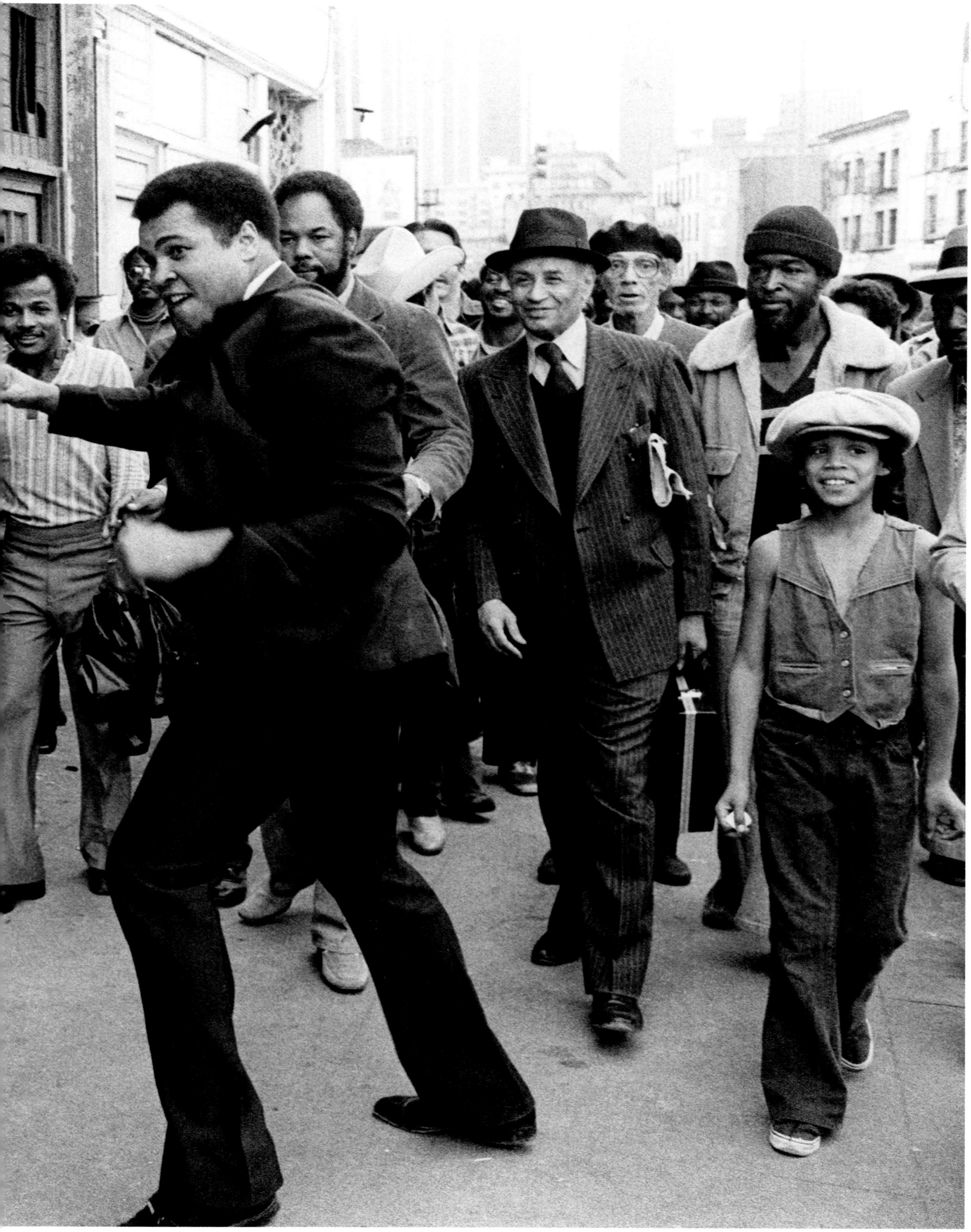

Bahamas

1981

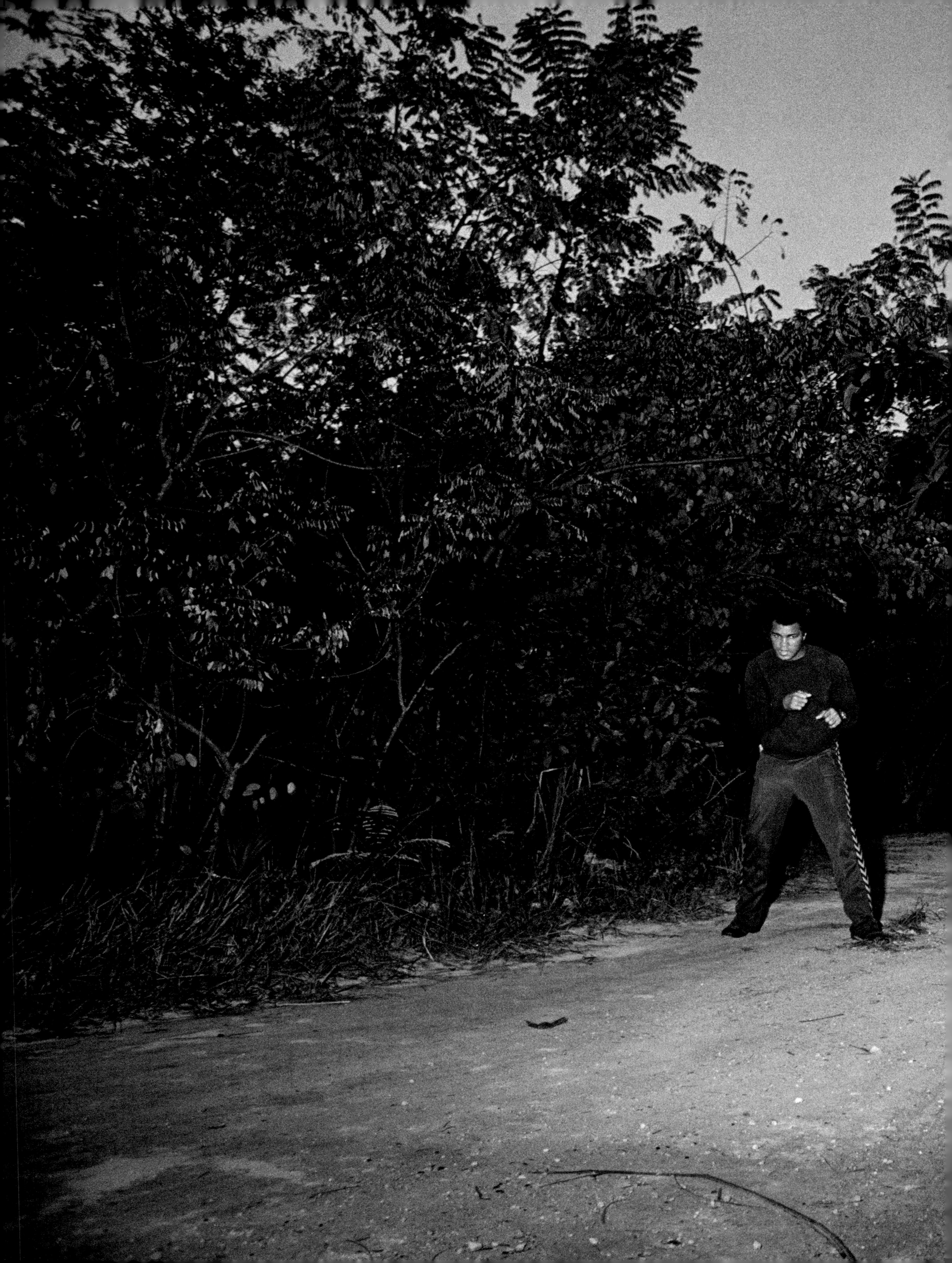

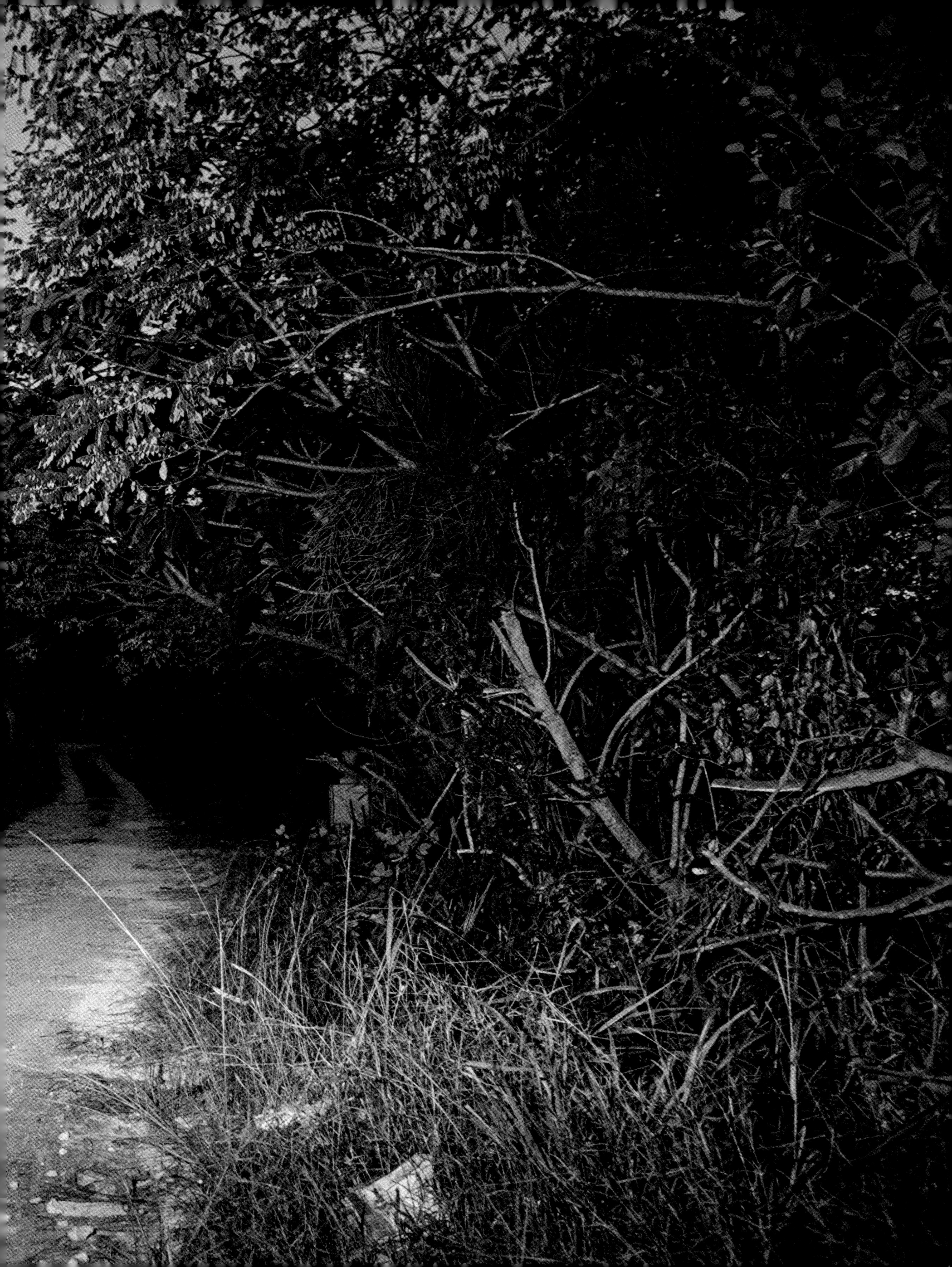

"I'M SO MEAN, I MAKE MEDICINE SICK."

252 —

← Jebb Harris
Muhmmad Ali shadow boxes during an early morning run while training in the Bahamas for his final heavyweight fight against Trevor Berbick.

December 1981

Muhammad Ali's last bout was in doubt hours before the bell, and it has been a source of regret ever since.

Unable to secure a boxing license from any major American commission – this time out of concerns arising from his dismal showing against Larry Holmes – Ali lost a listless bout to Trevor Berbick in the Bahamas on Dec. 11, 1981.

The slapdash production was promoted by an underfinanced felon named James Cornelius, and ticket sales were so slow that they would be deeply discounted and made available at local grocery stores.

Berbick refused to enter the ring until assured by a sponsor, one hour before the program was scheduled to start, that he would be paid. Don King contributed to the fight's farcical backdrop by showing up, claiming a contract with Berbick and alleging that he had been roughed up by associates of Cornelius while seeking to share in the proceeds.

When the bell finally sounded for the first round, the disorganized organizers relied on a cowbell. As the bout proceeded, the 39-year-old Ali found he could no longer rely on his once-incomparable reflexes.

"After Holmes, I had excuses," he said later. "I was too light. I had trouble breathing. But I had no excuses this time. I had 10 rounds to do what I wanted to do, but I couldn't do it. ... Father Time caught up with me. I'm finished. I've got to face facts."

Berbick won by unanimous decision. Jay Edson, one of the ringside judges, confessed that he had wanted to score one round for Ali, but couldn't.

"Berbick is the kind of lumbering, slow-armed swinger Ali would have first embarrassed and then demolished in his dazzling prime," Hugh McIlvanney wrote in The Observer. "To see Ali lose to such a moderate fighter in such a grubby context was like watching a king riding into permanent exile on the back of a garbage truck."

When Ali was diagnosed with Parkinson's disease three years later, the indignity of his last defeat was compounded by concerns that he had taken too many unnecessary blows in pursuit of the delusional dream of winning the heavyweight title a fourth time.

If there was any consolation, it was that the Berbick bout convinced Ali to abandon fighting altogether. He would make no more attempts at a comeback.

"It doesn't bother me to lose my last fight," Ali said. "People feel inferior when you're too good. They like to see you as human. I've got more fans now than I've ever had."

1 Jebb Harris
Muhammad Ali shadow boxes as the sun rises behind him after running and walking for an hour during a training session for his bout with Trevor Berbick.

December 1981

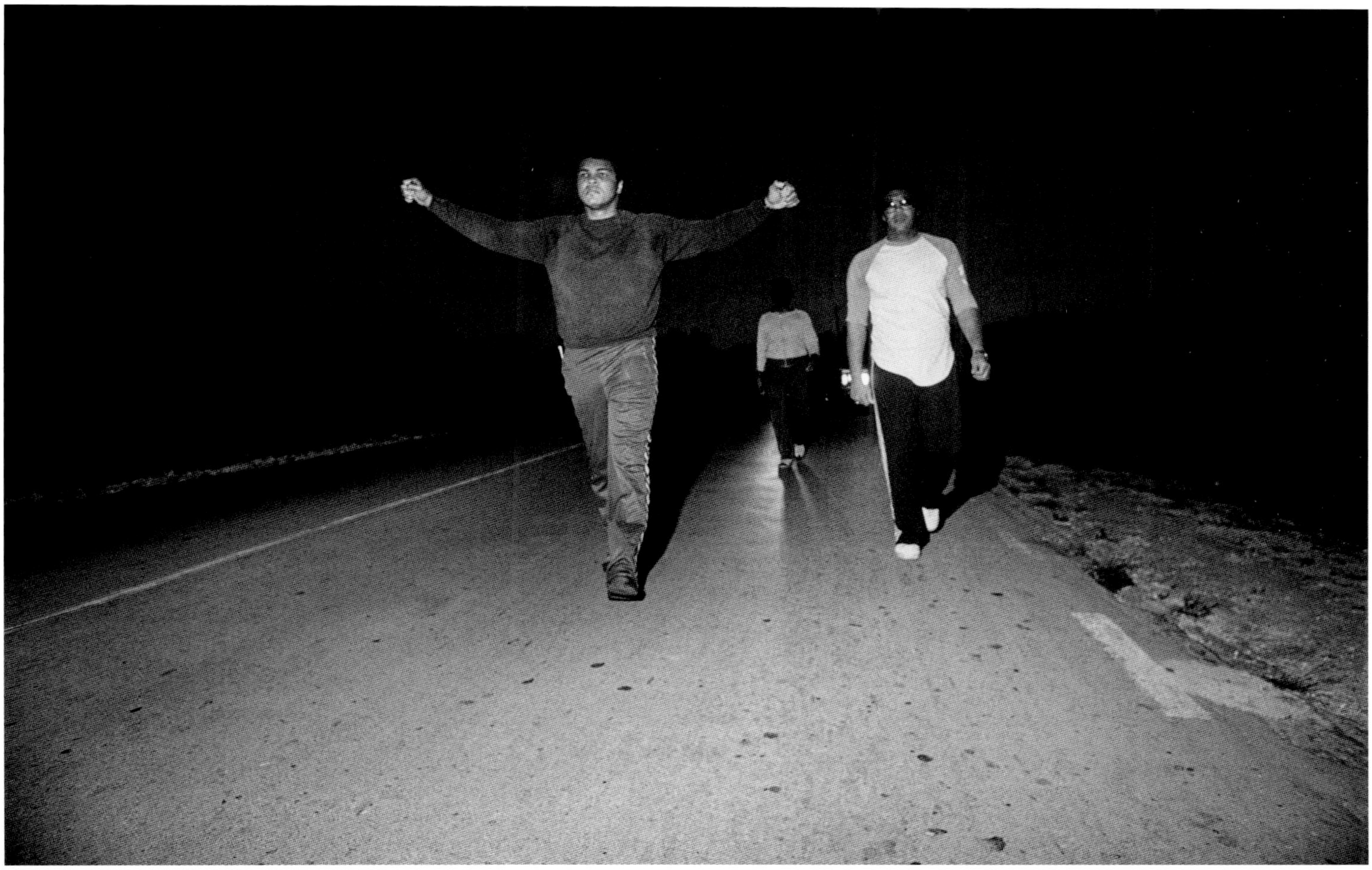

256 —

1 Jebb Harris
Muhammad Ali has a kiss for a member of
the hotel staff.

December 1981

1 Jebb Harris
Ali sits and waits for his meal to be served.

December 1981

258 —

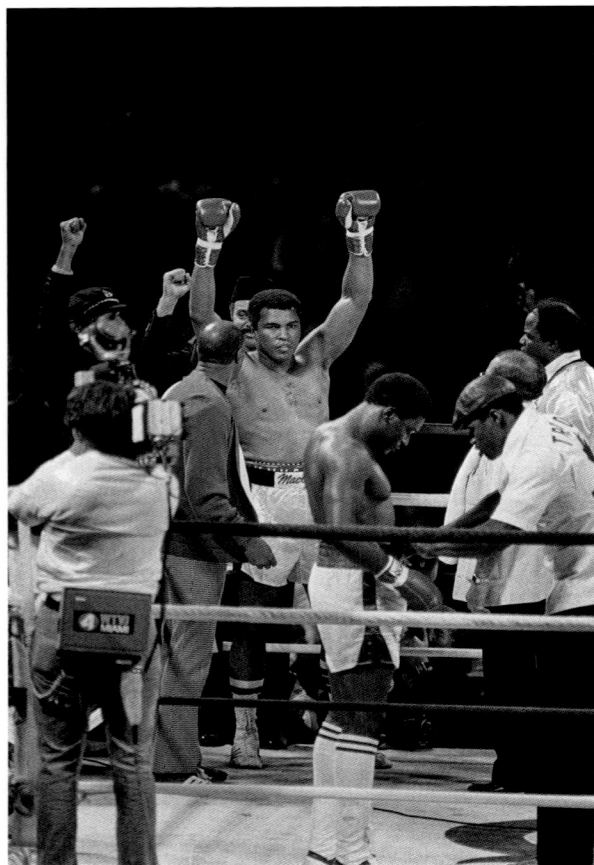

↑ Jebb Harris
Ali, 39, loses to Trevor Berbick, 27, in the 10-round match which turned out to be Ali's final fight.

December 11, 1981

→ Jebb Harris
Muhammad Ali, age 39, loses to Trevor Berbick, age 27, in the ten-round match. It would be Ali's last fight.

December 11, 1981

Page 260–261

Jebb Harris
Ali is swarmed by the media after losing to Trevor Berbick.

December 11, 1981

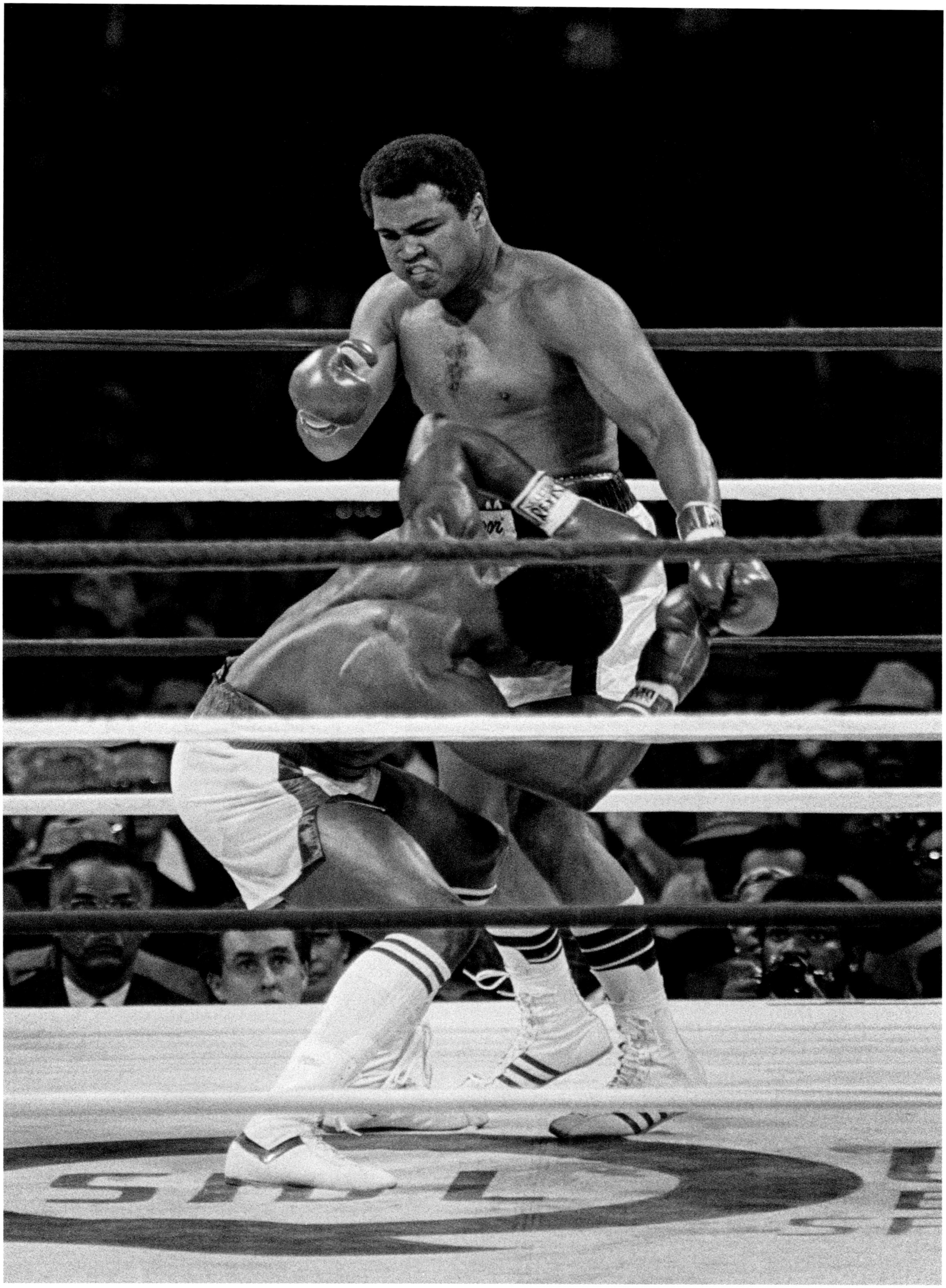

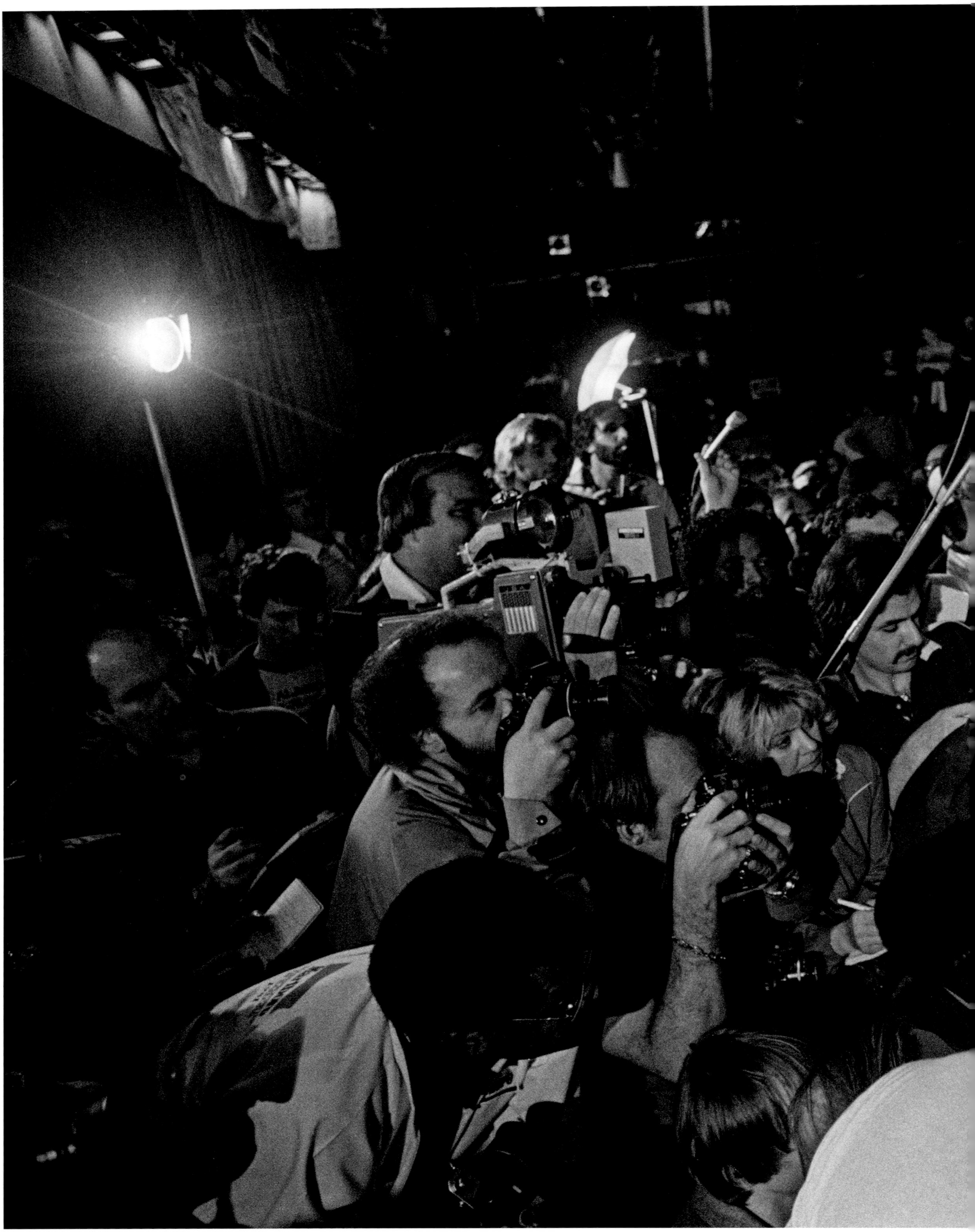

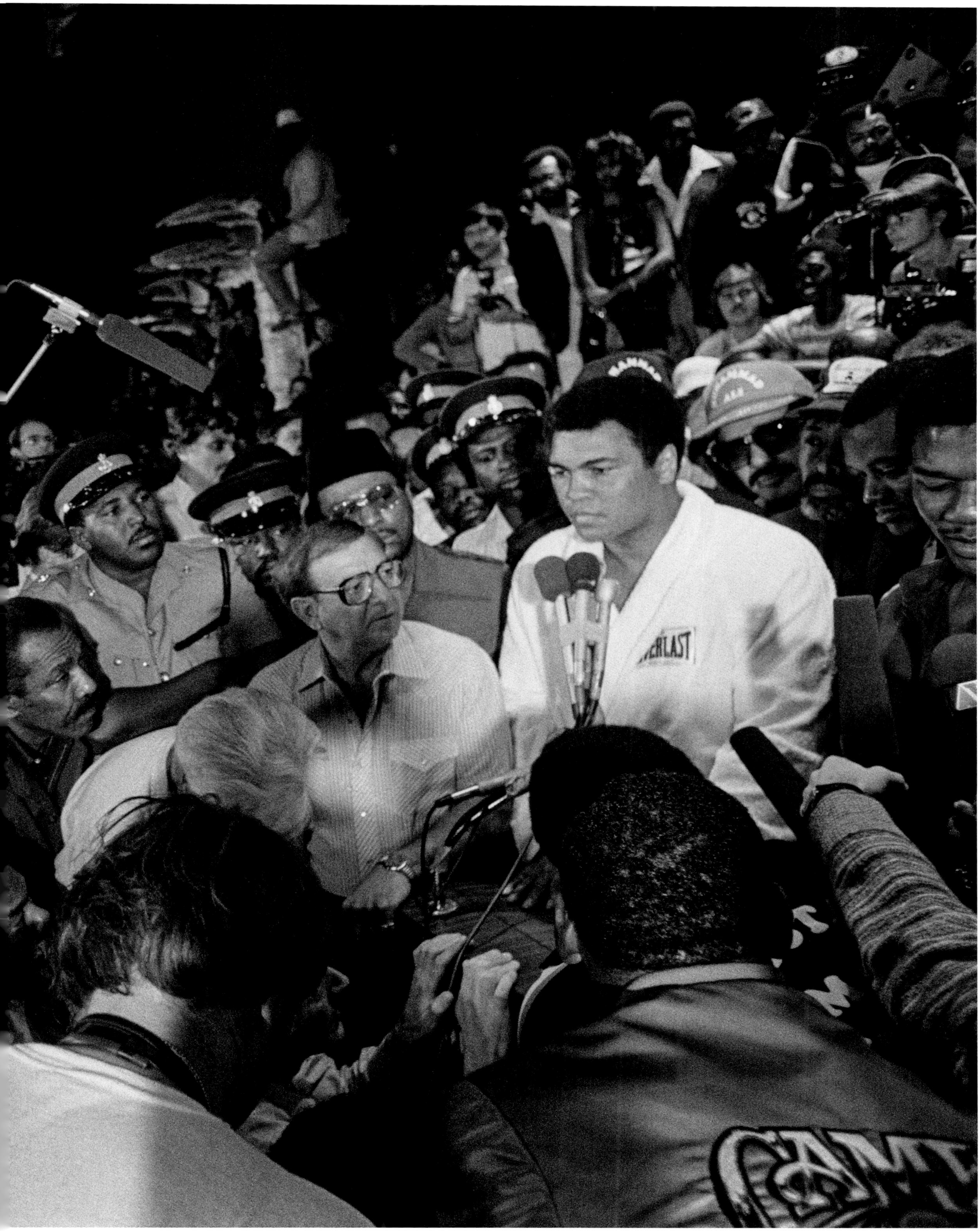
VERLAST

The Later Years

1984
— 2016

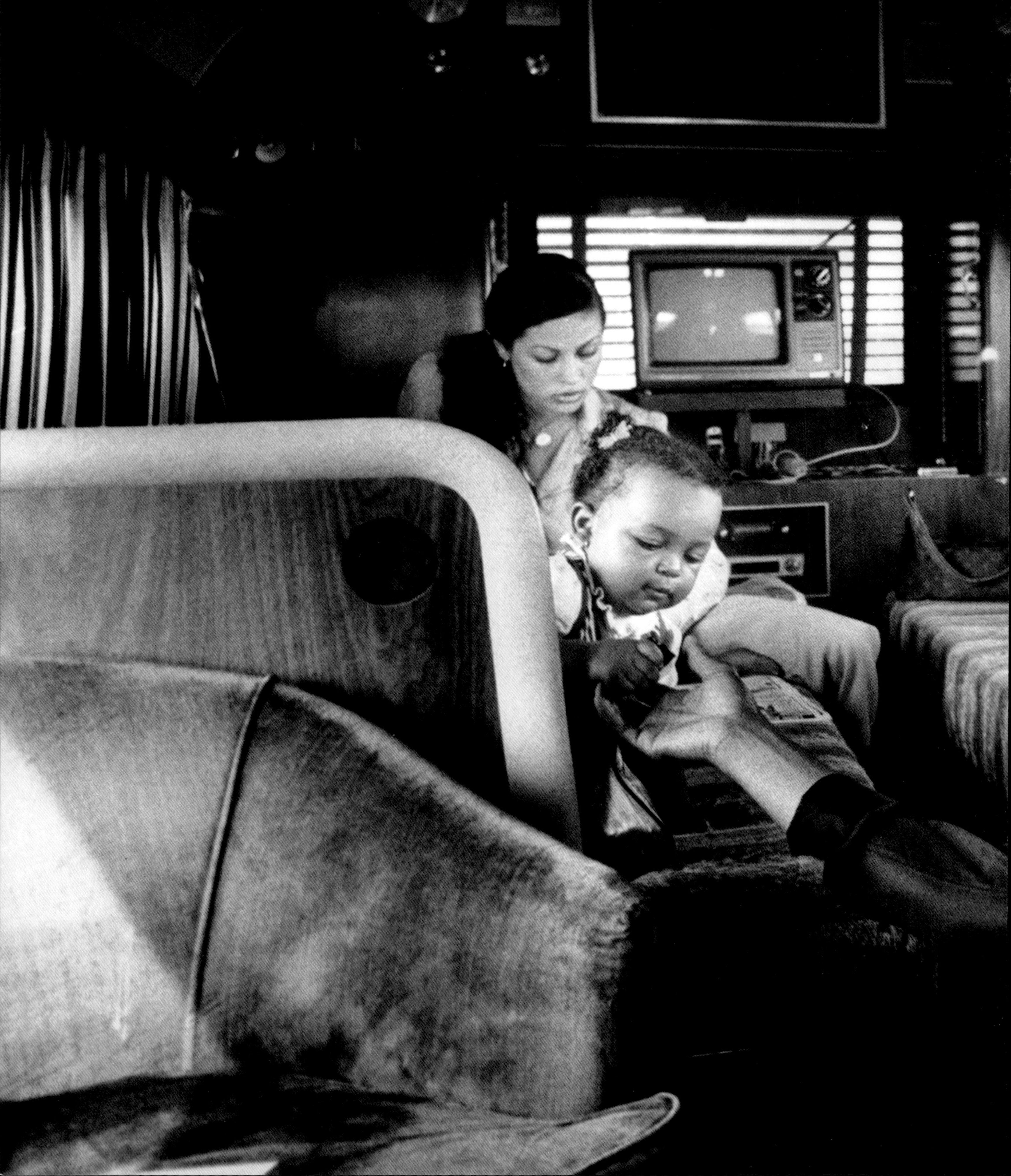

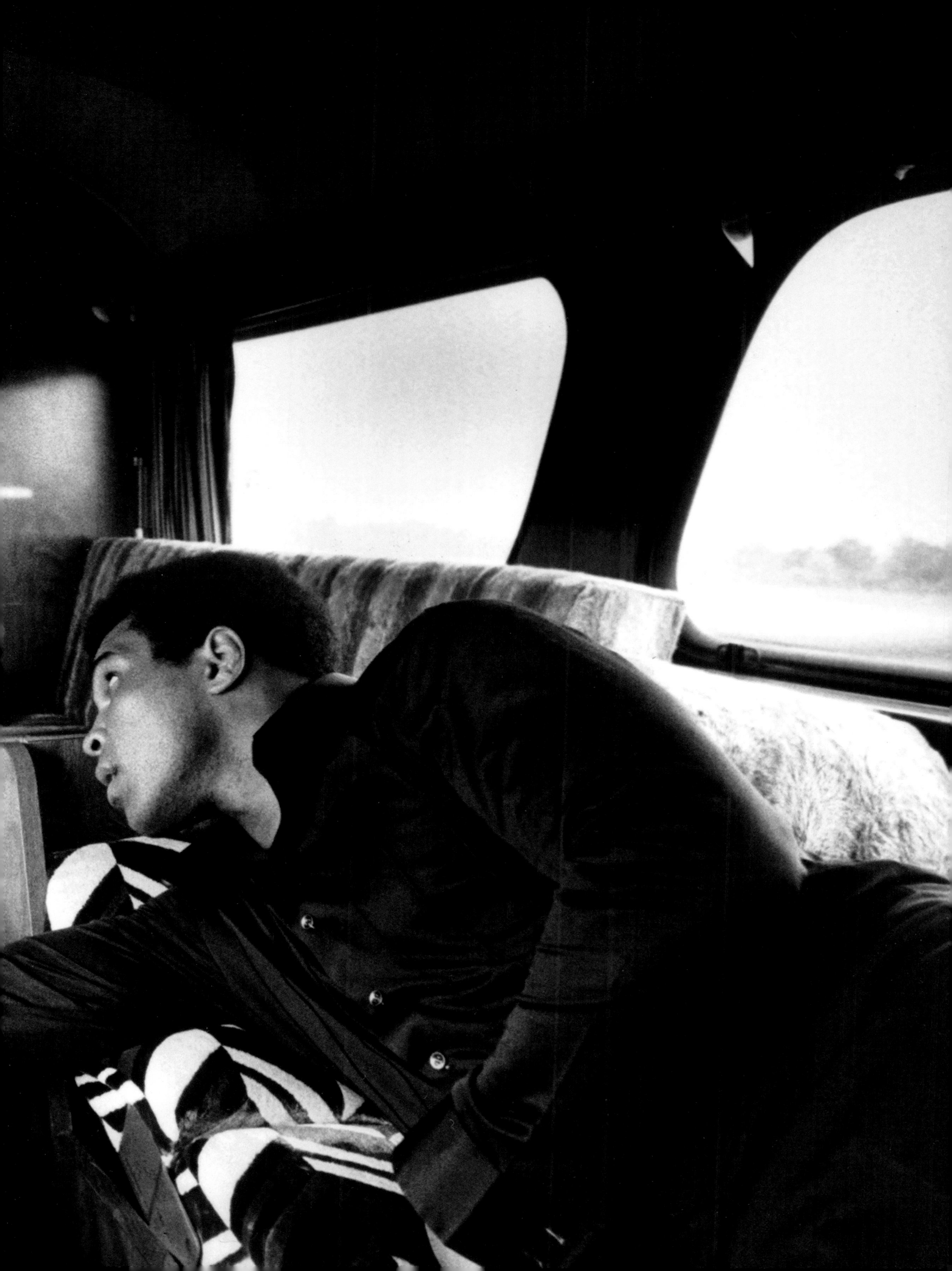

"LIVE EVERY DAY AS IF IT WERE YOUR LAST BECAUSE SOMEDAY YOU'RE GOING TO BE RIGHT."

← **Courier Journal Archive**
Muhammad Ali plays with
daughter Laila while traveling
by bus with his wife, Veronica.

1986

↑ **Keith Williams**
Ali gives a copy of an Islam prayer book, "Prayer and Al-Islam,"
to Arthur Robertson. He later gave out more than 900 of the
books in the lobby of the Courier Journal building.

April 25, 1986

The problem historians will have with Muhammad Ali is perspective.

He is a subject too broad and a character too colorful to be easily captured, much less capsulized. To reprise a sentence written upon his death, he floated like a butterfly, stung like a bee and left footprints befitting a brontosaurus.

"He's the most transforming figure of my time, certainly," promoter Bob Arum told the Associated Press upon Ali's death in 2016. "He did more to change race relations and the views of people than even Martin Luther King."

By trade, he was a boxer, and maybe the greatest of boxers. But to see Ali strictly as an athlete is to miss his broader significance, to trivialize his impact on culture and politics and to overlook his remarkable journey from reviled to revered.

The outrageous young fighter who adopted the name Muhammad Ali was once as polarizing a figure as any man in America.

An audacious braggart who happened to be black won the heavyweight title for the first time at the height of America's struggle for racial equality, 128 days before Lyndon Johnson signed the Civil Rights Act of 1964.

In embracing the Nation of Islam and rejecting the military draft as a conscientious objector, Ali stood on the front lines of the two most divisive issues of the day: race and the war in Vietnam.

For some, avoiding the draft made Ali permanently irredeemable. Yet as American attitudes shifted on the war, Ali's three-year exile from boxing was widely seen as an act of martyrdom. Biographer Jonathan Eig says attitudes about Ali began to change after Joe Frazier knocked him down in their epic 1971 bout in Madison Square Garden; that his image improved as his boxing skills declined.

By the time he lit the Olympic flame in Atlanta in 1996, his free hand trembling from Parkinson's disease, Ali was as beloved as he had been hated.

"I found Muhammad Ali to be one of the greatest human beings I've ever met in my life," former heavyweight champion George Foreman told the BBC. "... A big piece of me died when he passed away, and I call it the greatest piece."

270 —

1 Gary Bogdon
A fan reaches out to touch Muhammad Ali as he carries the Olympic torch through Louisville.

May 27, 1984

→ Gary Bogdon
Ali carries the Olympic torch through Louisville after retiring from boxing for the second time.

May 27, 1984

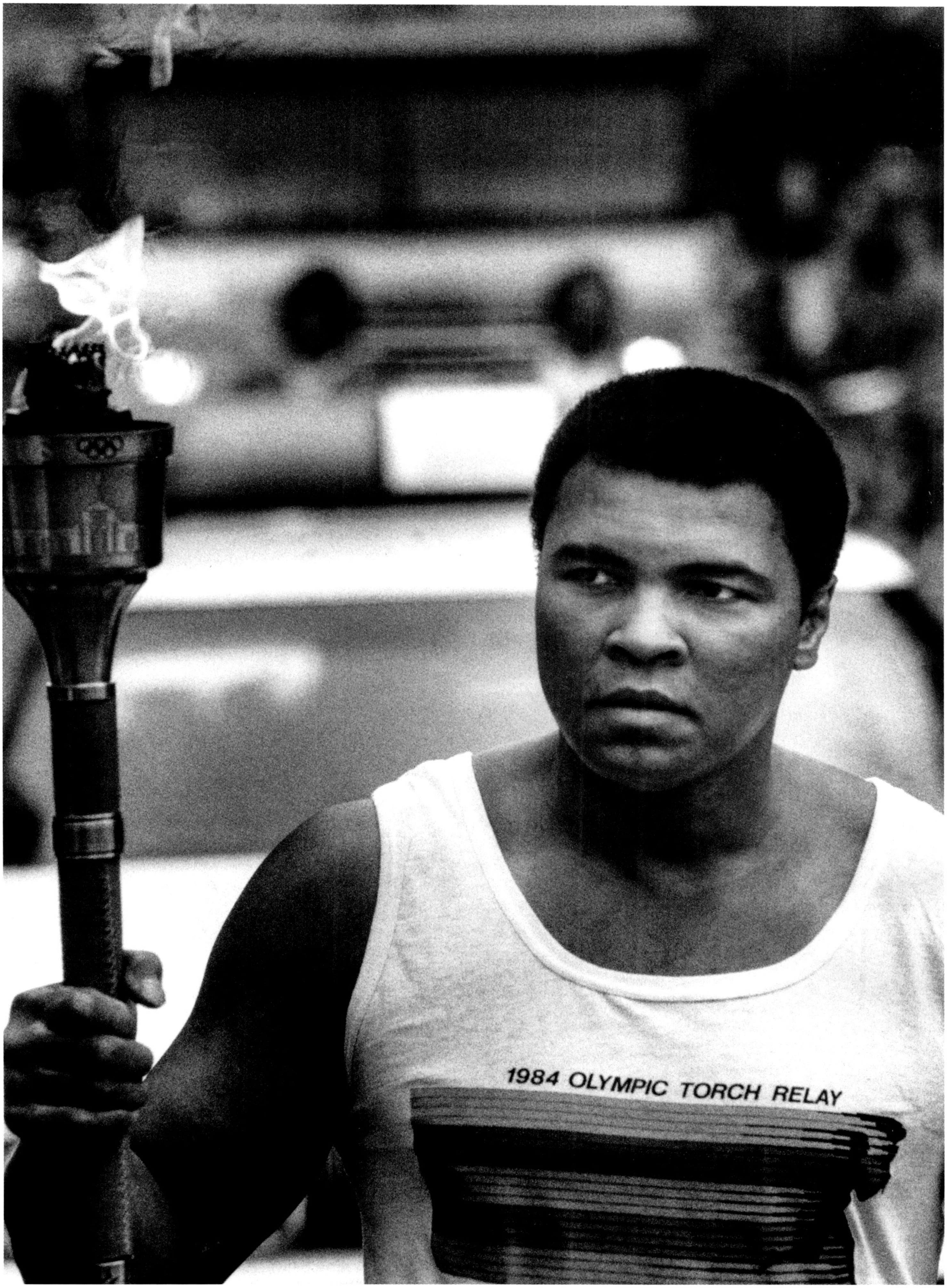
1984 OLYMPIC TORCH RELAY

272 —

"A man who views the world the same at 50 as he did at 20 has wasted 30 years of his life."

← Pat McDonogh
Muhammad Ali shakes hands with fans as he arrived at YUM! Brands headquarters to receive a $500,000 donation. The gift put the Ali Center project near its capital fundraising goal.

March 26, 2003

← Sam Upshaw
Ali greets U.S. Sen. Barack Obama at the Muhammad Ali Center. Obama called Ali "the quintessential American, with the ability to overcome barriers and to remake himself as a symbol of reconciliation."

September 14, 2006

274 —

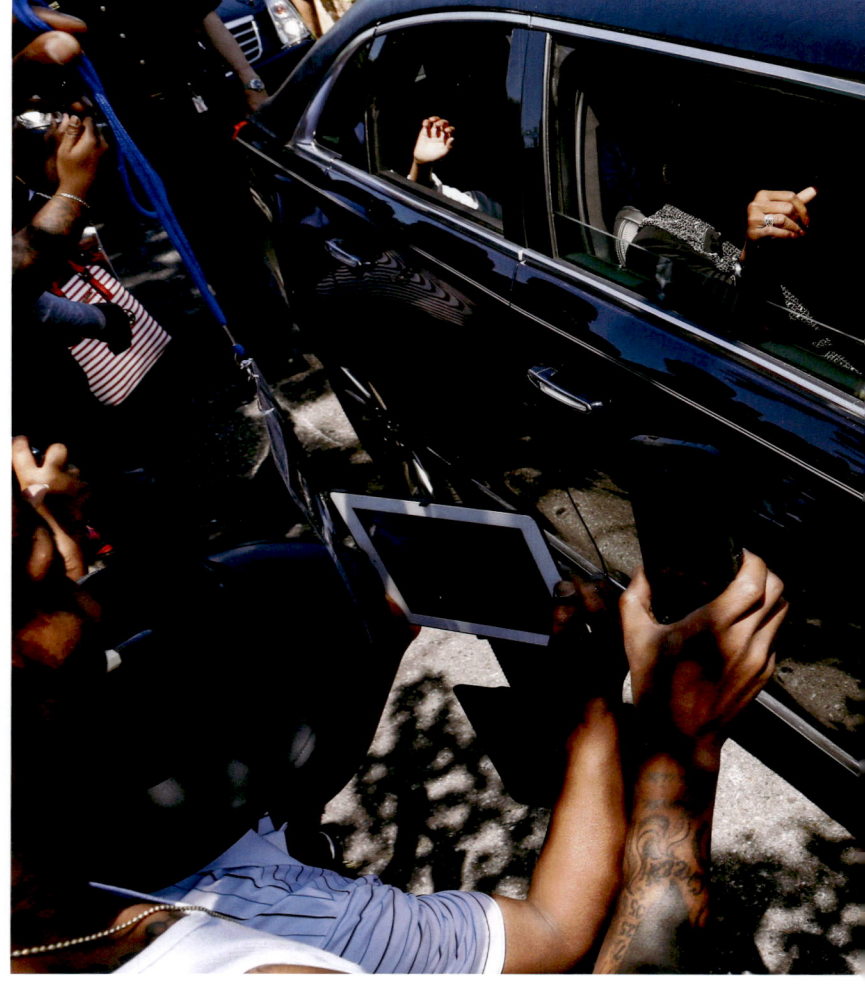

1 Sam Upshaw Jr.
A boxing robe Muhammad Ali wore as an amateur is one of the items that is stored in the archive of the Muhammad Ali Center in Louisville.

November 13, 2009

↑ **Alton Strupp**
A passenger in the funeral procession for Ali blows kisses to spectators as it makes its way past his boyhood home on Grand Ave. in Louisville.

June 10, 2016

↑ **Pat McDonogh**
Ali's funeral procession makes its way east on Broadway to Cave Hill Cemetery in Louisville.

June 10, 2016

— 275

1 Alton Strupp
Hundreds of fans line the streets for the funeral procession for Muhammad Ali as it makes its way past his boyhood home on Grand Avenue in Louisville.

June 10, 2016

— 277

1 Sam Upshaw Jr
Les Thomas kneels and prays before a makeshift memorial in honor of Ali at the Ali Center in Louisville.

June 4, 2016.

1 Pat McDonogh
Roddrick Monroe, 5, from Louisville, wears a boxing robe and gloves to a makeshift shrine at the Muhammad Ali Center honoring the late boxer.

June 8, 2016

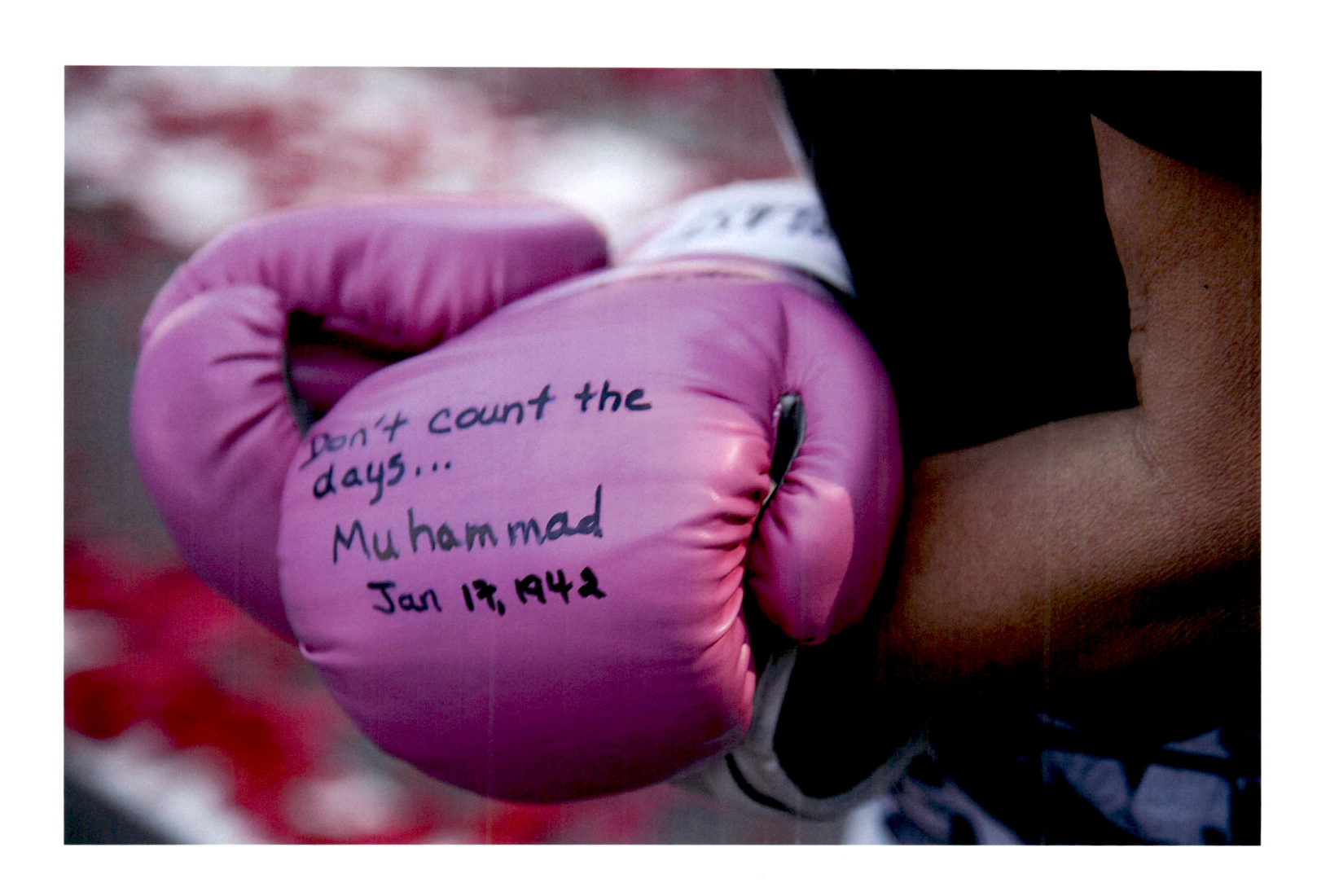

1 Lauren Nolan
Dianna Volpe wrote tributes to Muhammad Ali on pink boxing gloves on the day of his interment and brought them with her to see the funeral procession.

June 10, 2016

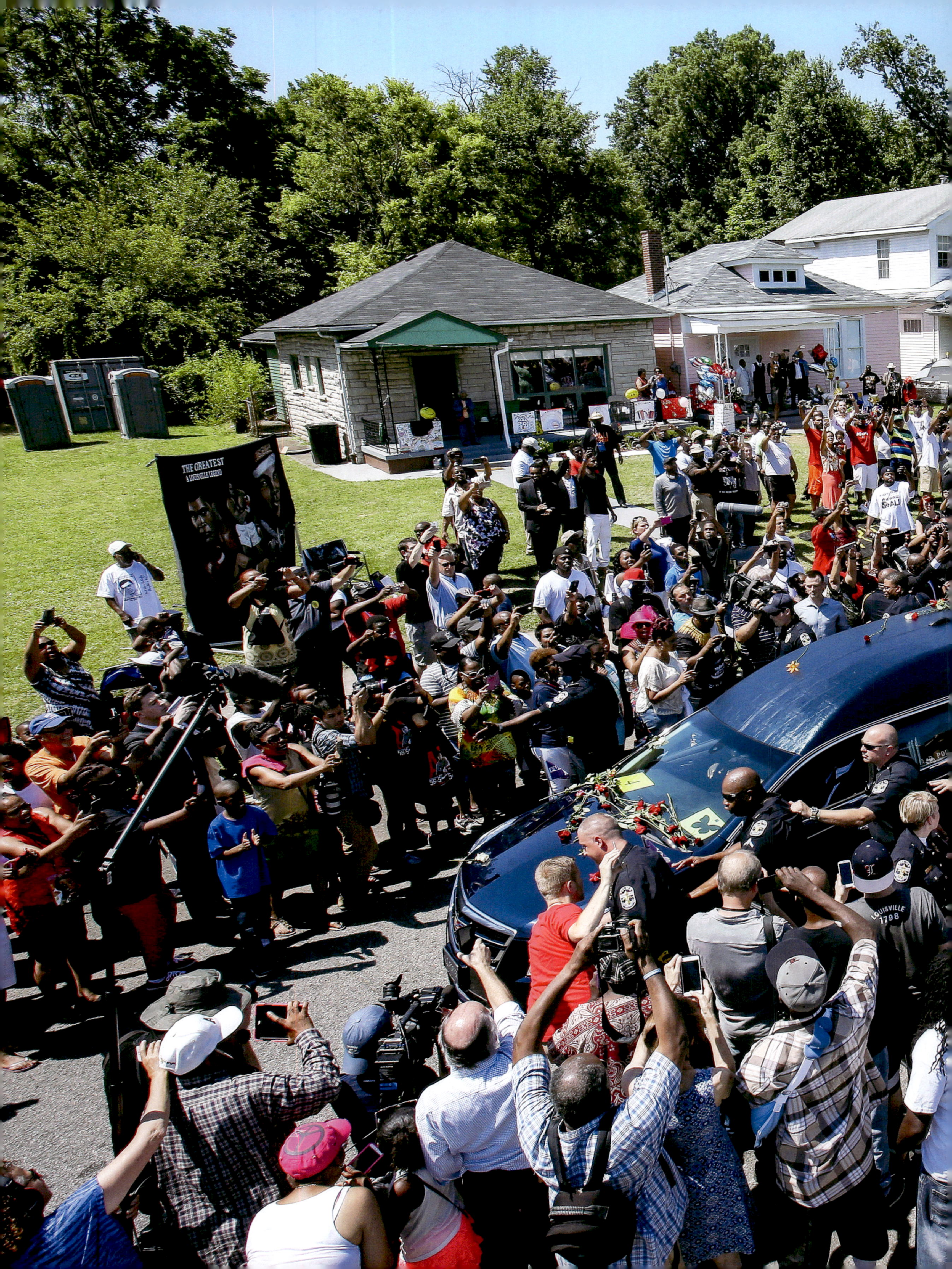
THE GREATEST
A LOUISVILLE LEGEND
LOUISVILLE
1798

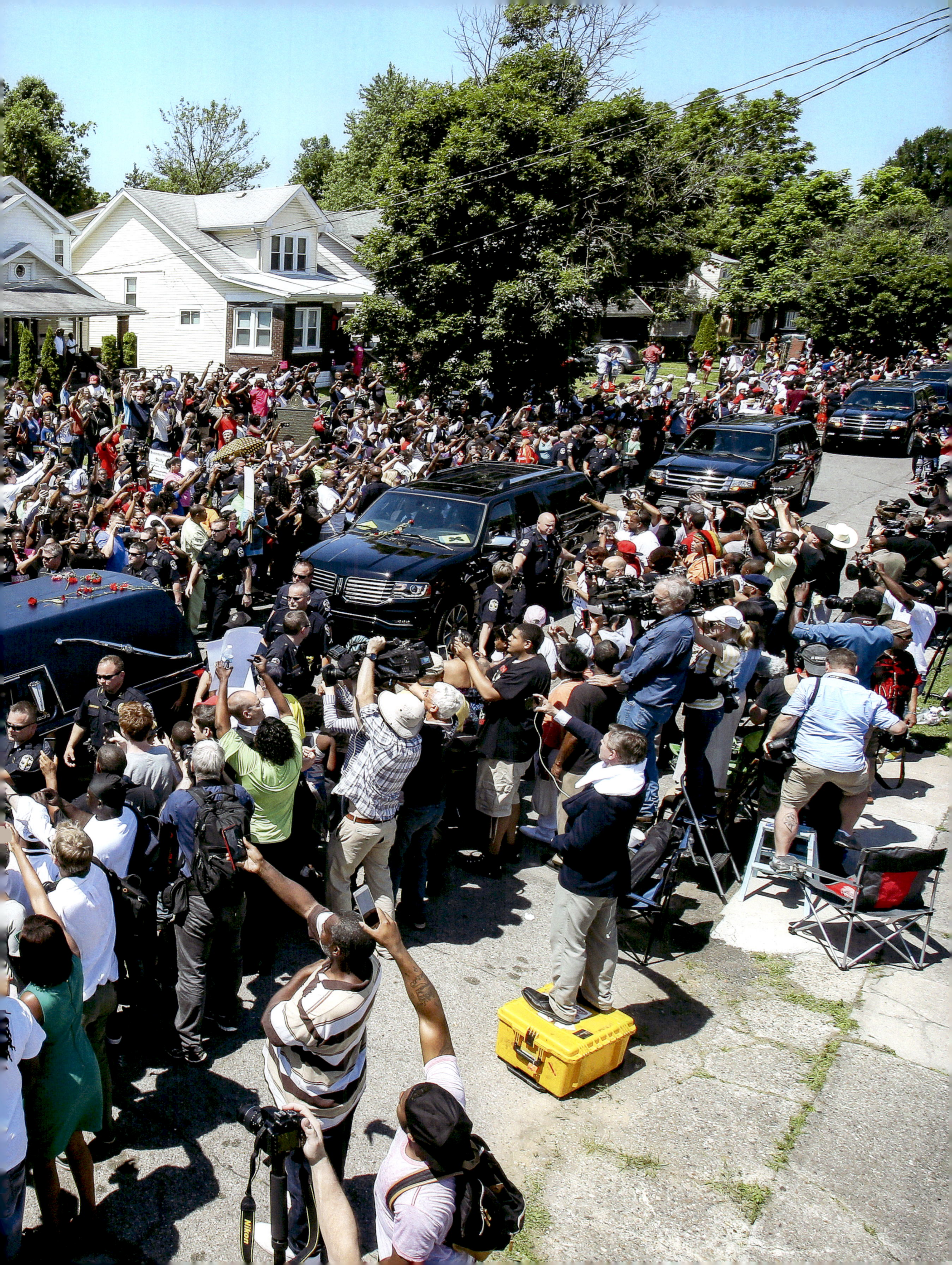

282

1 Michael Clevenger
A boy runs beside the hearse carrying the body of Ali as it drives down Broadway toward Cave Hill Cemetery in Louisville.

June 10, 2016

← Alton Strupp
The funeral procession for Muhammad Ali makes its way past his boyhood home on Grand Avenue in Louisville as hundreds of fans line the streets.

June 10, 2016

1 Pat McDonogh
Fans reach out to touch Ali's hearse as it drove the last few blocks on Broadway to Cave Hill Cemetery in Louisville.

June 10, 2016

1 Sam Upshaw Jr.
Participants arrive for the Jenazah, a Muslim funeral prayer service for Muhammad Ali at Freedom Hall in Louisville.

June 9, 2016

1 Sam Upshaw Jr.
Sayfullaah Ali reads from a collection of Muslim prayers before the Jenazah for Ali at Freedom Hall.

June 9, 2016

→ Michael Clevenger
Pall bearers place the casket of Ali into a hearse in Louisville.

June 10, 2016

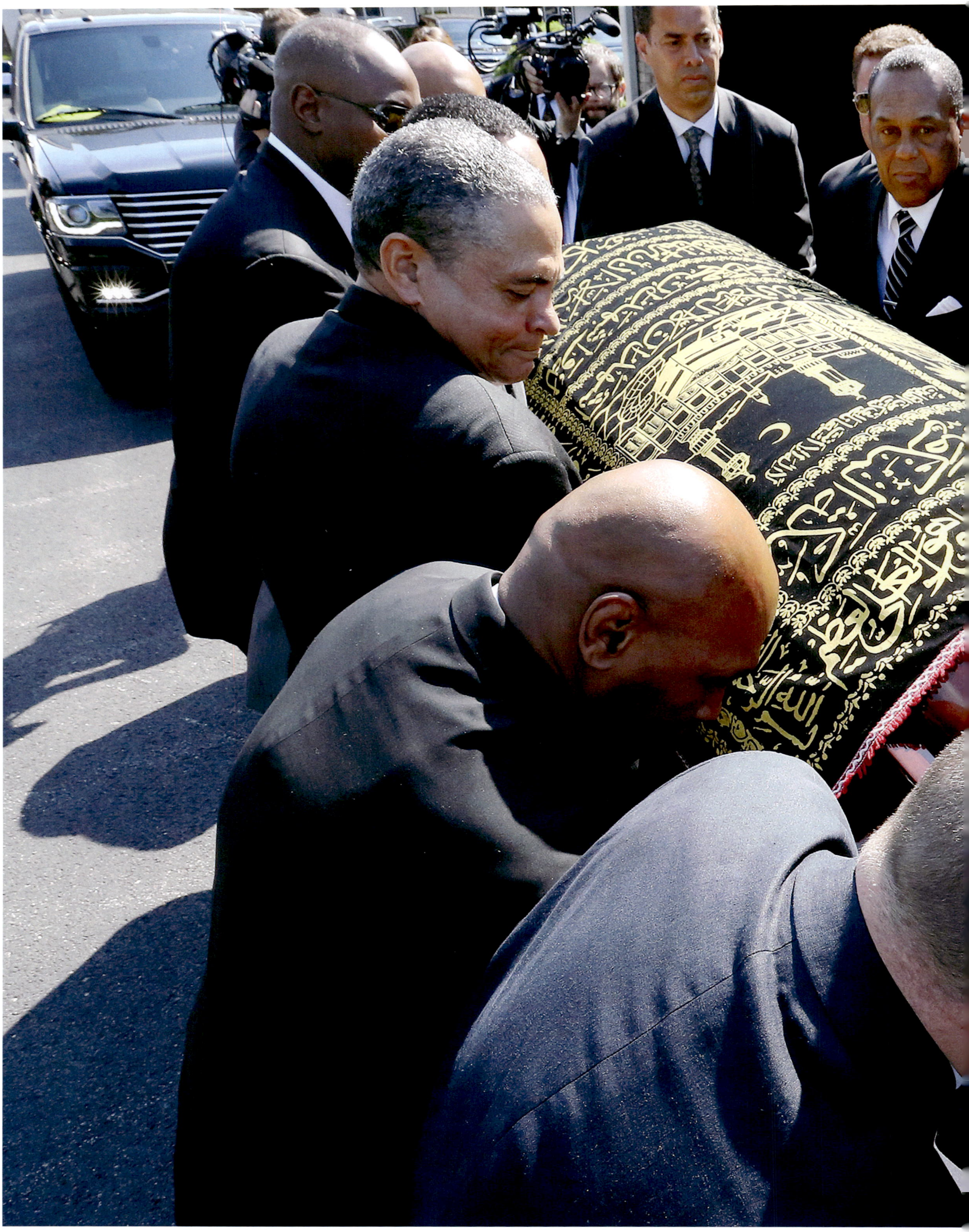

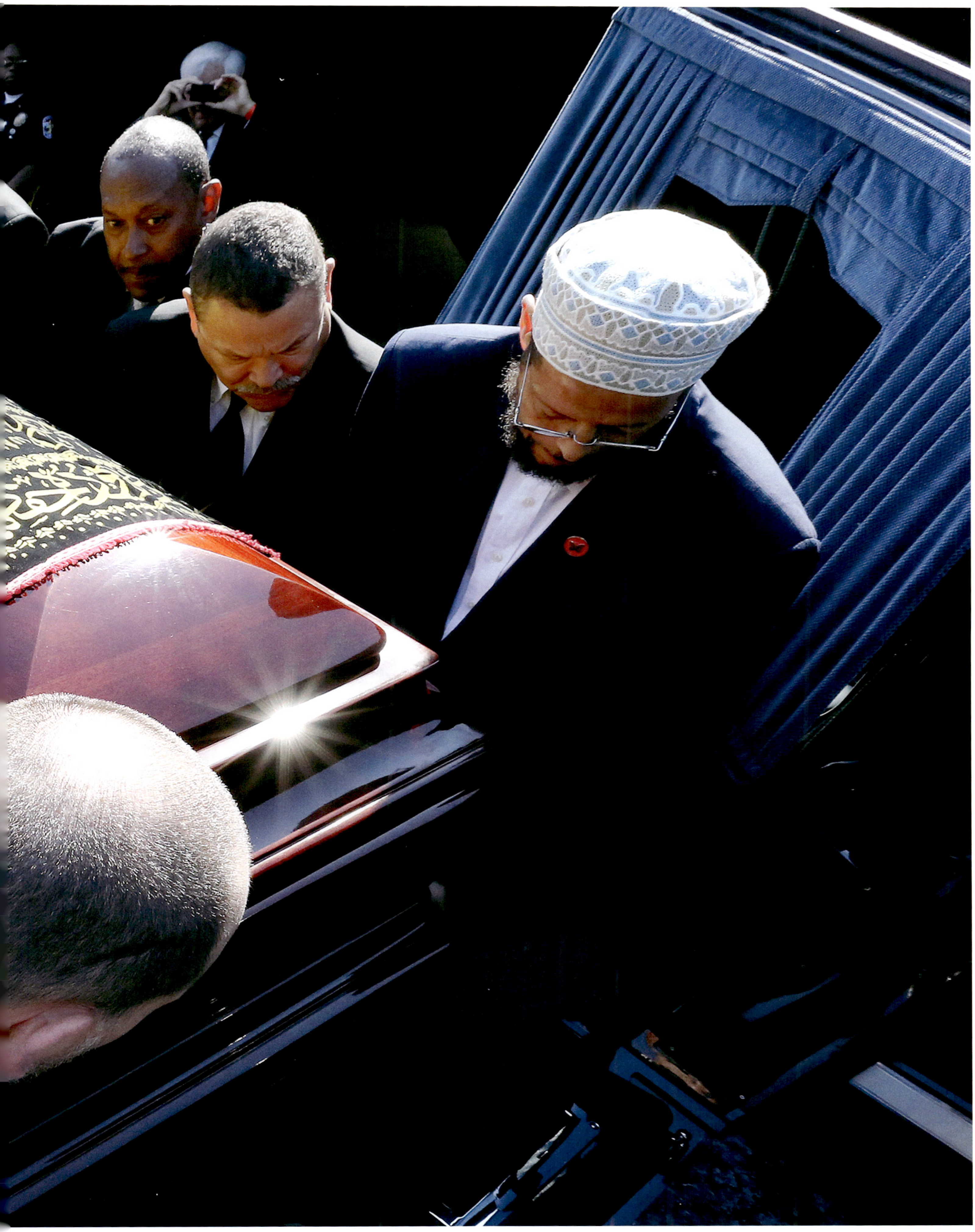

1 Sam Upshaw Jr.
Comedian Billy Crystal performs his famous Muhammad Ali impression during his remarks at the funeral for Ali at the KFC Yum! Center.

June 10, 2016

1 Matt Stone
Former President Bill Clinton becomes emotional when describing how he was 'weeping like a baby' when he watched Ali light the flame during the 1996 Olympics. Clinton spoke during a public memorial service at the KFC Yum! Center.

June 10, 2016

1 Sam Upshaw Jr.
Muhammad Ali's daughter Rasheda Ali-Walsh becomes emotional as she makes remarks during the funeral for Muhammad Ali at the KFC Yum! Center.

June 10, 2016

1 Sam Upshaw Jr.
Lonnie Ali, Muhammad Ali's widow, spoke of her late husband at Ali's public memorial service at the KFC Yum! Center, saying: "It was his religion that turned him away from violence. So even in death, Muhammad has something to say."

June 10, 2016

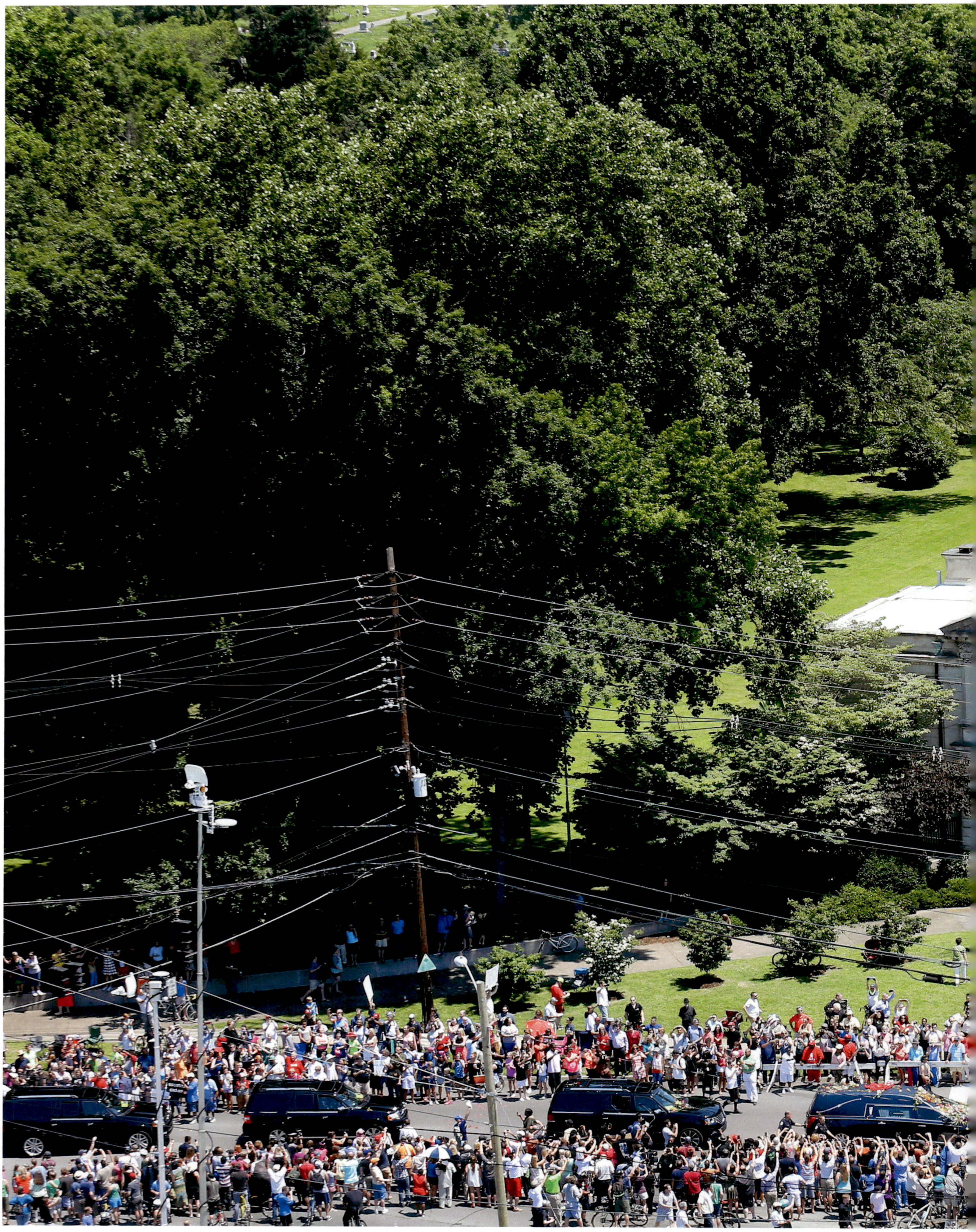

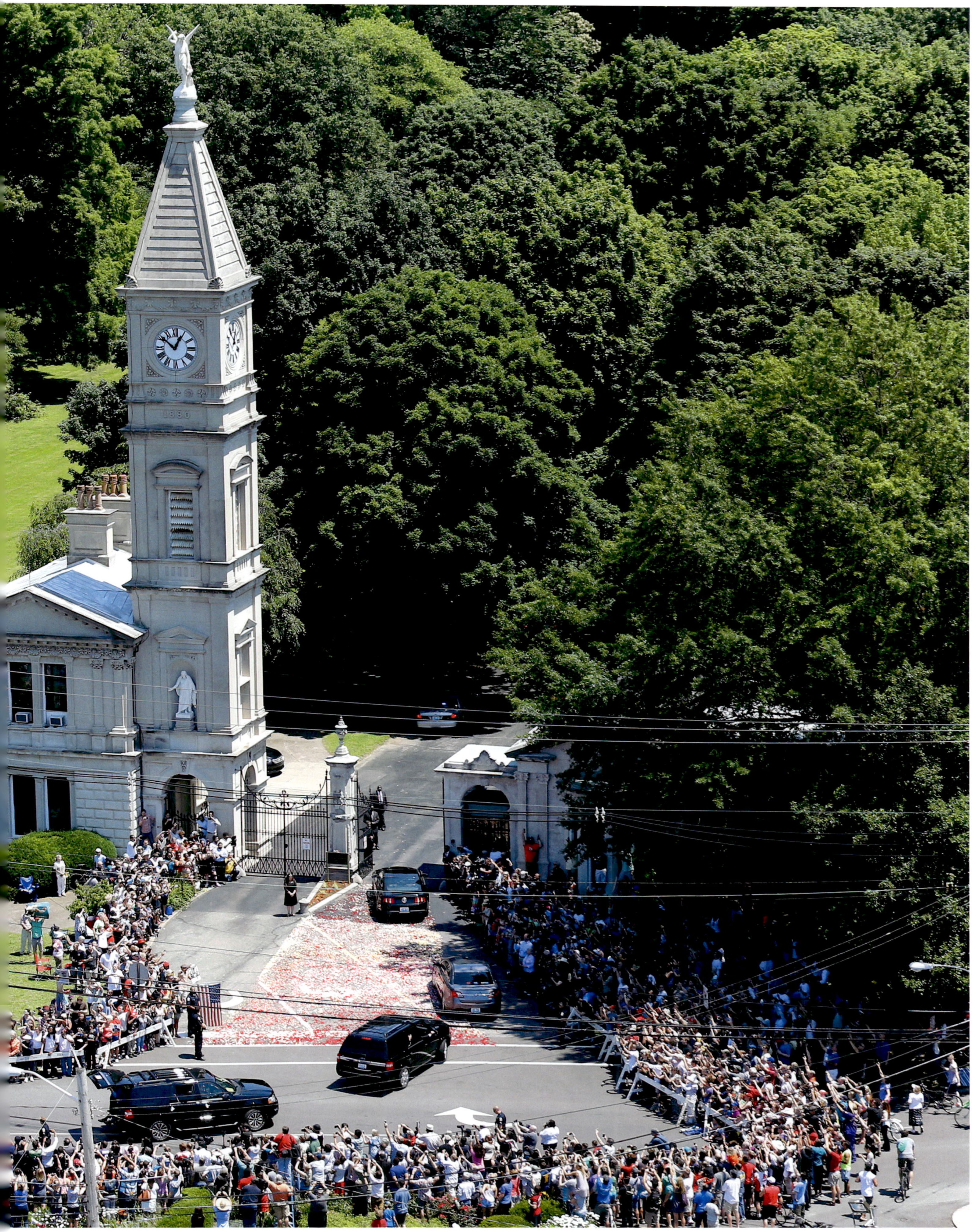

← **Pat McDonogh**
Muhammad Ali's funeral procession enters the gates of Cave Hill Cemetery in Louisville.

June 10, 2016

↑ **Pat McDonogh**
Allie Senn, 12, signs a large banner honoring Ali during the I Am Ali festival.

June 8, 2016

"I wish people would love everybody else the way they love me. It would be a better world."

Published by Press Syndication Group
2850 N. Pulaski Road, Suite 9
Chicago, Illinois 60641

www.cjbookproject.com
+646.325.3221
sales@cjbookproject.com

Rights and Licensing Contact :
N. Warren Winter
+646.325.3221
warren@psgwire.com

Editor : N. Warren Winter
Photo Editor : Pat McDonogh
Photo Editor Emeritus : C. Thomas Hardin
Written by : Tim Sullivan
Designer : de.MO design Ltd.

All photos in this book are ©1915-2018
the Louisville Courier Journal.

All rights are reserved under applicable Federal and
International copyright conventions and laws. No part of
this book may be reproduced or transmitted by any means
now known or hereafter developed without prior written
permission from Press Syndication Group.

$59.95

1st edition, 2018.
ISBN #9781732319615

Printed in China.